SOCIAL SCIENCE RESOURCES IN THE ELECTRONIC AGE

SOCIAL SCIENCE RESOURCES IN THE ELECTRONIC AGE

Volume I
World History

**Elizabeth H. Oakes and
Mehrdad Kia**

GREENWOOD PRESS
Westport, Connecticut • London

Library of Congress Cataloging-in-Publication Data

Oakes, Elizabeth H., 1964–
    Social science resources in the electronic age.
        p. cm.
    Includes bibliographical references and indexes.
        Contents: v. I. World history / Elizabeth H. Oakes and Mehrdad Kia — v. II. U.S. history / Elizabeth H. Oakes and Michael S. Mayer — v. III. Government and civics / Elizabeth H. Oakes and Jeffrey D. Greene — v. IV. Economics / Elizabeth H. Oakes and Michael H. Kupilik — v. V. Geography / Elizabeth H. Oakes and Jeffrey A. Gritzner.
        ISBN 1–57356–589–X (set : alk. paper) — ISBN 1–57356–474–5 (v. I : alk. paper) — ISBN 1–57356–473–7 (v. II : alk. paper) — ISBN 1–57356–476–1 (v. III : alk. paper) — ISBN 1–57356–477–X (v. IV : alk. paper) — ISBN 1–57356–475–3 (v. V : alk. paper)
        1. Social sciences—Computer network resources. 2. Humanities—Computer network resources. I. Title.

H61.95.O25   2004
025.06'3—dc22   2003060400

British Library Cataloguing in Publication Data is available.

Library of Congress Catalog Card Number: 2003060400
ISBN: 1–57356–589–X (set)
        1–57356–474–5 (vol. I)
        1–57356–473–7 (vol. II)
        1–57356–476–1 (vol. III)
        1–57356–477–X (vol. IV)
        1–57356–475–3 (vol. V)

First published in 2004

Greenwood Press, 88 Post Road West, Westport, CT 06881
An imprint of Greenwood Publishing Group, Inc.
www.greenwood.com

Printed in the United States of America

The paper used in this book complies with the Permanent Paper Standard issued by the National Information Standards Organization (Z39.48–1984).

10 9 8 7 6 5 4 3 2 1

Contents

Set Introduction

INFORMATION IN THE ELECTRONIC AGE

Tracking down quality information has always been the key to writing a good research paper. In the social sciences fields, that information comes in a multitude of forms—opinions, statistics, background material, biographical facts, detailed definitions, maps, and so forth. Until recent years, information typically filtered from its original source to a publisher, where it was reviewed, edited, and printed in a journal or book. The publication eventually made its way to library and bookstore shelves, where it would then, with any luck, find its way into your hands.

Most student researchers would agree that the computer revolution has changed all of that for the better, vastly improving our access to information. Today, you can gather material for a research project utilizing an array of electronic media. From your home computer, it's now possible—and easy—to download text and photographs from a digital library's collection, ask an expert a question, collect data from government documents, access a subject-specific commercial database, or watch live film from another part of the world.

As a student, you couldn't be in a better position for tapping into some of the most informative, reputable sources out there. The World Wide Web and its electronic cousins—CD-ROMs, specialized databases, e-mail, Usenet newsgroups, online journals, etc.—now represent a fundamental part of our lives, having overlapped or usurped the functions of the encyclopedia, reference desk, microfilm, and, let's face it, sometimes even pen and paper. And it's only going to improve. By the time you finish reading this chapter, technology whizzes will have undoubtedly figured out how to make even more kinds of information accessible from your computer.

In some instances, electronic media not only represents a new way to present information, but a new kind of information resource altogether. As we'll explore for social science disciplines, electronic media has created unprecedented opportunities for students to research and problem-solve in a collaborative mode. Students and teachers can communicate with one another beyond their classroom or even their countries.

Another notable strength and innovation in electronic media is its interconnectedness. Unlike print resources, where each book is an entity unto itself, resources on the Internet are literally one keystroke away from one another. For instance, if you initiate your research using your local library's home page as a jumping-off point, you can search the library's online catalog, then simply click to place a hold on a book or to request an interlibrary loan. From there, you can tap into one of the discipline-specific databases the library subscribes to, then click again to browse through an online academic subject directory devoted to topics in the discipline, and then click once more to visit a Web site.

So as you can see, there's simply no reason to conduct a research project that relies on the one or two books your library happens to have on its shelves. The information you need is out there in glorious abundance. But that very abundance can create its own stumbling blocks. Haven't you found yourself second-guessing whether you've searched thoroughly enough? Or wondering if the most relevant piece of information is still out there, eluding you? This set is meant to alleviate those concerns by showing you how to conduct your research with the best media available in today's electronic age. For this multivolume set of expert guides in the social sciences, we have sought out the best electronic research sources in world history, U.S. history, government and civics, economics, and geography—sources that are definitive, comprehensive, credible, and current.

Social Science Resources in the Electronic Age is designed as a one-stop resource for cutting through the chaos of the Internet to find authoritative, age-appropriate information on topics covered in the world history, U.S. history, government and civics, economics, and geography curricula.

SCOPE AND CONTENT

This *Social Science Resources in the Electronic Age* set comprises five volumes. This world history volume also contains a section on "The

Basics." *U.S. History, Government and Civics, Economics,* and *Geography* are the other volumes, and the *Geography* volume contains the set index. Each discipline also has its own index.

"The Basics" is to be used for the set and is meant for student, teacher, and parent use. This part provides you with the best in general Web sites and Web information to ground you and get you started. It offers something for everyone, whether you are new to computer research or computer-savvy. "The Basics" provides fundamental information about the Web, search engines and other search tools, Web material evaluation, and copyright and plagiarism issues that are unique to today's electronic resources. It also offers an invaluable introduction to the different kinds of electronic media. In addition to learning about the types of electronic resources, you'll also find general Web sites that can be mined for your research projects. In separate sections at the end, general Web resources are listed for educators and parents. Other broad sites are listed for summer programs for students and careers.

Each discipline is divided into five chapters.

Chapter 1: "Resources in . . . "

Here you are provided with a treasure map to quality information on the Web, which will save you hours of your own research time.

We have searched for and found the crème de la crème of Web sites providing specific information on each discipline. These sites include any pertinent ones from library electronic services and various types of Web resources, including reference, commercial, government, academic and educational, interactive/practical, maps, and primary sources.

Chapter 2: Researching Individual Topics on the Internet

This is the heart of each discipline's content. We gathered the individual topics listed from a detailed analysis of the national standards and leading subject texts, and all were screened by an expert in the field. These topics are listed alphabetically rather than by the name of Web sites so that you can immediately go to the information you need without guessing whether a site will be useful.

For each topic, you'll find reviews of several Web sites, giving you all of the information you need to know: the name, URL, appropriate grade range, and a thorough discussion of how to use the site for research. When you log on to the Web to find background information on the Green Revolution or to gain a fuller understanding of macroeconomics, for example, you'll now have a few handpicked sites, as opposed to the thousands that might turn up with a keyword search. In case you choose to conduct your own online search for a key topic, we let you know which search engine and keywords provide the best hits.

The number of Web sites reviewed in each entry is determined by the number of good Web sites that look at different aspects of the topic, not the importance of the topic. Some important topics have only one or two Web sites. In these cases, no other Web site we previewed could add anything significant to the offerings of the Web sites provided. For some topics, there are hundreds of great sites on the Web, but we couldn't include them all. We have limited the number of sites per topic to four, and we have chosen these four based on how closely they mirror what is covered in textbooks and the national geography curriculum.

Because space is limited, some important kinds of topics were necessarily omitted. For example, you won't find names of individuals or specific countries in the topic list. But we haven't left you hanging. "The Basics" section for the set is the place to go for general sites across disciplines. We've provided some good general sites here that will help you start your research. If you're looking for biographical information, there are biographical dictionary sites. If it's countries you want to learn about, try the *Library of Congress: Country Studies* site. The individual volume's and comprehensive set index will also lead you to topics not on the list.

Chapter 3: Materials and Resources for Teachers

With the abundance of resources available on the World Wide Web, teachers can expand students' learning in ways unheard of just 10 years ago. For starters, a teacher's circle of peers is no longer limited to the sundry crew in the teacher's lounge at school. These days, a social studies teacher at a small high school in Montana can log on to the Web to find economics lesson plans written by education specialists in New York, to research potential summer training seminars within her region, or to apply for grants or travel opportunities online. Even a green, first-year teacher who needs to put together his first comprehensive unit on accounting can come across to students as an old pro, simply by using the Web to gather relevant lesson plans, printable handouts, in-class exercises, field trip ideas, and to chat with other teachers about the subject.

"Materials and Resources" reviews a number of excellent subject-specific Web sites that offer materials and resources for parents and for educators, such as free maps, government document reprints, lesson plans, and downloadable software. "The Basics" lists the general sites, but a few are repeated in the individual volumes with added value in the specific tips for the particular discipline.

Chapter 4: Museums and Summer Programs for Students

This chapter surveys Web sites offering unique online museum exhibits, interpretive centers, summer programs, and other interactive opportunities for students. While nothing can replace the experience of walking through the corridors of a wonderful museum, today's museums are no longer reliant upon bricks and mortar. Many museum resources are now available online 24 hours a day, across the globe, to anyone with an Internet connection. Online exhibits can be constantly changed and expanded, and—unlike their physical counterparts—online exhibits need not be dismantled to make room for new ones. Likewise, a print brochure about an outstanding—but obscure—summer program might never find its way into your hands, but on the Web, you can learn about the summer program *and* apply for it, regardless of whether it takes place in your hometown or on another continent. We've found amazing sites that'll convince you to log off your computer—to spend the summer in Paris studying international relations or travel to the country of Peru where Internet connections are far and few between.

Chapter 5: Careers

Whether you're simply gathering information to help you turn your passion for geography, for example, into a livelihood or you're actively searching for your first job in the field, the World Wide Web can play an integral role in the development of your career. Regardless of the specific field you're interested in, you'll discover numerous Web sites with tools to help you determine your career aptitudes, match your academic interests with a university program, locate funding for a research project, find peers online, register for professional conferences or student workshops, and of course, you'll encounter dozens of job database sites, including those specific to geography-related careers.

We've selected what we consider to be the best career-building Web sites, with the needs of upper-level high school and college students firmly in mind. These sites, which include professional organizations and societies, federal and state agencies, private companies, and nonprofit groups, should give you a good jump start on your career.

HOW TO USE THIS SET

There are three ways you can find information in *Social Science Resources in the Electronic Age*. First you can look at the detailed table of contents for "The Basics," which will quickly lead you to such topics as copyright law or search strategies. Each discipline also has a contents page. If you are researching a particular topic in a discipline, you can immediately go to the alphabetical listing of topics in Chapter 2 for that discipline. Finally, you can use the volume or set index, which expands our coverage significantly. Because we had to limit the number of topics found in each discipline's Chapter 2, we added as much detail as possible to our site reviews. These include names of people and countries, events, and other topics covered in the Web site but not included in our topic list. All of these have been indexed. For example, in the Geography volume, the partition of India is not in the topic list, but if you look in the index, you will find that it is discussed in a site on boundary and boundary conflicts and in a site on the caste system. Therefore, if you don't find what you want in the topic list, go to the volume or set index.

So, when you are desperate for a quick, reliable Web site for a report on African independence movements, need to know about Boolean searching or citing electronic sources, or want to know what it's like to be an economist, reach for *Social Science Resources in the Electronic Age*. It will help you avoid the frustration of endless surfing and wasted time by taking you directly to the Web's best resources in the social sciences.

The Basics

"The Basics" offers a plethora of information about the Web. It introduces you to the fundamentals of the Web, the general format of resources, and types of Web resources with references to general sites. It also shows you ways to research, how to evaluate Web material, and how to present your research taken from the Web. Even the most Web-savvy users will glean some useful knowledge from the material offered here. It is especially informative to novice users and will prime all to get the most out of Web research.

"The Basics" also supplements subject-specific information from each of the disciplines with general sites for teachers, parents, and students that appeal to a broad range of interests. This supplementary material is divided into the following categories: "General Web Resources for Teachers," "General Hands-on Opportunities for Teachers," "General Web Resources for Parents," "General Summer Programs for Students," and "General Career Sites."

"The Basics" is meant to serve the whole set, and readers are encouraged to ground themselves here before delving into each of the subject volumes and to refer back to it when broad sites are sought.

WEB BASICS

Is the Web the Same Thing as the Internet?

You might be surprised to learn that there's more than just the Web on the Internet. The World Wide Web is *part* of the Internet, and clearly, it's the part that has grabbed the lion's share of the public interest. That's probably because the Web, unlike other systems running on the Internet, uses hypertext to create a complex, yet accessible, linkage of words, pictures, sounds, and animation. A great Web site not only provides you with information on a topic, but it also points you in the direction of other sites on the same topic.

What Are URLs?

An URL, or Uniform Resource Locator, is the address of a World Wide Web location. In the United States, six commonly used top-level domain codes will tell you the basic type of server where the site comes from:

.com—commercial

.edu—educational

.gov—government

.net—network

.org—nonprofit organization

.mil—military

Knowing the different top-level domain names is a good start in assessing a site's credibility. It's useful to learn a bit more about how to read URLs. Did you know, for instance, that an URL that includes a tilde (˜) is probably someone's personal page on a larger site? Let's take a look now at the parts of this fictitious URL: http://www.mapsgalore.com/spain/culture.html.

"http" stands for hypertext transfer protocol, the way in which computers exchange information on the Web

"www" is the host computer name

"mapsgalore" is the second-level domain name

"com" is the top-level domain name

"spain" is a sub-directory

"culture" is a file

"html" stands for hypertext markup language.

Here's another reason to understand how URLs are strung together. Have you ever clicked on a hyperlink only to have a "not found" error message pop up on the screen? You can often still find the information you need by removing parts of the URL, starting at the tail end. In the *MapsGalore* URL, you could remove "culture.html" for starters. If you don't find the information you want that way, chop the URL all the way down to http://www.mapsgalore.com/ and look at the site map or use the site's internal search mechanism.

What Are Browsers?

A browser is the software your computer uses to access Web sites. The most widely used browsers are Netscape Navigator from Netscape Communications and Internet Explorer from Microsoft. Browsers aren't hard to come by. Chances are, your computer came equipped with one, and if not, your Internet service provider will supply the software for you.

Before you begin a research project, you might want to customize your browser so that your favorite search engine or reference site comes up automatically when you sign on. By designating it as your start page or home page, you can go back to it easily by clicking on the browser's "Home" or "Start" button.

Browsers have all sorts of features that you can tinker with that can ease the research process. For example, all Web browsers let you choose to load text without pictures. Sure, this makes for less interesting, less colorful surfing. But turning off the graphics can speed up initial searches when you simply need to accumulate a list of sites that you plan to visit in their full glory later.

Finally, get to know how to use your browser's "Back," "Forward," and "History" buttons effectively so that you can stay on track during a research project. These tools help you retrace your steps so that you don't waste time just roaming around.

How Can I Use Favorites or Bookmarks?

When you find a Web site that looks promising, you can set a bookmark on Netscape or add the site to your favorites on Internet Explorer. This will store the URL address so that you can quickly access the site again without retyping the address.

As your collection of favorites or bookmarks grows, you can organize them into specific subject folders and even subfolders. You may, for instance, want to create a folder labeled "Search Engines" to keep all of your favorite search tools at hand. Some students like to handle their research chronologically, by creating a bookmarks or favorites folder labeled with the date, then reorganizing the collection under subject-headed folders later.

What Are Search Engines?

Search engines are Web sites that allow you to ask for a list of Web pages containing or pertaining to certain words or phrases. A search engine sends out spiders or robots—software programs that retrieve and index Web pages into massive databases. Depending upon the particular software the engine uses, it will search for a keyword in the URL, the title, the text, or from descriptions written by a Web site's author. When you use a search engine, you're not actually searching the entire Web, but rather the fraction of the Web that this particular engine has already indexed.

You'll quickly discover that search engines are like snowflakes—each one is a little different. While there is no single best search engine, some are clearly better than others for certain types of queries. In Chapter 2 of this book, we've singled out which search engine, metasearch engine, or subject directory produced the best results for each topic. Try a few out for yourself. If you're like most people, you'll find a handful of search engines that work for you and you'll stick with them.

Search engines are useful when you're searching for unique keywords or phrases that might be buried in the full text of Web pages. But if you dare to type in a very common word or phrase, you'll be snowed under by many irrelevant links. That's when you need to make your query more specific, and to take the time to read the search engine's advanced search instructions. The more you know about how to use a specific search engine, the better your results will be. Later in this section, we'll talk about how to conduct effective simple and advanced searches.

Some of the search engines used for researching topics in Chapter 2 include the following:

Google
http://www.google.com/

This engine uses link popularity (in other words, the number of other sites that link to the search result) to rank Web sites. This produces excellent results, even for very common queries, because other sites have already vouched for the sites by linking to them.

Ask Jeeves
http://www.askjeeves.com/

This service directs you to sites that try to answer your question, which you can phrase naturally (e.g., "What is the Green Revolution?").

Northern Light
http://www.northernlight.com/

A favorite among researchers because it indexes a large amount of
the Web, then clusters documents by topic. It also has fee-based special
collection documents from news wires, magazines, and database sources
that are not reached by other search engines.

Raging Search
http://www.raging.com/

This is operated by the larger, portal-type engine AltaVista. Raging
Search offers the same core index and ranking scheme as AltaVista,
without the portal extras (shopping, travel, headlines, etc.).

DirectHit
http://www.hotbot.com/

This engine determines the most relevant sites for your search request
by analyzing the activity of millions of previous Internet searchers.

Excite
http://www.excite.com/

Excite offers a large index and incorporates non-Web material such
as company information and sports scores into its results, when
appropriate.

How about Metasearch Engines?

Metasearch engines work by quickly searching the databases of many
search engines simultaneously, offering the cumulative results. Some of
the metasearch engines organize their results into categories such as educational sites, nonprofit sites, country sites, and so on. Others display
results ranked by relevancy, while others display each search engine's
results separately. While metasearches typically retrieve only about 10
percent of each individual engine's results, these returns are from the
top of each engine's list and are usually the most relevant.

Sounds great, right? The downside to metasearches lies in the fact
that each individual engine will read, or process, your query according
to its own search protocol (meaning that each engine may end up looking for something slightly different than the others). In addition, metasearches tend to time out—or run out of time—before every search
engine completes its database search. The result is a less comprehensive
list of links. The best time to use metasearch engines is when you are
conducting a search for a unique, simple term, or you want a quick

overview on a topic. Metasearches are also one way to see which engines are retrieving the best results for your topic.

Some of the metasearch engines that were used for researching topics in each volume's Chapter 2 include the following:

Dogpile
http://www.dogpile.com/

This site queries a customizable list of 18 search engines and specialty search sites, along with Dogpile's own catalog. It displays results from each engine separately.

Inference Find
http://www.infind.com/

This site sends your search to WebCrawler, Yahoo, Lycos, Alta Vista, InfoSeek, and Excite and then clusters the results into handy subjects.

MetaCrawler
http://www.metacrawler.com/

The granddaddy of metasearch engines, MetaCrawler started back in 1995. It sends queries to AltaVista, Excite, Google, GoTo, Infoseek, LookSmart, Lycos, Thunderstone, and WebCrawler, among others, then organizes the results according to relevance.

Ixquick
http://www.ixquick.com/

Ixquick lists results based on how often a site received a top-ten ranking from the various search engines.

What Are Subject Directories and Subject Catalogs?

Many search engines have grown and evolved into another beast, called a subject directory or subject catalog. Unlike search engines, the listings in a subject directory have been handpicked and categorized by human beings, rather than software programs. They are also sometimes called subject trees because of their hierarchical arrangement: they start with a few main categories and then branch out into subcategories, topics, and subtopics. To find information about African infant mortality rates at *Galaxy* (http://www.galaxy.com/), for example, select "Social Sciences" at the top level, "Geography" at the next level, "Country Studies" at the third level, and finally conduct a keyword search for "Africa infant mortality." Many subject directories include internal search engines that allow you to search the directory and link you to another search engine if an internal search is unsuccessful. Subject directories usually deliver a higher quality of research-friendly sites, and they are indispensable tools for narrowing down your project parameters or simply getting ideas. Most university libraries offer their own subject directories, which can be an excellent resource for students.

Now, a few caveats. Like everything you'll find on the Web, subject directories *do* have their weaknesses. Each subject directory has its own criteria for inclusion; in some cases, inclusion is not necessarily a badge of merit, but merely a reflection that the site was submitted to an editor there. You must also factor in the expertise and personal bias of the editor who chooses the links.

These are a few of the subject directories that provide excellent coverage of the social sciences:

Argus Clearinghouse
http://www.clearinghouse.net/

Argus maintains a comprehensive collection of subject guides, with Web links that are thoroughly described and evaluated. Its searchable listings are great when you really want to delve into a subject.

The Librarians' Index to the Internet
http://lii.org/

This is a searchable and browsable index to Internet resources, selected and annotated by librarians.

Academic Info
http://www.academicinfo.net/

Here's a searchable subject directory of Web resources selected for the college and university community. Each subject guide is an annotated listing of the best general Web sites in the field, plus a gateway to specialized and advanced research tools.

Yahoo!
http://www.yahoo.com/

Yahoo! is one of the most popular Internet subject directories. It contains over a million Web site listings, some evaluated, some reviewed, but most accepted as submitted. It can be searched directly or browsed by category. If no items are found within Yahoo! itself the query is automatically sent to Google's database.

FORMATS OF RESOURCES

Library Electronic Services

Portals

Library catalogs are a far cry from the dusty index cards they once were. Card catalogs have been replaced by computer systems that you can access at the library or online from home. These catalogs list not only the books in the library's collection, but magazines, films, government publications, videos, CD-ROMs, and other electronic formats as well. You can conduct your search by author, subject, or title, or limit your search by date or by a particular format, such as videos. To see a list of libraries that have web-accessible catalogs, visit *LIBWEB* at http://sunsite.berkeley.edu/Libweb/.

Your search for information can move seamlessly from the library's collection to the World Wide Web to commercial databases to which your library subscribes. Your library's portal (or home page) will likely provide a menu of the multitude of research options available. The Web portal for the Library of Congress (http://www.loc.gov/library/) typifies the kind of electronic smorgasbord available at libraries today. Here, you can search the complete collection of the Library of Congress, access the catalogs of hundreds of other libraries, find full-text digital resources, and utilize specialized bibliographies and indexes. You will also find topic-specific collections of Web resources prepared by subject specialists at the library.

Specialized Databases

Libraries pay for access to commercial databases from companies such as DIALOG, Ovid, and OCLC (Online Computer Library Center). Databases are collections of information drawn from scientific and technical literature, full-text trade journals, newspapers and news wires, demographic data, government statistics, and more. The cost of subscribing to these databases is prohibitive for most individuals, but as a card-carrying patron of a library, you have access to vast amounts of data simply not available elsewhere. (Keep in mind that many databases are available in print, CD-ROM, and/or online formats, depending on your library's preference.)

CD-ROMs

CD-ROMs allow libraries to store large collections of printed material in a small amount of space. Like other electronic media, CD-ROMs are searchable, so you can focus on the information you really want. To find articles in magazines, journals, and newspapers, you'll use periodical indexes stored on CD-ROM. These indexes are usually faster and easier to use than their print counterparts and cover a longer time span. Many CD-ROM indexes also include brief summaries of the articles, which can help you decide if an article truly pertains to your research.

Some common CD-ROM indexes owned by libraries include the *Readers' Guide to Periodical Literature*, *Books in Print*, *InfoTrac*, and *ProQuest's Periodical Abstracts*. At a university library, you will also find specialized subject indexes such as the *General Science Index* or the *Applied Science and Technology Index*. Find out if there are CD-ROM periodical indexes that cover the discipline you are researching at your library. Subject-specific CD-ROMs will naturally offer the most complete coverage of your topic.

CD-ROMs have also usurped other traditional print reference guides, such as dictionaries, encyclopedias, atlases, and statistical databases. CD-ROM dictionaries and encyclopedias offer a few unique advantages, chiefly sound and graphics. If you're not sure how to pronounce a word, many CD-ROM dictionaries, such as the *American Heritage Talking Dictionary*, let you hear for yourself. A CD-ROM's multimedia format incorporates color images, video, and sound, as well as the text you expect. When you search the CD-ROM version of the *World Book Encyclopedia*, for example, you'll find thousands of videos, animations, pictures, and sound clips.

Internet

The Internet is an interconnected network of networks linking people and organizations from across the globe. Web sites are a part of the Internet, but not the whole of it. There is also e-mail, chat rooms, FTP, gopher, telnet, newsgroups, and mailing lists, to name a handful. Granted, the boundaries between these Internet offerings have blurred. Most library catalogs, once available only through telnet, are now on the Web. Most gopher sites have converted into Web sites. Likewise, newsreaders are a standard part of today's browsers, making it possible to access newsgroups without stand-alone software.

The Internet is a warehouse of research goodies just waiting to be found. It can deliver an expert's thoughts on the underlying causes of illiteracy among children right to a high school student's desktop. It allows a college freshman in Kansas to review eighteenth-century documents housed in a Virginia library from the comfort of her dorm room. It offers some of the timeliest research data that's out there. Best of all, once you find one great information resource on the Internet, it often leads you to others.

But the Internet can also present a student with a great way to waste an afternoon chasing down elusive information. Some of the frustrations of spending time on the Internet include waiting for Web pages to load, clicking on extinct links, conducting fruitless keyword searches, and struggling to determine the quality of content found at a site. Later in this section, we'll look at research strategies to make your time on the Internet worthwhile and productive.

E-mail

Electronic mail, or e-mail, is still the most widely used Internet application. You can send messages to anyone on the Internet, including specialists in the area you're researching or students working on related projects. If you know the name of the person you'd like to e-mail but don't know his or her address, check out an e-mail directory site, such as *Switchboard* at http://www.switchboard.com/ or *Yahoo! People Search* at http://people.yahoo.com/.

Mailing Lists

A mailing list is a discussion group in which messages are distributed by e-mail. There are mailing lists—also called listservs, listprocs, or majordomos—on just about every distinct topic you could think of. *Liszt,* a directory of mailing lists, currently indexes almost 3,000 of them, many intended for academic or professional audiences.

To join a mailing list, you must subscribe. Once subscribed, you'll automatically receive the discussions of the group's members as e-mails. You can join in the conversation by replying to the entire list, or respond to an individual member. Remember, however, that these groups are indeed *groups*. Consider yourself an eavesdropper until you get a feel for the group. The best way to do this is to watch for a couple of weeks and see how the members act.

Mailing lists can be a good way to immerse yourself in a topic—perhaps appropriate if you're engaged in a long-term research project or thesis. Do your homework before you post a question. For example, don't ask for information that can readily be found with some basic research of your own. You could also try simply checking previous discussions of the group. A mailing list can also be a great way to locate experts who have an interesting angle on your subject. You can conduct your interview via e-mail or even by the old-fashioned telephone.

Check out these mailing list Web sites:

CataList: The Official Catalog of Listserv Lists: http://www.lsoft.com/lists/
   listref.html

Liszt: The Mailing List Directory: http://www.liszt.com/

Topica: The Email You Want: http://www.topica.com/

Usenet Newsgroups

Usenet newsgroups are another kind of online discussion, on thousands of subjects ranging from athlete's foot to Hitchcock movies. Like a mailing list, Usenet brings together experts, specialists, and zealots in a certain field of interest. The main difference between a mailing list and a Usenet newsgroup is that you *go* to the newsgroup to read the discussion, whereas a mailing list comes to you. All of today's Web browsers are equipped with a piece of software called a newsreader, which allows you to access Usenet groups.

Newsgroup names consist of words separated by periods, somewhat like a Web address. The first letters at the beginning of a newsgroup's name tell you what broad category the group falls into. These include the following:

alt (alternative)

k12 (k through 12)

soc (society)

sci (science)

rec (recreation)

comp (computers)

To find and subscribe to newsgroups that interest you, check out these two Web sites:

Deja News
http://www.deja.com/usenet/

CyberFiber Newsgroups
http://www.cyberfiber.com/index.html

Full-text Magazines and Newspapers

Thanks to the Internet, libraries aren't the only place you can go to track down articles or stories from periodicals. However, finding full-text magazines and newspapers online is still a bit of a hit-or-miss process. Some publications with an online presence offer free, fully searchable archives, some charge a fee for back issues, and others don't maintain an archive at all. For information or data that is several decades or centuries old, the Internet may not be your best bet. You'll typically find a more complete collection of old books, newspaper articles, and magazine features at the library, often preserved on microfiche.

Given these limitations, where should you start? If you're trying to locate articles from a particular publication, visit its Web site to see what sort of search options it offers. *NewsDirectory* (http://www.newsd. com/) has organized links that provide access to over 8,400 English-language periodicals worldwide. Another site called *e-journals* (http:// www.e-journals.org/), part of the World Wide Web Virtual Library, also provides links.

Your next step should be the *Electric Library* (http://www.elibrary. com/), an affordable commercial database geared to students and other researchers. At *Electric Library* you can conduct keyword searches to access full text from magazines, books, travel guides, subject dictionaries, the *World Almanac and Book of Facts*, and international newspapers, as well as photographs, maps, and radio and television manuscripts. Take them up on their free 30-day trial membership. If you're hooked after that, it's just $9.95 a month or $59.95 a year.

Digital Libraries

Digital libraries are an exciting initiative that's taking place on the Internet. They are libraries that store their entire, digitized collection on computers instead of on library shelves. Digital libraries provide broader public access to documents and artifacts such as rare photographs and manuscripts, maps, recorded sound, and motion pictures.

Visit *Digital Library.net* (http://www.digitallibrary.net/), *Berkeley Digital Library SunSITE* (http://sunsite.berkeley.edu/), or the *Digital Libraries Resource Page* (http://www.interlog.com/~klt/digital/) for lists of online digital libraries or to read more about digital libraries.

Web Sites

Web sites are the meat-and-potatoes of the Internet. A Web site for an organization, association, company, or school is typically made up of numerous Web pages. The home page is your entryway to a site and will guide you to your specific areas of interest at that site. A home page usually provides some history on the organization or person; a description of services; an organization or person's mission and projects; information on contacting the group or person; links to related sites; and perhaps even its own search engine within the site.

Biographies

If you're looking for biographical information on important people in any given field, there are numerous biographical dictionaries. Below is a short list of the best.

The Biographical Dictionary
http://s9.com/biography/

If you need a quick identification this is the site for you. It offers biographies of 28,000 notable men and women throughout history. You can search the directory by name or keyword. The site also says you can search by date, but this doesn't seem to work. Remember this will be the first stop in your research. You will need to go further for in-depth information on your subject.

Biography.com
http://www.biography.com/

Here's a site that contains biographies of over 25,000 people throughout history. The site is a snap to use. Just type in the name of the individual you want at the home page. Some of the biographies are quite short, but there are frequently links to related topics, which can help you dig deeper into your research.

Infoplease Biographies
http://www.infoplease.com/

This site contains biographies of over 30,000 individuals, which you can access easily from its home page. You can search all Infoplease sources on the site or limit your search. The most efficient way to get to a biography is to limit your search to "Biographies." This will lead you to a screen that asks you to choose the source you want—encyclopedia, dictionary, or almanac. If you want an identification click on "Dictionary." For a longer biography use "Encyclopedia" or "Almanac." The almanac has more detailed information on birth and death dates, but the encyclopedia has deeper coverage of the individual. The site also contains helpful biographical search tips.

FemBio—Notable Women International (English or German)
http://www.fembio.org/Archiv/dbsuche_e.shtml

This biographical database contains information on more than 30,000 notable women worldwide. Six hundred of these women are searchable online under "First Name," "Last Name," "Date of Birth," "Birthplace," "Date of Death," "Place of Death," "Nationality," "Profession," and 15 biographically relevant attributes like "was only child," "wrote autobiography," "loved a woman," and "emigrated."

The unique strength of this database is the information you can obtain by connecting different attributes in the search function. If you want to find a woman who was a writer, never married, lived in Italy, and died in the 1940s, you can search for her here.

Distinguished Women of Past and Present
http://www.distinguishedwomen.com/subject/field.html

Here you'll find biographies of writers, educators, scientists, heads of state, politicians, civil rights crusaders, artists, entertainers, astronomers, and others. Some were alive hundreds of years ago and some are living today. You can search by subject or by name. This is a really nice resource if you know you want to research a certain group of women, say women aviators or women explorers and adventurers. The categories are numerous and quite varied, so chances are you'll find something helpful and interesting here.

Education World—Biographies
http://www.education-world.com/awards/past/topics/history.
   shtml#Biographies

Education World has done a nice job of collecting biographical sites from all over the world and all time periods. This index mixes together all sorts of biographical sites, but the name of each site readily reveals what you'll find if you follow the link to the site. And some sites are a collection of biographies, like *4,000 Years of Women in Science,* while other sites are devoted to biographical information on one person, such as *Anne Frank Online* or *Long Walk of Nelson Mandela.*

It's fun to browse here, and the resources are all top-notch. You can be sure of that since it's an *Education World* page.

Reference Books

No matter how electronically savvy you are, your library's print resources will always play a role in a research project. In fact, it's not a bad idea to start at the library shelves to acquire some basic background information on your subject. Each book in this set suggests some specific references for that discipline.

TYPES OF WORLD WIDE WEB RESOURCES

The World Wide Web offers an abundance of sites, many of them packed full of good research material, if only you knew where to look.

And while you'll want to look under every (virtual) rock, there's a strong likelihood that most of the solid information you find during your research online will come from five types of Web sites: reference, commercial, government, academic/educational, and interactive/practical. To collect a comprehensive array of research material—including statistical data, factual background information, expert opinions, photographs, graphs—you'll probably need to utilize each type of Web site.

To some extent, defining these five types of Web sites creates arbitrary divisions, as there is a lot of overlap. A government site, for instance, could have a very strong educational program, and a commercial site might provide the best interactive quizzes on a particular topic. We've chosen to distinguish and define these five types of Web sites merely so that you can consider each type's inherent strengths and weaknesses.

Reference Sites

The Web is a tremendous reference library, with mainstream reference guides, as well as unique sites that fill every idiosyncratic research need. As we discussed in the previous section, encyclopedias and dictionaries have made themselves quite at ease on the Web, doing more than merely posting their text for retrieval.

As the Web has grown and grown, reference sites have sprung up that not only incorporate encyclopedia and dictionary information, but also take on the role of Web traffic cop, directing you to the best Web sites on particular subjects. A reference site's strength is in its breadth of unbiased information; its limitation is in the depth of coverage of any single topic area. Reference sites are usually well organized, easy to search, and provide excellent topical links.

StudyWeb
http://www.studyweb.com/

StudyWeb is a subject guide designed for student researchers who need to find information as easily as possible. With over 141,000 quality Web links reviewed and categorized into numerous subject areas, you can narrow in on a topic for a report, find background material for a project, begin research for a paper, or just increase your knowledge of a particular topic.

The home page for *StudyWeb* is clutter-free and easy to navigate. *StudyWeb* helps you decide if the link is appropriate for your research by giving the site a score for visual interest, describing its contents, and indicating which age group the material is geared toward.

InfoPlease
http://www.infoplease.com/

InfoPlease is the online spin-off of a company that's produced almanac publications and reference databases for more than 60 years. This colorful site lets you tap into a massive collection of almanacs on almost every imaginable topic—chockfull of millions of authoritative factoids.

You can search for keywords within *InfoPlease*'s almanac database and come up with an impressive amount of information—more than some general search engines provide. If you know the kind of information you need, you can use a pull-down menu to restrict your search to *InfoPlease*'s dictionary, biographies, or encyclopedia.

For more general research help, click on "Homework Center," a section designed to help K–12 students conduct their research and improve note-taking and writing techniques. This section will also direct students to other study-aid Web resources.

Britannica.com
http://www.britannica.com/

Britannica.com is a true hybrid: part subject directory, part encyclopedia, part Web portal. For researchers, you can't beat its integrated search capabilities. Your search query brings up information from the well-respected and authoritative *Encyclopaedia Britannica*, a list of relevant books and magazine articles, and a list of Web sites culled from *Britannica*'s *Internet Guide*—a collection of 130,000 sites selected, rated, and reviewed by Britannica editors. From the "Advanced Search" page, you'll also find handy links to other excellent reference sites that can provide data such as maps, world facts, statistical data, and U.S. government documents. A searchable version of *Merriam-Webster's Collegiate Dictionary* is also available here.

If you don't find what you need, you can simply click to extend your search to *Britannica.com*'s sponsors, which include Ask Jeeves, AltaVista, and Barnes and Noble Books. Remarkably, this site is free, unlike its granddaddy, the *Encyclopaedia Britannica* at http://www.eb.com/, where you have to pay $5 a month or $50 a year to get the goods.

As Web portals go, *Britannica.com* has more of an academic bent than most, with featured topics like history and humanities, science and technology, world and travel, health, and education. If you're in the market for a start page that also provides daily news, shopping, markets, sports, and weather updates, you might consider this one. If not, it's easy enough to dodge the more commercial aspects of this site to access its excellent search capabilities.

Encyclopedia.com
http://www.encyclopedia.com

This site bills itself as the premiere free Internet encyclopedia. With more than 50,000 articles, it's quite comprehensive, and it's also easy to use. Just type a keyword into the search box and sit back while the *Encyclopedia.com* does the work.

Commercial Sites

In the social sciences, you'll discover that there are superb Web sites produced by commercial enterprises. In general, you can expect sophisticated graphics and cutting-edge interactive features at commercial sites. You'll find that it's easy to search for a specific topic at these sites, since they typically have good search databases. Many of these companies or organizations have even established educational outreach programs specifically to help students find information and participate in group projects.

However, you can also expect that these companies are selling something, somewhere on the site. Keep that in mind as you collect information. While many commercial sites are well-respected, credible sources for factual information, you need to ask yourself, is the product being sold skewing the facts that are provided by this organization?

Government Sites

If you're under the impression that a government-sponsored Web site will be all facts and no fun, think again. Not only are government sites considered authoritative, credible sources for research, many of them have developed lively and interactive sites that students will want to return to even when their research is done.

No doubt about it: government sites provide some of the best geographical research data available on the Web. No matter what topic you're researching, you'll want to bolster opinions and theories with good old reliable statistics and facts, which the government generates in abundance. Government sites are almost uniformly well designed and easy to navigate and search.

Central Intelligence Agency (CIA)
http://www.odci.gov/

As you probably know, the CIA's mission is to collect foreign intelligence to assist the U.S. president and other policymakers in making decisions relating to national security. At this site, you can tap into some of their intensive research.

If you want to gain a fuller understanding of a country's dynamics, the CIA's *World Factbook* is a sound place to begin your investigations. Its full text is available on the Web site and can also be downloaded for use offline. In the *Factbook*, you'll find a detailed listing for every country in the world, providing background information and data on the country's geography, people, government, economy, communications, transportation, military, and transnational issues, along with reference maps.

U.S. Census Bureau
http://www.census.gov/

For housing such a wealth of data, the U.S. Census Bureau's Web site is reassuringly straightforward and easy to navigate. Use the A–Z index if you have a specific topic in mind. Otherwise, you can search by keyword or subject, or delve into the general sections, which include People, Business, Geography, News, and Special Topics. If you're looking for data about the population and socioeconomics of the United States, this is the preeminent source.

The Census Bureau is also a good source for maps, courtesy of the TIGER map server, which produces high-quality, detailed maps using public geographical data. You can generate maps of anywhere in the United States, right down to your street, using the TIGER database. These maps have simple GIS capabilities such as point display and statistical choropleth mapping.

Other good research tools at this site include the American Fact-Finder, an interactive database that can provide you with data from the 1997 Economic Census, the American Community Survey, the 1990 Census, the Census 2000 Dress Rehearsal, and Census 2000. To get information at the national, state, and county level, you should click on another tool called QuickFacts. Also be sure to check out the population clocks for the United States and the world that reveal, minute-by-minute, just how rapidly our populations are increasing. The site also provides excellent links to other government sites with useful social, demographic, and economic information.

Academic and Educational Sites

Some of the best sites on the Web to help you do your research exist for that very purpose. These academic and educational sites are usually designed to supplement, not supplant, the classroom, and they offer students and teachers great research material, interactive tools, and dynamic ideas for making social science topics come to life. These sites let you set the pace of learning. At an educational Web site, you can delve into a topic that your geography teacher skimmed over.

At their best, educational sites are a lively source for the latest educational resources. The weakness of some of these sites is that they are here today, gone tomorrow, usually due to lack of funding.

Interactive/Practical Sites

You'll find that many of the sites we've included in the commercial, government, and academic listings have interactive components, in which you can take a quiz, participate in a research study, or perhaps watch a movie online. But there are also a number of excellent sites maintained by individuals with enough passion about a subject to create a Web site and stock it full of games, quizzes, tutorials, and the like. Some of these sites have an amateur feel, while others are a bit more sophisticated. What they have in common is a can-do sensibility and an appreciation for fun. If you're using information from these sites for your research, be sure to verify it with other sources. If you're just visiting them for diversion, then go for it!

Organization Sites

World Bank
http://www.worldbank.org/

The World Bank collects and publishes social and economic data on most countries around the world. Click on "Data and Statistics" in the home page menu. You will be given the following choices: "Country Data," "Data by Topic," "Data Query," "Working with Data."

"Country Data" contains national statistics for countries and regions, including country-at-a-glance tables and data profiles. "Data by Topic" will put you in touch with indicator tables, sectorial data, and links to other data sites. You should also browse the box of special features. When we visited, it contained links to "Latest Stats on Gender" and "Health, Nutrition, and Population Stats," among other topics.

World Health Organization (WHO)
http://www.who.int/home-page/
high school and up

As the major organization concerned with world health, WHO has created a Web site that's a great starting point for research on disease. Use the "Information" section to find a multitude of WHO publications, such as the *Weekly Epidemiological Report* and the annual *World Health*

Report. The "Press Media" section also provides many useful resources, such as press releases, fact sheets, and multimedia clips.

Look in the "Disease Outbreaks" section to find information on current outbreaks or past outbreaks in the historical archives, which are arranged by year (1996 to 2000) and disease. The "News" section is another best bet for finding information about topical issues on disease.

Just click on "Data and Statistics" in the menu at the left-hand side of the home page for an analysis, complete with numerous charts and graphs, of the worldwide estimates for morbidity and mortality among children.

Or if you want statistics on human rights for children, child refugees, or child labor, you'll find sections here that contain documents and data of all types on these topics too.

Primary Sources

If you want to get your hands, or at least your eyes, on an original document, you'll be looking for primary sources, and may want to try the following sites.

Avalon Project at the Yale Law School
http://www.yale.edu/lawweb/avalon/avalon.htm

This site features documents from around the world in law, history, economics, politics, diplomacy and government from ancient times to the twenty-first century. You can access the material by time period, keyword, or collection. If you don't know the formal name of the document you want, try browsing under "Major Document Collections." This will give you a good idea of what's available on the site. You can also browse by time period.

Personal-Experience Accounts
http://www.libertynet.org/zelson/publish/list.html

For excerpts from personal letters, diaries, travel journals, and other such sources, try this site, which is accessible by categories such as contemporary daily life and general history.

READY TO RESEARCH

In Chapter 2 of each discipline, you'll be happy to see that we've already scouted the Web for you, locating quality research sites for key topics in the field. However, it's inevitable that there will be topics or concepts that you'll want to research on your own. If you've combed through the Web before, you know how alternately exhilarating and frustrating the process can be. One search hits the research jackpot, while the next brings you face-to-face with a computer screen of crummy returns. But searching the Web doesn't have to be such a bumpy ride. By understanding how to develop a search strategy and how to conduct simple and advanced searches, you'll find yourself spending less time spinning your wheels on the Web and more time writing your research paper.

Search Strategy

It's tempting to just dive in, find any old search engine, type in the word you're looking for, and hit "Search." If you're lucky, you'll find some useful information. But more often, you'll waste precious time. So unless you really want to retrieve 4,678 relevant documents, you need to slow down, breathe deep, and cultivate a search strategy. A search strategy defines what results you hope to find and what terminology will help you find them. Here are a few steps to help you break a big research project into manageable parts:

What is the basic question that you want to answer through your research?

What are the main concepts within that question?

How in-depth will your research go? Are you looking for general background information or for detailed facts and statistics?

What search terminology best describes those main concepts? Are there any synonyms, alternate spellings, or variations on that terminology? Remember, it's important to choose your words carefully. Too many words will result in an overly narrow search, and too few (or too general) words will result in a landslide of inane returns.

Once you've come up with a specific search terminology, you're ready to start searching!

Simple Queries

Earlier, in "Web Basics," we discussed how a search engine trolls the Web, creating its own unique database of Web pages. When you make a simple query, you're providing the search engine with one or more keywords with which to conduct a search of its database for relevant Web pages. A simple query is the easiest—if not always the most productive—way to find information on your subject. The downside to simple queries is that they can result in a large number of matches, many of which might be useless to you. You'll find that a simple search works remarkably well for specific or unusual keywords, but not so well for general or ambiguous terms.

Each search engine handles simple queries according to its own default setting. Some search engines find all the keywords that you type in, others find at least one of the keywords, while others consider any multiple-word query to be a phrase. For example, depending on the search engine's default setting, a query for "prime meridian" might find the following:

pages with the complete phrase

pages that contain both words

pages containing only one of the words

To configure queries that use each search engine to its best advantage, you'll need to investigate how that engine uses the keywords that you type in. Look for a link on the search engine's home page called "About," "Help," or "Search Tips," where you can read instructions for the system you're using.

Advanced Queries

To increase the precision of your search results, you'll want to conduct an advanced query. Advanced queries help you zero in on the specific information or type of Web sites you want to find. There's nothing to be intimidated about. Look on the search engine's home page for something called "advanced search"—also known as a power search, optimized search, or complex search—and click. Every search engine provides different options that give you more control over where the engine will look for information and how it will link two or more keywords.

Boolean Operators

Many search engines support Boolean operators, which means you can combine keywords in ways that exclude some words and include others. Before you conduct an advanced query, it's worth understanding what this Boolean business is all about. Boolean logic is derived from a system of logic created by mathematician George Boole in the 1800s. It uses the capitalized operators AND, OR, and NOT to link words and phrases for more precise queries.

When the operator AND is used, it narrows your search by finding documents that contain all of the keywords you enter. For example, if you type in *Congo AND independence AND*, the search engine will limit its results to Web pages where the words all appear, with no particular placement or order. Some search engines prefer the implied Boolean operator for AND, which is a plus (+) sign, with no space between the plus sign and the keyword.

The Boolean operator OR is used to expand your search results. When you use OR, the search engine returns pages with one keyword, several keywords, or all keywords. OR is useful when your search term has synonyms or alternate spellings. Some search engines require that you enclose the OR portion of your query in parentheses, while other search engines automatically default to OR.

The need for AND NOT often arises after you perform an initial search. When your search results contain irrelevant Web sites, you can use AND NOT to filter out the undesired results. AND NOT tells the search engine to retrieve Web pages containing one keyword but not the other. For example, if you're looking for information on Nazism, but you don't want to know about Germany. Some search engines use the term NOT, others AND NOT, while others prefer the minus (−) symbol.

Since each search engine handles Boolean operators differently, be sure to read the fine print. With IxQuick's power search, for instance, you can use either capitalized operators or their symbols. With Yahoo's advanced search, you'll want to stick with the symbols. If you're using a metasearch engine, bear in mind that Boolean operators are often ineffective, although some of the newer metasearch engines customize your search terminology to suit the individual engines they send your query to.

Phrase Searching

Phrase searching will help narrow your search results, particularly in combination with Boolean logic. Placing a group of words in double quotation marks tells the search engine to only retrieve documents in which those words appear as a phrase. For example, typing the phrase "children of Hiroshima" would cull more pertinent results for historians than typing the separate keywords. At certain search engines, you use a pull-down menu, rather than quotation marks, to indicate that you wish to search for a phrase.

Truncation or Wildcard Features

To conduct an advanced search that allows for variations in spelling and word form, you can use truncation or wildcard features at many search engines. The asterisk (*) symbol tells the search engine to return alternate spellings for a word at the point that the asterisk appears. For example, you could type in "geog*" to search for variations on the word geography, such as geographer, geographical, and so on.

Capitalization

Submit your search query in lowercase letters if you want the search engine to search for the words as either uppercase or lowercase. If you want to limit your results to initial capital letters (e.g., "North Atlantic Treaty Organization") or all uppercase letters (e.g., UNICEF) type your keywords in that way.

Singular/Plural

Like capitalization, most search engines interpret singular keywords as singular or plural. If you want plural forms only, make your keywords plural. Keep in mind, however, that some search engines will automatically stem plural forms of words.

Field Searching

To narrow your results, you can use an advanced feature at many search engines called field searching. Instead of searching entire Web sites, field searching lets you specify which part(s) of the document the engine should search for your terminology. Read the instructions for using field searching at any given engine. Some search engines use symbols, while others use a pull-down menu.

Some of the most commonly offered field search options include title, domain, URL, and text searches. A title search instructs the search engine to return Web pages where your keywords appear in the title. A domain search allows you to limit results to certain top-level or country domains such as educational sites (.edu), government sites (.gov), or sites based in the United Kingdom (.uk). An URL search finds pages with specified keywords anywhere in the URL. A text search searches within the text of Web sites for your keyword(s).

Beyond the common advanced search features discussed above, you'll discover innumerable, nifty ways to fine-tune your search to find exactly what you need. For instance, at certain engines, you can specify that your results be limited to sites that contain images, video, ActiveX, Shockwave, JavaScript, MP3 audio, and more! Many engines allow you to restrict your results to sites modified within a specified time range. Other search engines let you limit your results to sites containing broadcast news transcripts, city and regional newspapers, college newspapers, or press releases.

Natural Language Queries

Now that you have a handle on how to conduct simple and advanced queries, you can appreciate the intent behind natural language search engines. These systems allow you to ask the search engine a question, using the same phrasing you'd use to ask a friend.

A natural language search doesn't require you to use Boolean logic or other special commands. In theory, it uses relevance ranking and other artificial intelligence methods to parse your query down to its essence, conduct the search, and return with relevant goodies. But in reality, these search engines can come up with some oddball results to your questions, and you're sometimes better off resorting to those keywords. There are still only a smattering of search engines designed to support natural language queries, with Ask Jeeves at the forefront. Ask Jeeves' popularity certainly signals that, despite the shortcomings of natural language search systems, plenty of users will flock to it for its ease of use.

Evaluating Web Material

The World Wide Web has certainly changed the way we do research. Just ask any old-timer (a thirty-year-old will do) what it was like 15 years ago finding current, credible information to use in a research project. They'll describe a process that involved searching for misplaced library books and spending countless hours in front of a microfiche machine. The Web has delivered student researchers with desktop access to excellent information sources, but it's also delivered something they didn't bargain for: new responsibilities. Unlike traditional information tools—e.g., encyclopedias, reference books, periodicals—that go through a review and verification process before publication, Web sites can appear overnight, with little to indicate that anyone other than the author approved the site's content. Placing documents or pages on the Web is easy, cheap, and unregulated. That's why the responsibility of screening sites falls squarely on the shoulders of Web users. Whether you choose to use the contents of a site is up to you and only you.

You can expect the information you uncover on the Web to vary widely (and wildly) in its accuracy, reliability, and value. When a search engine provides you with results for your keyword search, it's not recommending the sites that are listed; it's merely telling you that they exist and seem to match your criteria. A typical search query will return a handful of excellent resource sites, but it will also cough up sites that contain biased reporting, inexact science, or rambling diatribes.

Books like this one are designed to point you to the good stuff, so that you can dodge the dogs of the Web. Another way to hone in on good research sites is to use a reliable online subject directory that utilizes experts and educators who evaluate and rate Web pages. *Argus Clearinghouse* (http://www.clearinghouse.net/), for instance, gives you a hand in judging the credibility of a site. Other good subject directories in the social sciences include *Librarians' Index to the Internet* (http://lii.org/), the *Scout Report* (http://scout.cs.wisc.edu/report/), Infomine (http://infomine.ucr.edu/Main.html), and *Academic Info* (http://www.academicinfo.net/).

Ultimately, though, you need to develop your own radar for sites that provide valid information. Ask yourself which sources are likely to be objective, lack hidden motives, and maintain quality control. With experience, you'll train yourself to identify dubious or unreliable sources easily. Again, a clear search strategy that lays the foundation for what you *want* to find is instrumental. Take a minute to ask yourself what you are looking for so that you can quickly weed out irrelevant Web sites. Do you want facts, opinions, statistics, and/or descriptions? Do you have a unique position you want to support, are you looking for new theories, or are you looking for the establishment's position?

The Web can be a great place to accomplish research on a multitude of topics in the social sciences. But it's your job to pick the *right* sites. In this section, we'll help you sharpen your Web-smarts, so that you can confidently examine and judge every site's authority, accuracy, and timeliness.

Authority

One of the first things to evaluate is the authority of a Web site. Reading the URL will tell you what type of domain the site comes from (educational, government, commercial, etc.). Analyze whether or not the source seems appropriate for the content. For instance, a commercial site might be less reliable for statistical information than a government site, and an educational site might provide more trustworthy comparative data on universities than a personal site. By looking at the home page, you should also be able to quickly discern the identity of the publisher, organization, or author behind the information presented. If a site allows its contributors to be anonymous, that should send up a red flag for you. Ideally, you will also find clear contact information, including an e-mail address, postal address, and a phone number.

In general, a well-established organization (i.e., a corporate, governmental, or nonprofit organization) is more likely to provide valid, accurate information than a Web site hosted by an individual. However, consider the organization's reputation, purpose, and overall perspective. If it is biased in a known way, its Web site will likely reflect that bias. Any bias needs to be taken into consideration when interpreting and using the information. For example, information about air pollution on the Web site of an environmental organization will present a different perspective than information from the Web site of a major automaker. Ask yourself who the intended audience for a site is and what the purpose of the site is. In other words, why was it created? Was it meant to inform, explain, persuade, promote, sell, or antagonize? If there are sponsors, do they have a vested interest in the viewpoint presented? Look for any links called "Sponsors," "About Us," "Philosophy," and the like to get a sense of the purpose behind the site.

URLs for sites that are hosted by individuals often contain a personal name, following a tilde (˜), or contain the word "users" or "people." Exercise caution in using personal sites for research: after all, would you implicitly trust the contents of a pamphlet somebody handed you on the street? While personal sites need to be scrutinized closely before using for research, you will find some gems amidst the scrap. The Web has given a voice to worthy enthusiasts in every discipline of the social sciences, many of them teachers and professors who've identified and tried to fill a research void on their subject. But you need to be wary. Ask yourself the same questions about possible bias as you would for an organizational site, along with the following: Is the person a specialist in the field? Does he or she have appropriate education, training, and/ or experience? What is his or her title or position of employment? Can you evaluate this person's reputation or standing among peers?

In addition to making your own judgments about a site, check out what others have to say about it. It carries a great deal of clout, for instance, if a respected professional association has awarded or cited the site. Have other esteemed organizations linked to the site? Has it received citations or awards from educational sites, directories, or guides?

Accuracy

If you feel comfortable about the authorship of the site, now it's time to evaluate the specific content more closely. Your gut instinct and critical thinking skills will carry you a long way. Look for an explanation of the site's quality control or peer review process. Has the information been screened or reviewed by experts in the field? Many online journals in the social sciences use qualified peer editors. What criteria must be met for information to appear at this site? Is it objective? Biased? What sort of reputation does that organization or person have for producing reliable, credible publications and/or data?

The sources of information should be identified clearly. In other words, *how* does the author or organization know this information and why should you believe it? Citing the sources strengthens the credibility of the information, particularly for statistics and claims of fact, which often come from third-party sources. A red flag should go up in her head when numbers or statistics are presented without an identified source or corroboration. Otherwise, someone may be fiddling with the numbers, or simply making them up to suit his or her argument.

If the tone or style of the writing is inappropriate, trust your suspicions. The writing should be in an objective tone that presents other points of view fairly. It shouldn't be argumentative or manipulative. Be wary of sweeping generalizations or vague assertions, particularly if they contradict the facts you have gathered from reputable sources. Since most good sites proofread their material carefully before it appears online, you should question the legitimacy of sites that contain misspelled words or poor grammar, as these errors might reflect a more hazardous carelessness with the facts.

Is the information provided complete, and does it present a balanced, reasoned argument? While no single information source can guarantee the whole story, some Web sites deliberately omit important details. In a perfect world, you would only use sites that present two sides of a controversial issue. However, that is not always possible. Just keep in mind that it's never wise to rely too heavily on any one source, and that holds doubly true for Web sources. If an idea is presented that is surprising or hard to believe, use caution and seek at least two, unrelated sources that corroborate that claim. If you cannot find any other sources confirming or acknowledging the information, you should refrain from using it or present it accordingly.

Timeliness

One of the chief advantages of using the Web is that you can find up-to-date information easily. The best Web sites for a research project are those that are maintained with regularity. Look to see when a Web site was last updated and consider whether or not the information provided is appropriately current. In some fields of research, information becomes outdated rapidly. Does the content seem passé on a time-sensitive or evolving topic? If you can't find a date indicating when the site was created and/or updated, keep shopping for a better source.

Finally, remember that Web pages, even at reputable sites, have a habit of shifting around. When you're using Web pages as source material, keep a print backup so that you can verify sources later if needed.

Plagiarism and Copyright Issues

What Is Plagiarism?

Plagiarism in the age of electronic media is still called plagiarism. It's trying to pass off someone else's ideas or words as your own. The purpose of any research writing you do is to show your own thinking and analysis of the materials you have gathered, not to cobble together a collection of borrowed ideas. When you properly integrate sources in your writing, you attribute ideas or words so that readers have no uncertainty about where the words or ideas came from and how they might find the source themselves.

Obviously, it's plagiarism when you buy research papers or copy someone else's work verbatim, but it's also verboten to borrow brief passages from books, articles, or Web sites without identifying them. Unfortunately, with the ease of information gathering on the Web, the ranks of accidental plagiarists have swelled. The temptation to cut and paste can make a cheater out of even a well-intentioned student, but don't let it happen to you. All schools and universities have clear, stringent rules about plagiarism and its consequences, which you should familiarize yourself with. The bottom line is that you must provide appropriate references for all the research you've done and all the ideas you've soaked up from other sources.

Facts that are considered common knowledge in your subject probably do not need to have sources identified. However, when you are presenting facts that are new, uncommon, or controversial, you need to attribute these to a credible source. If you're unsure about whether a fact requires attribution, play it safe and provide source information within the paragraph. Without proper citations, your writing might fall into one of the three most common forms of plagiarism: direct, patchwork, or paraphrase.

Direct plagiarism is the most blatant. Here, direct passages are taken from the original source and used in your work. It's not adequate for you to simply list the sources in the bibliography. If you choose to use the exact words of someone else, you must enclose them in quotation marks and give credit to the author. It's a good idea to use quotes only when the original words are truly interesting or add punch to your paper. Otherwise, try to summarize the idea, mentioning the original author's name and credentials.

In patchwork plagiarism, passages from the original text are not necessarily copied verbatim. Instead, the student intertwines paraphrased source material with his or her own observations, without giving credit to the original sources. This kind of plagiarism can largely be avoided by taking careful notes and making printouts of Web pages as you conduct your research so that you can keep track of which sources provided which specific ideas. When you take notes, try to summarize the text in your own words, putting quotation marks around anything you write down word-for-word.

Sometimes, after immersing yourself in a subject, ideas that you gleaned elsewhere begin to seem like your own. That's when the risk of paraphrase plagiarism arises. In this form of plagiarism, you absorb the concept presented by someone else and then rephrase it. It may be in your own words, but it doesn't represent your original thinking. Here, you need to simply acknowledge the source where your ideas came from. You can also avoid this form of plagiarism by not overly relying on one expert's ideas. The best research papers make extensive use of multiple—perhaps even contradictory—sources. Your research paper should truly reflect the critical thinking *you* put into sorting out the topic.

Formats for Electronic Source Citations

Okay, so the *reason* for citing your sources is pretty clear, right? You need to give credit to the original author, establish credibility for your own ideas, and provide a way for readers to find the source material themselves. Here comes the murky part: what should these citations look like?

There is no single standardized format for citations, but the Modern Language Association (MLA), American Psychological Association (APA), and the University of Chicago Press (e.g., Turabian) documentation styles are generally recognized as the big three. Ask your teachers or professors which style they prefer. However, each of these styles offers limited guidance on citing electronic sources such as Web pages, CD-ROMs, and online databases. To get detailed information on citing electronic sources, you'll need to turn to one of the style guides developed specifically for electronic sources. You'll find that the *elements* in a bibliographic reference for electronic sources are similar for all of the documentation styles, although the *order* in which they appear varies. These elements typically include the name of the author (if provided), the title of the document, the title of the site, the last revision of the document, the full URL, and the date of your visit to the site. For later reference, you should print out any Web pages that contain information you intend to incorporate into your paper.

The following are some of the best style guides for electronic sources:

Online! Citation Styles
http://www.bedfordstmartins.com/online/citex.html

This site offers excellent adaptations on the MLA, APA, and the Chicago/Turabian style.

Electronic Styles: A Handbook for Citing Electronic Information
http://www.uvm.edu/~ncrane/estyles/apa.html or
    http://www.uvm.edu/~ncrane/estyles/mla.html

This was one of the first style guides written to address the needs of the electronic age. Revised in 1996, it bases its recommendations on the essential principles of the MLA and APA style manuals.

Library of Congress: Citing Electronic Sources
http://lcweb2.loc.gov/ammem/ndlpedu/cite.html

The Library of Congress provides examples of citations using the MLA and the Chicago/Turabian styles for unique sources you might find in digital libraries, such as films, maps, recorded sounds, and special presentations as well as electronic text sources.

The Columbia Guide to Online Style
http://www.columbia.edu/cu/cup/cgos/idx_basic.html

This site offers comprehensive solutions for documenting your electronic sources in either the humanities style (MLA or Chicago/Turabian) or scientific (APA) style.

Copyright Law

Copyright law was established to give the author of a work (i.e., books, videos, songs, charts, graphs, words, etc.) the sole rights to copy, modify, distribute, perform, and display an original work for a certain time period. The World Wide Web, by making it so easy to find and use information, has also made it tempting to forget that much of that information is copyright protected.

Sometimes the symbol © appears on work protected by copyright, but often it doesn't. In the United States, a work becomes copyrighted by the author at the time it is created, so the symbol isn't necessary. Your general rule of thumb is this: If you didn't write it, design it, draw it, and so on, then you need to pay or get permission to copy or distribute the work. To request permission to use copyrighted material, you need to contact the copyright owner and describe specifically how the material will be used or copied. If you are given permission to use the material, you must still include a citation that says "Copyright used with permission from [the copyright holder]."

There are certain instances when it's okay to use material that you haven't obtained permission for. You can legitimately copy works in the public domain, which means works that are more than 75 years old and not subsequently updated. You can also use works that were first published before January 1, 1978, and do not have a copyright notice. It's also okay to use most U.S. government documents.

Some copyrighted works fall within the fair use category. The fair use privilege allows limited copying, without permission of the copyright holder, for purposes such as criticism, news reporting, parody, teaching, and research. Fair use is determined by a four-factor test:

1. Purpose and character of use (commercial or not)
2. Nature of the copyrighted work (factual or creative)
3. Amount and substantiality of copying
4. Effect of the use of the work (how will copying affect potential profits for the copyright owner?)

If you're looking for more information about copyright law, the University of Texas System offers an excellent and entertaining crash-course tutorial online at http://www.utsystem.edu/OGC/IntellectualProperty/cprtindx.htm. It covers fair use, how to figure out who owns what, multimedia creation, copyright management, licensing resources, and online presentations tailored to faculty, students, librarians, artists, and administrators.

GENERAL WEB RESOURCES FOR TEACHERS

American Memory: The Learning Page
http://memory.loc.gov/ammem/ndlpedu/lessons/index.html

The *American Memory* site, created by the Library of Congress, provides access to over five million historical items, such as unique and rare documents, photographs, films, and audio recordings.

The "Learning Page" section was created to help educators use the *American Memory* site to teach about United States history. Here, you'll find tips and tricks for using the collections, as well as frameworks, activities, and lessons that provide context for their use. The lesson plans, arranged by grade level, encompass topics such as child labor, transportation and the marketplace, and the Great Depression that would be pertinent for certain economics classes.

Be sure to click on "Educators" to read about a range of professional development programs for teachers, such as the yearlong American Memory Fellows Program, numerous hands-on workshops in Washington, D.C., do-it-yourself workshops online, and regional presentations.

AskERIC
http://ericir.syr.edu/

AskERIC is a personalized Web service providing education information to teachers, librarians, counselors, administrators, and parents. It's part of the vast Educational Resources Information Center (ERIC), a federally-funded national information system.

The centerpiece of this site is the Q&A, where you submit an education question. Within two business days, you'll receive a personal e-mail response from an ERIC information specialist, along with a list of ERIC database citations that deal with your topic and referrals to other Internet resources for additional information. The ERIC database, which is updated monthly, contains more than one million abstracts of documents and journal articles on education research and practice.

At the site, you can also tap into the "Resource Collection," which has over 3,000 resources on a variety of educational issues, including Web sites, educational organizations, and electronic discussion groups. You might also want to check out the site's "Lesson Plan Collection," with more than 1,100 unique lesson plans written and submitted by teachers from all over the United States.

Busy Teacher's Web Site
http://www.ceismc.gatech.edu/busyt/homepg.htm

This site, which has been praised by numerous education groups, provides teachers with direct source materials, lesson plans, and classroom activities, all with a minimum of site-to-site linking. You'll find "General Reference and Search Tools," "Education Programs," "Lesson Plans/Classroom Activities," and other specific resources to help you teach your students.

The Copernicus Education Gateway
http://www.edgate.com/

The *Copernicus Education Gateway* has good resources that are earmarked for educators, parents, and students, but the real highlight of the site (at least for teachers) is the "Curriculum Matrix," which presents each state's curriculum standards. These standards are linked to related lesson plans, assessments, and resources. A flexible array of search options allows you to hone in precisely on the topic, grade level, and tools that you need. You can even customize the databank of lesson plans, assessments, and resources to reflect local curriculum requirements.

Education World
http://www.education-world.com/

This site provides a place where educators can start each day to find lesson plans and research materials. *Education World*'s internal search engine is for educational Web sites only, which allows you to find trustworthy information without searching the entire World Wide Web.

At the site, you'll also find original content such as lesson plans created by *Education World* staff, articles written by education experts, employment listings for teachers, and information on how to make the best use of technology in the classroom.

The Gateway to Educational Materials
http://www.thegateway.org/

This is a must visit for busy teachers. Sponsored by the U.S. Department of Education, this site provides teachers, administrators, and parents with quick access to high-quality lesson plans, curriculum units, and other education resources on the Internet.

You can browse through lists organized by subject or keyword, or conduct a search by subject, keyword, title, or grade level. Under "Economics," for instance, you'll find 1,386 classroom resources, described in brief and rated for appropriate grade levels.

Lightspan
http://www.lightspan.com/

Lightspan serves as an education portal for educators, parents, and students, providing resources, research tools, and grade-specific activities. It has recently become a subscription-only service, so you'll have to register for a free, 30-day trial subscription if you're not already a subscriber. Use the "Learning Search" tool on the home page to find Web sites for learning and teaching a specific discipline.

The "Teachers Channel" points educators to the best online resources for their students' grade level and offers a one-stop resource for more than 1,500 online lesson plans. At the "Parents Channel," moms and dads will find a helpful "Homework Center" and a "Grade by Grade" assessment of what your kids should be learning, according to state and national standards.

The New York Times Learning Network
http://www.nytimes.com/learning/

This site will quickly become a favorite among teachers who want to enhance classroom learning with topical, real-world information. The *New York Times Learning Network*, which is updated five days a week, provides an outstanding service for students in grades 3 through 12 and their teachers and parents.

The "Teacher Connections" section provides daily lesson plans for grades 6 through 12. These comprehensive plans, written in partnership with the Bank Street College of Education in New York City, also provide reference articles that can be printed out for classroom use. You can find pertinent lessons by searching under a particular topic. Under the topic of "Math and Economics," for example, you'll discover an impressive collection of lesson plans, covering timely issues such as "And Now, A Word from Our Sponsor," a lesson in understanding the connection between sponsorships and special events; "Trading Off," which examines the multiple perspectives on the effects of NAFTA on Mexico and the United States; and "A Fallen Giant," about understanding and assessing the collapse of Enron.

Parents can expand their children's understanding of current happenings by tapping into the site's "Conversation Starters," reading the special news indexes on both current and historic events, or joining in an online discussion about education.

PBS Teacher Source
http://www.pbs.org/teachersource/

Don't worry anymore about your lesson plans matching your state's standards. This stellar site is searchable by keyword, subject, or grade and offers standards matching for each of its lesson plans. Its more than 2,500 lesson plans and activities are correlated to more than 230 sets of state and national curriculum standards. Just go to "Social Studies" and choose a grade level to begin your search. What makes this site truly wonderful is its knack for connecting current events, as current as yesterday's news, with its other offerings.

Kathy Schrock's Guide for Educators
http://school.discovery.com/schrockguide/

One of the best-known Web sites for educators, *Kathy Schrock's Guide* is self-described as a "categorized list of sites useful for enhancing curriculum and professional growth. It is updated often to include the best sites for teaching and learning." *Schrock's* covers the whole range of subjects.

In addition to the list of Web resources, the site provides sections for "Lesson Plans," "Teaching Tools," "Custom Classroom," "Conversations," and a "Teacher's Store." Other fun resources include "Brainbusters" and a "Clip Art Gallery."

The Library in the Sky
http://www.nwrel.org/sky/

Here's a database of 1,585 interesting and useful Web sites for educators. You can search by keyword, by user tab (teacher, student, parent, etc.), by materials needed, or by subject.

"Economics" is a subsection under "Social Studies." You might also be interested in "Civics," "Current Events," or "Countries," depending upon the topic you wish to research. Check out the "Editor's Pick" each week for a fun introduction to a new site.

Odyssey World Trek: Teachers' Zone
http://www.worldtrek.org/odyssey/teachers/index.html

This is a fabulous site for high school social science teachers. At the *Odyssey* Web site, your students can follow a team of educators in their two-year trek around the world, learning about diverse cultures, critical global issues, and ways that they can help create positive change in the world.

The experiences of the traveling team are documented online in video, audio, photos, and text, posted twice a week. Students can also interact with the team, the people they meet, and each other. As a teacher, you have online access to excellent teacher's guides and lesson plans for the countries and regions the team has visited, including Mexico, Belize, Guatemala, Central and South America, southern Africa, West Africa, and Egypt. These lessons can be used in conjunction with the Web site or independently when they tie in with your own curriculum.

Some lesson plans fit better with government and civics than others, but most explore a range of social issues that might effectively be tied to government questions facing your students. The lesson on "Youth and Society" in Mexico and Zimbabwe is a wonderful resource for exploring the rights and responsibilities of youth around the globe, as well as the important role youth play in social change. See the outline for this lesson at the Web site, as well as a handful of other lessons that might interest your class, such as "The Global Community," which is explored on a trek through India; "Social Change in Theory and Practice," which is explored in China and Mali; and "Community," a trek through Iran that explores the significance of community life to individuals.

You can also use the message board to interact with other teachers—ask questions, schedule live chats with other classes, learn about what other teachers are doing, and share your own suggestions.

RFE:Teaching Resources
http://www.aeaweb.org/RFE/Teaching/index.html

This guide is slightly more geared to the college-level instructor, but the section on guides for undergraduate students should still be quite useful for high school students and teachers as well. The links are divided into the following categories: classroom experiments, copyright issues, course packs, course support software, distance learning, guides for grad students, guide for undergraduate students, online markets, plagiarism, syllabi, and other resources.

Social Studies School Service
http://www.socialstudies.com/

This commercial site will entice you to research (and purchase) new teaching materials and texts and explore professional development programs, but its list of activities, broken down by discipline, is the best reason to visit. Go to the "On-line Activities" page and click on "Economics and Consumer Education." You'll be given 39 links to concise, curriculum-specific activities to teach your students about everything from international trade to entrepreneurship. A sampling of activity titles includes "Chester Town Tea Party," "Fixitup Faucet Company's Overseas Move," and "Land Use Competition."

Each activity includes an introduction, description of the activity, list of resources to use, directions, an explanation of how to evaluate student work, and the complete lesson plan from which the activity is drawn. Thorough and varied, this site is easy to use and fully searchable.

GENERAL HANDS-ON OPPORTUNITIES FOR TEACHERS

AFS Global Educators Program
http://www.socialstudies.org/profdev/profdev1.html#opportunities

If you want to go abroad with one of the oldest and most established international organizations, AFS (American Field Service) is for you. Open to teachers, librarians, and education administrators at any stage of their careers, these programs take you for one month or an entire semester to China, France, Argentina, Mexico, South Africa, or Spain.

AFS aims to provide educators with intercultural experiences that will affect the way they teach and learn throughout their careers. Your experience will combine classroom teaching with cultural immersion, allowing you to gain insight into a different way of life and educational system. There are also opportunities to meet with community leaders and local government officials to exchange ideas on education and culture.

If you'd like more information or an application, just contact AFS using the e-mail address or phone number provided at the bottom of the Web page.

Global Volunteers
http://www.globalvolunteers.org/

If you'd like your hands-on experience to involve doing some good for people in another part of the world, Global Volunteers can help you make it happen. They coordinate service-learning programs that offer educators the opportunity to participate in short-term human and economic development projects in more than 15 countries worldwide, including Mexico, Poland, Spain, Vietnam, Greece, Ecuador, Ireland, Ghana, Tanzania, Romania, and Italy. Projects typically involve building community facilities, painting and repairing homes, teaching conversational English, providing health care services, and assisting in environmental projects.

Green World Center Study Retreat
http://www.greenworldcenter.org/content.html

Here's a more contemplative, low-key opportunity for those of you who might want some time to work on writing a book or article or developing a new curriculum. A residential program in the Appalachian mountains of Quebec, the Study Retreat brings together students, teachers, scholars, writers, artists, and others who need to take some time for themselves and their work. The center is especially interested in environmental civics; human ecology; literature and philosophy; cinema; photography; multimedia; peace studies; animals and society; anthropology; nature writing; and environmental education.

Click on "Study Retreat" on the home page to read more about the center's resources and the faculty, which includes such folks as Jane Goodall, Noam Chomsky, and Francis Moore Lappe.

St. Johnsbury Advanced Placement Summer Institute for Secondary Teachers
http://www.stj.k12.vt.us/other/apinstitute.html

Does Vermont in July sound good to you? If you teach Advanced Placement classes, you just might want to consider the St. Johnsbury workshops. These workshops, which were founded 17 years ago, cover nearly every subject offered in Advanced Placement. Four sessions are offered through the month of July, and all of them cover test development and reading, new developments with AP curricula, developing AP assignments, and sharing problems and approaches in teaching.

See the Web site for more information. If interested, you'll need to e-mail the school for application details.

Working with Historical Documents at the National Archives
http://www.nara.gov/education/classrm.html

This summer workshop offers you the opportunity to gather primary-source material from the nation's premier storehouse of history. During the National Archives' one-week "Primarily Teaching" program, teachers research a topic of their choice, create classroom materials from historical records, and discuss how to present primary documents to students. Teachers have their pick of the complete Archives collection. In the summer of 2002, the dates for the workshop were June 24 through July 3. Graduate credit is available from the University of Virginia for an additional fee.

Travel 2 Learn Rainforest Workshops for Educators and Naturalists
http://www.travel2learn.com/

Want a little adventure in the guise of continuing education? These workshops held in places like Belize and the Amazon give you the chance to work side by side with a spirited and engaging faculty in some of the most biologically diverse areas of the world. The faculty includes specialists in ornithology, botany, marine biology, archaeology, and entomology. Participants gain experience using hand lenses, binoculars, headlamps, maps, field guides, water testing equipment, and other simple field equipment. You may also be able to earn graduate credit or qualify for scholarship help. The program is open to anyone with an interest in the rainforest and a desire to explore.

Just scroll down the page to read comments from workshop alumni on every aspect of the workshops. Quotes are organized under the following categories: workshop leaders, resources, inspiration, adventure, and group dynamics. Links on the menu will take you to information about grants, slides from previous workshops, and detailed biographies of the faculty members.

GENERAL WEB RESOURCES FOR PARENTS

Parents can use the Web to play a greater role in their children's education. The mother of a student who is studying labor unions can go on the Web to read and download a relevant news article, come up with weekend activities linked to the subject, or locate an article that will help bring her up to date on the topic. Some of the Web resources available to parents go beyond mere homework helpers; a handful of sites offer conversation starters for parents who want to reconnect with their kids, using curricula as a springboard. Parents are also using the Web to stay current on national and state education standards for subjects their children are studying.

Parent Council: Social Studies Resources
http://www.parentcouncil.com/TPS_SocS.htm

The motto for the Parent Council—"Because Children Learn from Everything They See, Hear, Read, and Do"—captures the spirit of this organization. This site is a great resource for parents who want to positively infuse their child's education with good extracurricular reading material.

The site contains parent/teacher reviews of outstanding books, CD-ROMs, and other resources. These resources are sorted into social studies topic categories. Pick a category and then read all the book reviews that fall under that general subject. Each book review includes the appropriate age range, a brief description, and information on purchasing the item.

Publications for Parents
http://www.ed.gov/pubs/parents/

This straightforward site offers you quick access to the vast majority of Department of Education publications that were designed specifically for parents. Publications are sorted into the following subjects: "College/Early Preparation," "College/Financial Aid," "Early Childhood Education," "Educational Excellence," "Educational Resources," "Family Involvement in Education," "The *Helping Your Child* Publication Series," "Internet Guide," "Learning Activities," and "Reading Improvement."

Each of these sections contains links to excellent publications that can help parents participate in and direct their children's education. For instance, in "Learning Activities," you'll find four age- and grade-appropriate brochures offering new ideas for developing math, reading, and science skills. In "Educational Resources," you can access the Educational Resources Information Center's (ERIC) online "Parent Brochures," which offer concise research-based answers to parents' frequently asked questions.

ParentSoup: Education Central
http://www.parentsoup.com/edcentral/

This engaging site is a fun visit for parents with children of all ages. It offers an interesting potpourri of expert articles, quizzes, and, of course, ParentSoup's well-respected chat rooms and message boards.

Choose the specific grade level of interest to you (preschool through 12th grade) and click "go." We chose tenth grade and were offered information on developmental milestones, tools to help kids prepare for junior year, curriculum suggestions, college planning ideas, and links to relevant chat rooms and message boards. From the home page, you can also choose to explore special topics, such as homeschooling, parent-teacher relations, fun learning, and standardized testing.

The Parents' Guide to the Information Superhighway
http://www.childrenspartnership.org/bbar/pbpg.html

This site provides rules and tools for families online from the Children's Partnership. It gives a comprehensive look at the information superhighway and what parents should know to help their children use it safely and wisely.

Parents' Guide to the Internet
http://www.ed.gov/pubs/parents/internet/

From the U.S. Department of Education, this guide suggests how parents can help their children tap into the wonders of the Internet while safeguarding them from its potential hazards.

GENERAL SUMMER PROGRAMS FOR STUDENTS

AFS
http://www.afs.org/

AFS, formerly the American Field Service, offers student exchange programs in more than 50 countries around the world. For students 16 to 18, programs involve attending school in a community abroad for a semester or a year, while living with a host family. There are some programs that allow students to spend their vacation from school studying the language and living with a host family in another country. Young adults 18 and over work in community service organizations or businesses in countries abroad while learning new skills, the language, and the culture.

At the Web site, click on "Go Abroad with AFS" to learn more about programs and host countries. You can also listen to an audio recording of former AFS participants talking about their experiences abroad or read "Postcard from France," the account of one AFS participant's year in France. If these don't get you excited to travel, nothing will.

AIPT: Association for International Practical Training
http://www.aipt.org/

AIPT promotes international understanding through cross-cultural, on-the-job, practical training exchanges for students and professionals in more than 50 countries around the world. Most full-time internships last for 8 to 12 weeks during the summer, but longer stays are available. AIPT programs include the International Association for the Exchange of Students for Technical Experience (IAESTE) to assist students majoring in technical subjects, the Student Exchanges program (mostly hospitality/tourism) to assist students in nontechnical majors, and the Career Development program for professionals and recent graduates in nearly any career field.

At the Web site, click on "Programs and Services" to explore the multitude of options available for students and other participants.

Center for Global Education at Augsburg College
http://www.augsburg.edu/global/studyabd.html

This center offers semester-long programs for college students who want to integrate solid academic work in their field with hands-on experience in the community. The programs emphasize encountering the culture both inside and outside the classroom.

Regional travel, family stays, and community involvement, in addition to your studies, are the hallmark of these special programs. Travel to Mexico, Central America, or southern Africa. Check the Web site for complete details on the programs and qualifications, as well as application materials.

National Institutes of Health (NIH) Summer Internship Opportunities Program
http://www.jobs.nih.gov/welcomeletter.htm

This program includes internship opportunities in the administrative, management, clerical, and information technology (IT) career fields. Many employees at the NIH work in scientific occupations. However, it also takes support staff working in the administrative, management, clerical, and IT occupations to carry out the NIH research mission effectively. Sample occupations included in this year's internship program were computer specialists, social science analysts, program analysts, and office automation assistants/clerks. This program provides students with valuable work experience and the opportunity to support the NIH and the advancement of biomedical research. Students in high school, college, and graduate school are invited to apply.

StudyAbroad.com
http://www.studyabroad.com/

If you're looking for a study abroad program that matches your specific educational needs, *StudyAbroad*'s search engine will prove to be a huge timesaver. Those of you who have a certain country in mind can simply use the "country portals" to find student programs, travel information, maps, and more. You can also easily search by subject area, using a pull-down menu to select from such choices as international relations, political science, cultural/regional studies, and more.

In addition to full academic year and semester programs, you can find information here about summer programs abroad, internship and volunteer opportunities, high school programs, and intersession programs.

Yahoo! Directory of Summer Programs
http://dir.yahoo.com/Education/Programs/Summer_Programs/

So many opportunities exist to study political science and international relations abroad in an academic setting. If this is the type of summer program you're looking for, check out the long list of programs at the *Yahoo! Directory of Summer Programs*. We've included a few such programs in our list, but this directory of programs may have what you're searching for if our list doesn't have it.

Young Writers' Workshop
http://www.people.virginia.edu/~eds-yww/about.html

If your love of history is accompanied by a strong desire to write, you may find that combining the two will lead you down an interesting path. This summer workshop for high school students in the foothills of the Blue Ridge Mountains of Virginia brings together a community of writers with a common purpose: to create a supportive and noncompetitive environment where teenagers can live and work as artists.

The Young Writers' Workshop strives to create a broad yet focused atmosphere that allows young writers to concentrate in a specific genre for daily intensive workshops, yet also experience other genres through elective and evening activities. These genres include songwriting, creative nonfiction, fiction, poetry, and playwriting.

Check out the Web site to read examples of student work from past workshops, to apply online for next summer's workshop, or to find a short but good list of links geared toward young writers.

GENERAL CAREER SITES

America's Career Infonet
http://www.acinet.org/acinet/library.htm

"Dream it. Find it. Get it" is the motto of this career service that's geared to help you along the path as you try to figure out what you want to do. If you're looking for ideas, give this site a try. It can connect you to resources that will help answer all your career-related questions. Just type in a keyword, and let the search begin.

Sections of the site include "Job and Resume Banks," "Job Search Aids," "Occupational Information," "Relocation Information," and "State Resources."

Career Services
http://www.rci.rutgers.edu/~cswebpg/

This Rutgers University site is geared toward helping its students, but you don't need to be attending Rutgers to take advantage of its stellar offerings. The site will help you choose a major, plan your career, find an internship or job, and make successful transitions from school to work.

MyFuture.com
http://www.myfuture.com/beyond.html

Here's a great resource if you're a high school student interested in exploring all the various possibilities, other than college, that exist just for you after graduation. This Web site is geared toward helping you learn about finding a job, doing volunteer work, joining the military, getting an internship, going to a vocational or technical school, or completing an apprenticeship program.

Each section of the site provides hands-on, practical advice for securing the type of opportunity you want, whether it's a paid position or a training program of some sort. You won't find information on specific jobs or schools, but you will find useful definitions and step-by-step guidelines for pursuing each of these types of post–high school experiences. So if you're not sure you want to attend a traditional four-year college or university, and you need to get a handle on all the other options out there, this is a great place to begin.

Peace Corps Master's Program
http://www.peacecorps.gov/volunteer/masters/index.html

Trying to decide between graduate school and the Peace Corps? The Peace Corps has come up with a way so you don't have to choose.

Thanks to partnerships with more than 40 campuses across the United States, the Peace Corps Master's International (MI) program allows you to incorporate Peace Corps service into a master's degree program.

Students apply to both the Peace Corps and the participating graduate school, and must be accepted by both. You would typically complete one year of graduate studies before starting a Peace Corps assignment. Your Peace Corps assignment then serves as the foundation for a thesis or other culminating project.

Introduction

Social Science Resources in the Electronic Age: World History was designed as a one-stop resource for cutting through the chaos of the Internet to find authoritative, age-appropriate information. The book is divided into five chapters. The first chapter, "Resources in World History," provides you with a treasure map to quality information on the Web, which will save you hours of your own research time. Here, we point you to the Web's top-notch general world history sites and also provide a list of relevant CD-ROMs, subscription databases, and other resources.

In Chapter 2, "Researching Individual World History Topics on the Internet," we searched for and found the crème de la crème of Web sites that provide specific information on key topics in world history. These topics were chosen based on a review of national curriculum standards and screened by an expert in the field of world history.

For each topic, you'll find an entry that lists and reviews four or five Web sites, giving you all of the goodies you need to know: the name, URL, appropriate grade range, and a thorough discussion of how to use the site for research. When you log on to the Web to find a tidbit about the Franco-Prussian War, you'll now have four or five handpicked sites, as opposed to the thousands that might turn up with a keyword search. In case you choose to conduct your own online search for a key topic, we have revealed which search engine and keywords provided the best hits.

The following chapter, "Materials and Resources for World History Teachers," reviews a number of excellent Web sites that offer world history–related materials and resources for teachers, such as free maps, government document reprints, lesson plans, and downloadable world history software.

"Museums and Summer Programs for World History Students" surveys Web sites offering unique online museum exhibits, interpretive centers, summer programs, mentoring programs, student chapters, and other interactive opportunities for students of world history, and the final chapter of the book, "Careers," turns its attention to Web sites that provide students with career information in the field of world history. Here, we've reviewed sites with specific career information, as well as sites for professional associations, academic groups, conferences, workshops, programs, clubs, and other outlets for students interested in working in the area of world history.

HOW TO USE THIS BOOK

There are two ways you can find information in *Social Science Resources in the Electronic Age: World History*. First you can look at the detailed table of contents. If you are researching a particular topic in world history, you can immediately go to the alphabetical listing of topics in Chapter 2. You can also use the index, which expands our coverage significantly. Because we had to limit the number of topics in Chapter 2, we added as much detail as possible to our site reviews. These include names of people and countries, events, and other topics covered in the Web site but not included in our topic list. All of these have been indexed. For example, the partition of India is not in the topic list, but if you look in the index, you will find that it is discussed in a site on boundary and boundary conflicts and in a site on the caste system. Therefore, if you don't find what you want in the topic list, go to the index. Also, don't forget to refer to "The Basics" section in this volume for general information.

1

⊶∞∞

Resources in World History

FORMATS OF RESOURCES

Library Electronic Services

Portals

See "The Basics" section in Volume 1 of this set for general information and sites.

Specialized Databases

A number of topic-specific databases are popular among world history students and researchers. The following represents just a handful of those you might find at your library. Check with the library staff about which databases would be useful for your project.

DISCovering World History. Provides comprehensive coverage of over 60 historical eras from prehistory to present day. Includes over 18 hundred encyclopedia-length essays on political, cultural, and historical events and over 17 hundred extensive biographies of key historical figures. Contains over one hundred full-text primary documents.

Historical Abstracts. Contains over five hundred thousand full-text articles from over two thousand historical journals. Provides annotated references to information on topics ranging from the Renaissance to Tiananmen Square (1450 to the present). Does not include material on the United States or Canada.

World History on File. Perfect for middle- and high-school students. Includes hundreds of maps, timelines, charts, drawings, and articles on different topics of world history. Organized chronologically and covers diverse cultures.

ITER. Bibliography of 230,000 full-text journal articles from five hundred scholarly journals on topics related to the Middle Ages and the Renaissance. Also contains bibliography of over 44 thousand records from books about the Middle Ages and Renaissance. Easy to navigate, but not intended for younger students.

CD-ROMs

Several reference librarians have noted that subject-specific CD-ROMs are gradually being phased out in favor of Web-based content. Nevertheless, there are many CD-ROMs that will help you in your world history research. Use *Ancient Greece* to learn about the political, intellectual, and social history of the ancient world. *Notable Women in History* offers detailed biographical information about individual women from different historical periods and geographical areas who impacted their culture. Unlike print reference tools, CD-ROMs can combine material from different media for a unique interactive experience. *Renaissance of Florence,* for example, synthesizes photographs, animation, video, sound, and text to create a multimedia presentation that will take you back in time. You can listen to Renaissance music, embark on a virtual tour of an art museum, and explore interactive maps of Renaissance Florence.

E-mail

If you have a specific question and need an expert to answer it, check out a great site maintained by the Center for Improved Engineering and Science Education (CIESE) (http://njnie.dl.stevens-tech.edu/askanexpert.html), with hundreds of links to ask-an-expert sites, including the following.

Ask-a-Holocaust Survivor (http://www.wiesenthal.com/surviv.htm) provides a unique opportunity for students to pose questions and thoughts directly to Holocaust survivors.

Another Web site that can locate experts for you is http://www.allexperts.com/. Follow the links from "Higher Learning" to "History." You can then pick the area of world history you want to explore. You'll find "Asian/Middle Eastern History," "Central/South American History," "European History," and "General History" sections. Click on one of these headings to choose from among several scholars with different areas of expertise.

Mailing Lists

Here are a few examples of world history–related mailing lists:

H-NET List for World History

> To subscribe, send mail to LISTSERV@H-NETMSU.EDU with the command: SUBSCRIBE H-WORLD

ANCIEN-L

> History of the ancient Mediterranean world

> To subscribe, send mail to LISTSERV@LISTSERVLOUISVILLE.EDU with the command: SUBSCRIBE ANCIEN-L

FRENCH-L

> Covers French history from the early Middle Ages to the twentieth century

> To subscribe, send mail to LISTSERV@WEBBEROUP.CO.Uk with the command: SUBSCRIBE FRENCH-L

H-AFRICA

> H-Net List for African history and culture

> To subscribe, send mail to LISTSERV@H-NETMSU.EDU with the command: H-AFRICA

To find other mailing lists of interest, check these Web sites:

CataList: The Official Catalog of Listserv Lists: http://wwwlsoft.com/lists/listref.html

Liszt: The Mailing List Directory: http://www.liszt.com/

Topica: The Email You Want: http://wwwtopica.com/

Usenet Newsgroups

Some newsgroups of interest to world historians include the following:

soc.history.ancient Discussion about the ancient world, especially ancient Greece

alt.history General discussion about history topics

soc.history.medieval Discussion about topics related to medieval history

soc.history.war.world-war-ii Discussion about topics related to the history of World War II

To find and subscribe to newsgroups that interest you, check out these two Web sites:

Deja News: http://wwwdeja.com/usenet/

CyberFiber Newsgroups: http://wwwcyberfiber.com/index.html

E-Journals

A couple e-journals of interest to world history researchers include the following:

Electronic Antiquity. Communicating the Classics (http://scholar.lib.vt.edu/ejournals/ElAnt/) provides papers, articles, and book reviews focusing on the culture, history, and society of the ancient world.

Historicom (http://wwwgeocities.com/historicom/) publishes articles on any aspect of world, national, or local history. The material is written by history laypeople and academics.

Digital Libraries

Some digitized collections that provide images and texts of interest to world history students and teachers include the following:

National Archives of Ireland: http://wwwnationalarchives.ie/

Eighteenth-Century Studies: http://eserverorg/18th/

Early Manuscripts at Oxford University: http://imageox.ac.uk/

Paging through Medieval Lives: http://www2art.utah.edu/Paging_Through/index.html

Reference Books

You will find a great deal of both background information and specific topical material in general dictionaries and encyclopedias. These include the *Dictionary of World Biography, Chronology of World History, Historical Dictionary of the Holocaust, Oxford Encyclopedia of World History, Dictionary of the Middle Ages, Cambridge History of Latin America, Cambridge History of Africa, History of Russia,* and the *Hutchinson Illustrated Encyclopedia of British History.*

If you're looking for biographical information on important historians, three are particularly helpful: *The Blackwell Dictionary of Historians, Great Historians from Antiquity to 1800,* and *Great Historians of the Modern Age: An International Directory of Historians.*

TYPES OF WORLD WIDE WEB RESOURCES

Reference Sites

InfoPlease
http://www.infoplease.com/

InfoPlease is the online spin-off of a company that's produced almanac publications and reference databases for more than 60 years. This colorful site lets you tap into a massive collection of almanacs, encyclopedias, and dictionaries to find almost every imaginable topic—chock-full of millions of informative factoids. For instance, by using the site's nifty "Year-by-Year Chronology," you can quickly discover key events that happened in each year, such as the Boxer Rebellion in China that occurred in 1900.

Click on the subject area "History & Government" and then on "World History" and you'll find subject headings that include "Ancient History," "1–999 A.D. World History," "1000–1999 A.D. World History," and "Millennium Milestones." Within "100–999 A.D. World History," you can find brief overviews of century-long periods within this millennium. There's also a section on the "Twentieth Century in Detail." Important people, events, and terms are in hypertext. All you need to do is click to learn more.

You can also search for keywords within *InfoPlease*'s almanac database and come up with an impressive amount of information—more than some general search engines provide. For example, the keywords "Winston Churchill" will turn up several relevant hits in *InfoPlease*'s dictionaries and encyclopedias, including brief articles on British history, World War II, and political events of the times of this influential British prime minister. If you know the kind of information you need, you can use a pull-down menu to restrict your search to *InfoPlease*'s dictionary, biographies, or encyclopedia.

StudyWeb: History and Social Sciences
http://www.studyweb.com/History__Social_Studies/tocUSstud.htm

This site is a great general resource. It covers a lot of the same ground as *America's Story*, but at a somewhat higher level and with some more detail. *StudyWeb: History and Social Sciences* is arranged according to general topics, and also allows you to access some primary documents. Click on the headings that interest you in the index, and you can read a brief essay on that subject. Better still, the site refers you to related Web sites on each topic. Each recommended Web site is reviewed and described, so you can easily determine whether it will be helpful to your research.

Commercial Sites

Britannia
http://www.britannia.com/history/

If you're focusing on British history, you won't want to miss this site, which boasts that it provides "the Internet's most comprehensive treatment of Britain's history from the prehistoric era to modern times." Whether or not it's in fact the most comprehensive, this site is truly a terrific resource. Its history section is divided into six major areas: "Monarchs," "King Arthur," "Church History," "Timelines," "Biographies," and "Documents." Simply select one of these topics from the menu at the top of the home page screen.

For a look at Britain's royal leadership, go to the "Monarchs" section, where you'll find biographies of all of Britain's kings and queens from Egbert (802) to current sovereign Elizabeth II. Each biography gives the high (and low) points of the ruler's career along with a detailed genealogy. The section also has lists of legendary kings and historical lists of the rulers from different areas of Britain. Go to the "Biographies" section for material on nonroyalty. There are dozens of brief biographies on people who made significant contributions to Britain. You can either search by category ("Prime Ministers," "Archbishops of Canterbury," "Great Scotsmen," or "Saints") or browse the "A–Z Index."

Those of you researching King Arthur will love the King Arthur section, which contains articles on whether Arthur actually lived, overviews of the Arthurian legend in literature, an Arthurian timeline, historical maps, biographies of key Arthurian figures, and much more. The section on church history has some excellent articles on the history of Christianity in Britain (including one on the structure of the English church), as well as biographies of dozens of bishops and abbots. Don't overlook the "Timelines" and "Documents" sections either. The site contains several detailed timelines of various periods of British history, such as Anglo-Saxon England and the age of empire, that contain a lot of information. What's great about these chronologies is that they not only identify important events in British history, but they also explain the events and their significance. And the "Documents" section is vast. In it, you'll find full-text versions of everything from "The Confession of St. Patrick" to Winston Churchill's "Sinews of Peace" speech.

As you enjoy the benefits of the Britannia site, don't forget that it is a commercial site. The ads are fairly easy to ignore, but one annoying feature is the pop-up that appears from time to time exhorting you to join Britannia (which books tours to Britain). The site is good enough to make it worthwhile to deal with these drawbacks, though.

Footnotes to History
http://www.buckyogi.addr.com/footnotes/index.htm

For everything you never studied in geography, try this site, which provides overviews of little-known states, countries, and governments, from Maryland in Africa to the Republic of West Florida to the Centro-

Caspian dictatorship. It also presents the "Atlas of Forgotten Nations," so that you can see just where they are in the world.

The History Channel
http://www.thehistorychannel.com/

This Web site, which is a companion to the cable television channel of the same name, is comprehensive and easy to use. This is a great site to visit whether you have a specific question about a topic or just want to trigger ideas for research.

One of the site's most useful features is its search capacity. Click on "Search Any Topic in History" on the home page, and you can access a ton of information. If you already have a topic, simply type it in. For example, if you're researching the fascist Italian dictator Benito Mussolini, a search for his name will bring up several articles about him that you can click on to read. One gives biographical data, while another provides a more general look at World War II. From here, you can opt to "Continue Your Search." One possibility, a search for "Related People on Biography.com," will take you to articles about other Italian prime ministers and Adolf Hitler. You can also peruse "Related Historical Places" or "Related Web Sites."

If you don't have a narrowly defined topic yet, you'll enjoy the "Search by Timeline" feature on the home page. After choosing a period from the pull-down menu that interests you, say 900–999, the Web site compiles a detailed list of key events for each year. For instance, you'll learn that Arabs introduced modern arithmetic notation to Europeans in the year 975. Want to learn more? No problem! Just click on the links to read brief essays on the Arabic people, Europeans, and numerals.

Another fascinating aspect of this Web site is its "What Happened Today" section, a terrific resource for both students and teachers. Instead of just giving you one key event, *The History Channel* allows you to read about "This Day in Automotive History," "This Day in Civil War History," "This Day in Cold War History," "This Day in Crime History," "This Day in Literary History," "This Day in Old West History," "This Day in Technology History," "This Day in Vietnam War History," "This Day in Wall Street History," and "This Day in World War II History."

Because this is a commercial site, you'll have plenty of opportunities to buy videos and books that relate to *The History Channel* features. If you're not in the market for these kinds of materials, just ignore the sales pitch.

History House
http://fromusalive.com/history/

If you have a speedy Internet connection and a good computer, you should check out the latest from the USAlive.com Internet TV network. *History House* is a show designed to give a current perspective on historical events. The show is on-demand, which means that all episodes are accessible to the audience at any time. To view a list of episodes, just click on the button at the top left of the home page.

Topics are from both American and world history and tend to focus on such things as social movements, war, industrial periods, architecture, philosophy, art, historical fiction, and the history of women. Past guests have included Harry Readshaw, from the Pennsylvania House of Representatives; Professor Perry Blatz, chairman of the History Department at Duquesne University; Kathy Ayers, author of historical novels for children; and University of Akron Law Professor Jane Moriarty, an expert on the Salem witch trials.

Regardless of the topic, the show explores the causes that drove historical events and takes an in-depth look into the backgrounds of the people who made history. David Cook, the host of *History House*, is a history professor who earned his master's degree at Boston College. Cook specializes in modern European intellectual history and hopes the show will spark interest in what others often perceive as boring. "Everything around you has a history, and my goal is to explain it in an interesting way," he says. "I want to get beyond the stereotype that it's just names and dates. History can help inform viewers in lots of ways. It's a road map that can help chart their course."

The History Net
http://www.historynet.com/

The History Net lives up to its motto: "Where History Lives on the Web." This site, which is operated by Primedia History Group (the publisher of several history-related periodicals), offers you access to over 760 articles. Use this site to trawl for research ideas or to look for specific information.

If you're in the market for a paper topic, you can start with *The History Net*'s current articles, listed on the home page under "This Week's Features." These essays cover a range of topics—not all of them about world history—but you'll find some interesting reading in any event. If you're looking for specific information by contrast, try searching the site's extensive archives. Just click on "Site Search" in the toolbar at the top of the home page. Although *The History Net* is not as comprehensive as a pure reference site like the *Encyclopaedia Britannica*, you'll still find plenty of information. For instance, searching for the keywords "Alexander the Great" brings up a list of useful articles, including several book reviews and essays on this ancient monarch, the history of his reign, and military history.

You can also browse the archives by topic. Click on the area that interests you from the toolbar on the left-hand side of the home page. Those that probably will be most relevant to you are "World History," "Personality Profiles," "Great Battles," "World War II," "Interviews," "Arms, Armies and Intrigues," "Eye Witness Accounts," and "Aviation & Technology." Click on "Additional Articles" at the bottom of each of these subject headings to find a complete list of all *The History Net*'s articles about that topic. For instance, the "World History" archives contain interesting essays on such things as the 1456 Siege of Belgrade, Buckingham Palace, the Great Fire of London, and Joan of Arc.

The site has other useful features as well, which can be accessed by clicking on the appropriate heading in the toolbar at the left-hand side of the home page. "THN Recommends" provides links to other Web sites. "Talk about History" is an interactive forum where you can enter into a discussion with—or pose questions to—other students and the editors of the site. The "THN Picture Gallery" has (as the name suggests) an archive of photographs of events and people.

The History Net is trying to sell you the magazines from which it culls its material. It's easy to avoid the ads, though, and the site is a good resource.

World History Archives
http://www.hartford-hwp.com/archives/

For secondary sources to bolster your research, try this huge collection of documents organized to support the study and teaching of world history and history in general. What we like most about this site is its library-like organization. There are five geographic sections—"The World," "Asia and Oceania," "The Americas," "Africa," and "Europe." Under each of these are numerous links, also geographically organized. Once you arrive at a list of documents on the history of, let's say, Belize, you might be given choices like "documents on political history of Belize," "documents on social history of Belize," and "documents on working-class history of Belize." Choose one, and you're in. The four documents that popped up when we clicked on "working-class history," were from a major Belize newspaper and an online magazine.

World History: HyperHistory Online
http://www.hyperhistory.com/online_n2/History_n2/a.html

Try this site if you're looking for a visual representation of fairly main-stream history. It's comprehensive but not especially in-depth. "People,"

"History," "Events," and "Maps" are the main buttons that let you access 3,000 years of world history with a combination of colorful graphics, lifelines, timelines, and maps. If you go to the "People" index, for example, you'll be asked to select a broad time period and then a colorful timeline will appear, illustrating the famous people who lived during those years with links to each person and to supporting resources, such as maps. Click on a person's name and you're give a brief biography.

Eighteenth Century History: The Age of Reason and Change
http://www.history1700s.com/

You'll find a myriad of subjects at this Web site that is probably the most informative guide to sites covering the eighteenth century. You'll find an encyclopedia of the century, historical overviews, special reports, numerous articles, and an extensive list of subjects that include such topics as "French Revolution," "Succession Wars," "Military History," "Science," "Biographies," "Law and Order," "Documents," and much more.

Although it does include some subdued advertising, called sponsors here, the site is visually pleasing, if a little haphazard in layout. You'll find it relatively easy to navigate. If your topic is an eighteenth-century one, this should definitely be one of your starting points for research on the Web.

Government Sites

African Voices
http://www.mnh.si.edu/africanvoices/

African Voices is the online version of a permanent exhibition at the Smithsonian Institution's National Museum of Natural History. This terrific Web site helps bring African history to life. If your research needs to go beyond European topics, you'll really appreciate this site's breadth. Don't expect a virtual version of dusty halls and dull exhibits, though! This site provides an inside look at the vibrant history and culture of Africa.

You'll be able to navigate this site with ease. Just use the toolbar on the home page. The best place to begin your online voyage is in the history section, where you'll find an interactive timeline that charts the history of Africa from the first humans to the present day. You pick the period of time that interests you: "Humans Arise," "Nile Valley," "Mali," "Africans in Spain," "Slave Trade," "Central African Trade," "Ethiopia," "Colonialism," "South Africa," and "Today." Each of these timelines allows you to examine artifacts from the actual Smithsonian exhibit. For example, in the "Slave Trade" section, you can look at a pair of shackles that were used to imprison Africans as they were captured and sold into slavery.

For a different view of African culture, visit the "Themes" section of the site. Here, many items from the exhibit are used to illuminate different topics about Africa's history and present: "Wealth in Africa," "Market Crossroads," "Working in Africa," "Living in Africa," "Kongo Crossroads," and "Global Africa." In the site's "Focus Gallery," you can take a closer look at the life and work of Lamidi Fakeye, a fifth-generation Nigerian woodcarver. As you browse this virtual retrospective, you'll learn about this individual and his craft, and you'll also get a sense of what it's like to be an African. "The Learning Center" provides a bibliography of print sources as well as a number of Web links for those of you in search of more information on African history.

Ancient Egypt
http://www.ancientegypt.co.uk/

This Web site, which was created by the British Museum, is one of the best Internet resources about ancient Egyptian history and culture. It presents an incredible amount of information in a fun, interactive, and truly educational way.

Ancient Egypt is organized into 10 thematic sections: "Egyptian Life," "Geography," "Gods and Goddesses," "Mummification," "Pharaohs," "Pyramids," "Temples," "Time," "Trades," and "Writing." You can access all of them from the home page. Unlike a lot of other Internet sites, this one really tries to use the capabilities that the Internet provides. So don't expect to sit back and passively soak up facts on this site! Instead you'll play an active role in learning about ancient Egypt. There are games and interactive stories where you get to choose where the character goes. You'll even be able to translate Egyptian hieroglyphics.

Each of the main sections has three parts: "Story," "Explore," and "Challenge." In the story areas, you'll find a narrative about each topic. For instance, the story in "Egyptian Life" relates a day in the life of two ancient Egyptians, one a wealthy nobleman, the other a subsistence farmer. In "Gods and Goddesses," the story takes you through the ancient Egyptian creation mythology and pantheon. In the "Mummification" story, you'll learn about the ancient Egyptian practice of embalming and wrapping corpses. Each of these story narratives is accompanied by items from the British Museum's collections. So you can look at artifacts that correspond to each story, such as a wooden box that an Egyptian nobleman used to store his money and an actual mummy!

After you've read the story in each section, you'll want to check out the "Explore" and "Challenge" parts. The "Explore" parts allow you to hone in on an area of the main topic. In "Geography," for instance, you can view various maps; in "Mummification," you can click on a sample coffin, a mummy, and other objects to learn more about them. The challenges are the most fun part of the Web site. There you get to test the knowledge you've acquired in the "Story" and "Explore" areas. For instance, in the "Geography" challenge, you play the part of an ancient Egyptian jeweler's assistant who has to read maps in order to travel to various places in Egypt and locate different items. In the "Mummification" challenge, you have to use spells from the Book of the Dead to navigate the next world. In the "Time" challenge, you are asked to put artifacts in their chronological order.

If you're in the market for easy to access historical information, go to the "Time" section. Once you're there, click on "Explore" and you'll find several interactive and detailed timelines. The ones on ancient Egyptian history and the history of the pyramids are particularly useful.

Creating French Culture: Treasures of the Bibliothèque Nationale de France
http://lcweb.loc.gov/exhibits/bnf/

The Library of Congress is renowned for its fantastic Web site *American Memory*, which makes available thousands of American history primary source documents to Internet surfers like you. It should thus come as no surprise that your friends at the Library of Congress have created another masterpiece about French history and culture. The Library of Congress teamed up with the Bibliothèque Nationale de France to build this excellent Web site charting the history of French politics and culture from the time of Emperor Charlemagne (eighth century) to Charles de Gaulle (twentieth century). Many of the items on display at this site have never been viewed outside France before!

Creating French Culture is divided into seven major sections that combine historical essays with over two hundred unique artifacts from the Bibliothèque Nationale de France. The items presented truly make the topic come alive. You can view a hymnal from the eleventh century, check out Victor Hugo's handwritten draft of *Les Misérables,* or look at a three-dimensional model used in the production of Verdi's opera, *Aida.* There are also dozens of paintings and photographs. You can either read through the entire site or simply pick the sections that appeal to you: "Introduction," "Monarchs and Monasteries," "Path to Royal Absolutism," "Rise and Fall of the Absolute Monarchy," "From Empire to Democracy," and "Conclusion." *Creating French Culture* is incredibly easy to navigate. Just use the menu on the home page to skip among sections if you want.

The Library of Congress: Country Studies
http://lcweb2.loc.gov/frd/cs/

This link takes you directly to the home page for the *Country Studies* published by the Federal Research Division of the Library of Congress. Most resources at the library pertain to American history, but the *Country Studies* handbooks present a description and analysis of the historical setting and the social, economic, political, and national security systems and institutions of countries throughout the world. They also examine the interrelationships of those systems and the ways they are shaped by cultural factors. Roughly 101 countries and regions are covered. Notable omissions include Canada, France, the United Kingdom, as well as other Western and African nations. The date of information for each country appears on the title page of each country and at the end of each section of text.

Tour: The Early Renaissance in Florence
http://www.nga.gov/collection/gallery/gg4/gg4-main1.html

Sometimes the best way to learn about a culture is to examine the works of art it produced. This is especially true when studying the Renaissance—that period of Western history when art, science, architecture, and philosophy underwent radical changes whose effects are still with us today. This National Gallery of Art Web site allows you to take an online tour of some of the artistic masterpieces of the Italian Renaissance. Even better, you can access a short (but thorough) history of the Renaissance and read detailed explanations of each painting.

Select "Overview" from the home page to read about the Renaissance as a whole. From within the essay you can click on the names of artists in hypertext to learn about them, their work, and the impact they had on other artists. Return to the home page when you're ready to enter the world of Renaissance art itself. If you want to view the entire exhibit, simply click on "Start Tour," and you'll be taken through a series of paintings. Each work is accompanied by a lengthy discussion of the piece. Reading these, you'll not only learn about the painting, along with the techniques and themes presented in it, but you'll also gain an understanding of the impact that each painting had on later artists and the broader culture. For those of you in a hurry, you can skip the virtual tour and view only the paintings that interest you.

Although *Tour: The Early Renaissance in Florence* focuses on only a small aspect of world history, the Web site will be invaluable to those of you researching the Renaissance. It might also be useful to students studying other topics in European history, since the Renaissance (and its art) had such a profound impact on Western thought and culture. Despite its apparent focus on one subject, this site actually provides an insightful view of world history.

Academic and Educational Sites

EuroDocs: Primary Historical Documents from Western Europe
http://www.lib.byu.edu/~rdh/eurodocs/index.html

This Web site is a gold mine for students researching European history. It contains hundreds of translated and full-text versions of documents that impacted Western and world history. It does not contain interpretive material that will help you make sense of the documents, though, so you'll need to use this site in conjunction with other resources that give you the background to put the documents you'll find here into context. Nevertheless, this Web site—which was created by a Brigham Young University professor—is one of a kind. It makes available a vast array of documents on a number of different topics. Its only downside is that it does not have an internal search engine, so you'll need to scan through the different sections to find the material you're looking for.

EuroDocs is divided into different categories. There's a collection of documents from "Medieval and Renaissance Europe," as well as one that deals with "Europe as a Supernational Region." Each European country has its own section, too, so you can scan through the site's holdings from, say, Denmark or France.

Be prepared to spend some time navigating this site. Once you've entered a collection, you won't just find individual documents, since some of the entries are for subcollections. For instance, when you are browsing the "Medieval and Renaissance Europe" section, you'll see that one entry is for "Historical Documents of the Franciscan Archive," which itself contains dozens of documents—spanning from 1221 to 1992.

The collection on "Europe as a Supernational Region" presents material that deals with Europe as a whole—not just an individual nation. Here you'll find an assortment of documents such as the 802 Capitulary of Charlemagne, World War I soldiers' memoirs, World War II treaties, material on the Marshall Plan, and recent documents that pertain to the European Union. If you want a document about a specific country, skip "Europe as a Supernational Region," and go to that country's own document collection instead. For instance, if you want to read the Irish

Constitution, simply select "Ireland" on the home page, and scan through its documents to find the constitution.

China Page
http://www.chinapage.org/china.html

All you students of Chinese history will love this vast Web site that examines Chinese history and culture from many different angles. *China Page*—which contains over 13 hundred individual Web pages—is the brainchild of one man, emeritus professor Dr. M. L. Pei. This gem of a site allows you to view detailed chronologies of ancient Chinese history, learn about Zen Buddhism, listen to famous poems being read in Chinese, read full-text versions of Chinese novels (translated into English), and much more. The site's only omission is that it does not deal with the history of Communist China.

Unless you want to read the site in Chinese characters, select "China Room" from the home page to access an easy-to-read English index. Once you're in the "China Room," simply scroll down the screen and select the headings that interest you. Do you want to learn about the Chinese language? Piece of cake. Just look in the section on "Calligraphy," where you'll find an essay on the history of Chinese calligraphy, samples from the masters of the art, and a piece on how to appreciate it. Maybe you're more of a literary bent. Once again, this site has you covered. In the "Poetry" section, you can read English translations of famous Chinese poems. To experience the poem more fully, go to "Poetry Reading" in the "Poetry" section. Click on any poem, and you can hear it being read in Chinese. Or, scroll down to the "Novels" section, where you'll be able to read classic Chinese novels in English (or if you're in a hurry, just a short translation). Go to the "History/Culture" section to read the *Ballad of Mulan*. (No, it wasn't originally a Disney movie!)

What if you want some hard facts for a history paper? Don't sweat it. Check out the site's "History/Culture" section, which contains several different chronologies of Chinese history as well as timelines of the dynasties. There are tons of maps in this section, as well as links to other Internet resources on the Opium Wars and the Silk Road. For a taste of Chinese philosophy, go to the "Philosophy/Religion" section, where you can read about Buddhism. You'll also find translations of the Zen Koans and some frequently asked questions about Zen.

For those with some time to spare, visit the "Tattoos" section, where you can learn why so many National Basketball Association players have gotten Chinese characters tattooed on their arms, as well as the history of tattoos in Chinese culture. The Web site also contains numerous links to related Internet resources. Go to the "General" section, and select "Links to Other Sites" to continue your research.

Histoire de France
http://instruct1.cit.cornell.edu/Courses/french_history/

If it's information about French history you're after, be sure to visit this Cornell University site. *Histoire de France* doesn't provide its own historical information; it's a clearinghouse for material about French history—it refers you to other Web sites on specific topics of French history. *Histoire de France* is well organized and trustworthy, since all the recommended sites have been carefully selected and reviewed. Simply scroll down the page and pick the links you want.

To start out, it helps to narrow down your topic a bit. The site is organized into several main sections: "Generalities," "Middle Ages," "Renaissance," "17th Century," "18th Century," "Revolution," "First Empire," "1814–1914," "1914–," and "Cinema." Within each of these headings, you'll find links to dozens of wonderful Web sites. What's doubly fantastic is that *Histoire de France* covers French history from a number of different angles. The sites it recommends are quite diverse— some contain primary documents, others are biographical, still others present broad histories of a period. For instance, in the "Revolution" section, you'll find links to a site that contains digitized versions of Revolutionary pamphlets as well as a more straightforward biographical site on Marie Antoinette and her role in the Revolution. In the section, "1814–1914," there's a link to a site on French Romanticism and another that examines the Paris Commune in the broader context of the history of anarchism. One word of caution is in order: while the majority of these linked sites are in English, some are in French.

Horus Web Links to History Resources (H-GIG)
http://horus.ucr.edu/horuslinks.html

H-GIG stands for "Horus gets in gear," which is pertinent to understanding the scope of this great history index. Its creation is at the core of an experiment by the history faculty at the University of California, Riverside, in using the Internet for research and instruction. Part of this experiment involves the submission of Internet resources to *Horus* from people and institutions all over the world. You'll find a great diversity of resources here—academic and nonacademic alike—all organized in a tried-and-true academic format. That's why *Horus* has won so many awards. Just take a peek on the home page to see the list.

Search the more than one thousand sites linked to *Horus* in one of two ways—using the alphabetical index, which allows you to browse by category (see the menu on the left-hand side of the screen), or using the search function.

Internet Resources in History
http://www2.tntech.edu/history/resources.html

This is an index site from the Department of History at the University of Tennessee with sections for the following subject areas: social science, social welfare, political science, government, international studies, history sites by subject, history sites by time period, and more. Although the links are not annotated, they are well organized and up to date, so you won't waste time chasing sites that have changed their focus or no longer exist.

Perseus Project
http://www.perseus.tufts.edu/

This rich site, produced by members of the Tufts University Classics Department, provides visitors with a wealth of information about the classical Western world. The site includes an atlas, encyclopedia, introductory essays to ancient Greek and Roman life, English-to-Greek and English-to-Latin dictionaries, classical texts, and images of art and archeology.

The table of contents for this evolving digital library includes "Classics," "Papyri," "English Renaissance," "London," "California," "Upper Midwest," "Chesapeake," "Tufts History," "Boyle Paper (History of Science)," and more. Just click on the subject that interests you in the left-hand column of the home page and let the explorations begin.

Resources for the Study of World Civilizations
http://www.wsu.edu/~wldciv/

This wonderful Washington State University site contains lots of great information for studying world civilizations. You'll find interactive learning modules, online courses, a two-volume reader that covers ancient Mesopotamia through the southern European Renaissance in the first volume and the northern European Renaissance to the present in the second. There are also resources for teachers and course syllabi for the online courses.

Rulers
http://rulers.org/

Rulers lists past and present heads of state of all countries and territories going back to 1700. Birth and death dates are provided, as well as the dates in which the person was in office.

Interactive/Practical Sites

Middle Ages
http://www.learner.org/exhibits/middleages/

Here's a nifty Web site that allows you to experience what it was like to live in the Middle Ages. The site aims to counter the myth that the medieval era was about knights in shining armor and beautiful ladies. Instead it lets you learn about what everyday life was like in the period.

Once you've entered the site, choose the area that interests you: "Feudal Life," "Religion," "Homes," "Clothing," "Health," "Arts and Entertainment," or "Town Life." Each of these sections is loaded with fun facts and asks quiz questions, such as "What kind of hat would you wear in the Middle Ages?" and "Which of these four cathedrals collapsed before it was completed?" Once you submit your answers, you'll find out whether you were correct. The site is a little long on information, but it does a good job of presenting its material.

Egypt Fun Guide
http://www.seaworld.org/Egypt/egypt.html

This Web site, designed by Sea World/Busch Gardens, is the perfect place for younger students to test their knowledge about ancient Egyptian civilization. *Egypt Fun Guide* has several great exercises that incorporate ancient Egyptian history. Select "Hieroglyphics" from the home page to learn about the Egyptian alphabet. Once you're finished, you'll be able to write your name on your own Rosetta stone. "Crossword Clues" contains a crossword puzzle whose clues deal with facts about ancient Egyptian geography, history, and culture. Click on "Answers" at the bottom of the screen when you're ready to check your work.

For those of you who want to play some Egyptian-themed games without being quizzed, check out the "Mummy Maze," in which you have to navigate yourself through a mummy's wrappings to find a precious amulet hidden inside. Likewise, "Mumminals" is a word game, and "Archaeologist's Challenge" makes you the archaeologist and asks you to solve some problems (most of which rely more on math than history to answer). Again, select "Answers" at the bottom of each screen to get your results.

The site also has some strictly educational material. Go to "Vocabulary" to brush up on the key terms of ancient Egyptian history. "A Nation of Irrigation," "Pyramid Power," and "Secrets of the Nile" provide information about these topics as well.

Ye Olde Renaissance Map
http://library.thinkquest.org/3588/Renaissance/GeneralFiles/Map.html

Although this Web site might seem a bit drab at first, it's actually a great way to learn about Renaissance culture in a painless way. It's fairly interactive and engaging, as well as easy to use.

The home page looks like a hand drawn map. It contains several drawings of important Renaissance buildings that include the Cathedral of Santa Maria del Fiore, the University of Padua, the Globe Theater, the Tower of London, ViRen Castle, the Sistine Chapel, and the Hospital of the Innocents. There's also a town and a courthouse. Click on any of these locations, and you'll be taken on a guided tour by a special host. Click on "Globe Theater," for instance, and you'll meet Richard Burbage, a friend of William Shakespeare, who proposes a number of topics to talk about, including the history of the Globe Theater, the Bard himself, and the Black Plague. He also introduces you to Mouse Allyn (who tells you about the Plague), and Anne Shakespeare, who shares her letters with you. Or stop by the Hospital of the Innocents to meet Father Frederick, one of the hospital's caretakers. He'll offer to take you on a tour of the surgical ward. You can also meet several practitioners of Renaissance medicine to learn about possible cures for a medical condition. Each location will offer you a unique perspective on an aspect of Renaissance history.

Nazi Germany: 1933–1945
http://www.rjtarr.freeserve.co.uk/Miscellaneous/hotpots/gcse/hitler/hitler1.
  htm

Visit this no-frills Web site for one reason only—to test your knowledge about Nazi Germany. The site consists of a two-part multiple-choice quiz that explains correct answers at the top of the screen after you've selected them. It also keeps a running score for you. The quiz is fairly detailed, and is definitely not for younger students. But it does provide a thorough overview of one of the most important periods in Western (and world) history.

Biographies

See "The Basics" section in Volume 1 of this set for information and sites.

Map Collections

Historical Atlas of the Twentieth Century
http://users.erols.com/mwhite28/20centry.htm

If you want a good general atlas of the twentieth century, turn to this site. It has hundreds of maps, charts, and graphs dealing with historical topics worldwide. To find the sites, click on "Links" under "Broad Outline" at the left of the home page. Then scroll down to find what you're looking for. Just about everything is covered.

Historical Map Web Sites
http://www.lib.utexas.edu/maps/map_sites/hist_sites.html#general

The Perry-Casteñada Library Map Collection at the University of Texas at Austin is the most extensive online map collection on the Internet. From the home page, just choose a part of the world to search the site's collection or browse the extensive list of links to other historical map sites. This is no small feat. There are hundreds of map sites, but chances are very good that you'll find what you're looking for without ever venturing beyond the borders of this site.

United States Military Academy (West Point)—Department of History Map Library
http://www.dean.usma.edu/history/dhistorymaps/MapsHome.htm

This site contains nearly 1,000 maps that were created over many years for a course entitled History of Military Art. Some of the maps you'll find here are Ancient Warfare; Dawn of Modern Warfare; Colonial Wars; Napoleonic Wars; War of 1812; Mexican War; Spanish-American War; Chinese Civil War; World War I; World War II—European Theater; World War II—Asia Theater; Korean War; Arab-Israeli Wars; Vietnam War; Wars and Conflicts since 1958.

Be forewarned that the files for these maps are quite large and thus slow to load. If you want to do some research here, use the fastest machine you can find, and leave yourself plenty of time.

Primary Sources

The Islamic Texts and Resources Metapage
http://wings.buffalo.edu/student-life/sa/muslim/isl/isl.html

Located at the University of Buffalo, this site includes a section of introductory texts, followed by sections dedicated to scriptures and prophetic traditions, Islamic thought, and Islamic language and art resources. It is, in its own words, "an attempt to provide a 'springboard' for exploring texts and resources on Islam and Islamic thought, ideas, and related issues."

The Introductory section may be especially useful if you're looking to get acquainted with the ideas and practices of Islam. These texts are written for those with little exposure to Islam, so they cover the basics very well.

Among the other resources found here is a FAQ section, which covers questions on women, marriage laws, and human rights, among other topics.

Avalon Project at the Yale Law School
http://www.yale.edu/lawweb/avalon/avalon.htm

The site features documents from around the world in law, history, economics, politics, diplomacy, and government from ancient times to the twenty-first century. You can access the material by time period, keyword, or collection. If you don't know the formal name of the document you want, try browsing under "Major Document Collections." This will give you a good idea of what's available on the site. You can also browse by time period.

Internet History Sourcebooks
http://www.fordham.edu/halsall/

Paul Halsall of Fordham University has collected primary source material and secondary texts in a number of different subject areas, each of which is called a sourcebook. These sourcebooks include some of the largest collections of subject-specific online textual sources, and they are presented in an easy-to-follow chronological outline for educational use. There's no advertising or fancy graphics to get in your way, just a rich array of primary source material, with annotated links so that you can efficiently pick and choose your resources.

His sourcebooks include the Internet Ancient History Sourcebook, Internet Medieval Sourcebook, Internet Modern History Sourcebook, and nine subsidiary sourcebooks in the following subject areas: African, East Asian, Indian, Global, Jewish, Islamic, Lesbian/Gay, Science, and Women.

Historical Text Archive
http://historicaltextarchive.com/links.php

Don Mabry's Historical Text Archive boasts 5,090 links to texts on a wide range of subjects. You'll find the usual sections (Africa, Asia, Latin America, Mexico, Islamic History, etc.) as well as the unusual—History of Mathematics, Internet History, Psychohistory, New Zealand, and Rock 'n' Roll. There's also a good section on maps.

Just follow the table of contents on the home page and choose the subject that interests you. Not all of the links provided are to sites with primary source material, but many primary sources, as well as some excellent secondary material can be located here.

Center for World Indigenous Studies
http://www.cwis.org/

This site aims, in its own words, "to present the online community with the greatest possible access to Fourth World documents and resources." The Fourth World Documentation Project is an online library of texts that record and preserve the struggles of Fourth World people to regain their rightful place in the international community. These texts include Tribal and Inter-Tribal Resolutions and Papers; African Documents; UN Documents; Treaties; and documents from each region throughout the world.

The site is searchable from the home page and available in French, Spanish, Portuguese, Dutch, Italian, and Norwegian, as well as English.

EuroDocs: Primary Historical Documents from Western Europe
http://www.lib.byu.edu/~rdh/eurodocs/index.html

This Web site is a gold mine for students researching European history. It contains hundreds of translated and full-text versions of documents that impacted Western and World History. It does not contain interpretive material that will help you make sense of the documents, though, so you'll need to use this site in conjunction with other resources that give you the background to put the documents you'll find here into context. Nevertheless, this Web site—which was created by a Brigham Young University professor—is one-of-a-kind. It makes available a vast array of documents on a number of different topics. Its only downsize is that it does not have an internal search engine, so you'll need to scan through the different sections to find the material you're looking for.

EuroDocs is divided into different categories. There's a collection of documents from Medieval and Renaissance Europe, as well as one that deals with Europe as a Supernational Region. Each European country has its own section, too, so you can scan through the site's holdings from, say, Denmark or France.

Be prepared to spend some time navigating this site. Once you've entered a collection, you won't just find individual documents, since some of the entries are for subcollections. For instance, when you are browsing the Medieval and Renaissance Europe section, you'll see that one entry is for Historical Documents of the Franciscan Archive, which itself contains dozens of documents spanning from 1221 to 1992.

The collection on Europe as a Supernational Region presents material that deals with Europe as a whole—not just an individual nation. Here you'll find an assortment of documents such as the 802 Capitulary of Charlemagne, World War I soldiers' memoirs, World War II treaties, material on the Marshall Plan, and recent documents that pertain to the European Union. If you want a document about a specific country, skip Europe as a Supernational Region, and go to that country's own document collection instead. For instance, if you wanted to read the Irish Constitution, simply select Ireland on the home page, and scan through its documents to find the constitution.

Hanover Texts and Documents Project
http://history.hanover.edu/texts.htm

While the Hanover Texts and Documents Archive is no longer as extensive as it once was, it remains a very well organized collection of electronic resources for historians of all levels. The scope of the Archive originally included texts from every major civilization from ancient times to the present, but the faculty and students working on the project were unable to keep the hundreds of pages updated and checked for accuracy. As of July 15, 2000, the project was reduced to a small number of pages: the Italian Renaissance, Protestant Reformation, Catholic Reformation, Witch Hunts in Europe, and for Asia, two pages . . . one on China and one on Japan.

If any of these subjects fall into your research domain, and you're searching for primary sources, check out the Hanover Archive. You'll find it a snap to search and navigate this site, and because it's not as huge as EuroDocs and its topics are more focused, you'll probably find it easier to use.

Slave Movement during the Eighteenth and Nineteenth Centuries
http://dpls.dacc.wisc.edu/slavedata/index.html

This site from the Data and Program Library Service at the University of Wisconsin provides access to the raw data and documentation that contains information on the following slave trade topics from the eighteenth and nineteenth centuries: records of slave ship movement between Africa and the Americas; slave ships of eighteenth-century France; slave trade to Rio de Janeiro; Virginia slave trade in the eighteenth century; English slave trade (House of Lords Survey); Angola slave trade in the eighteenth century; internal slave trade to Rio de Janeiro; slave trade to Havana, Cuba; Nantes slave trade in the eighteenth century; and slave trade to Jamaica.

A handy-dandy link at the top of the page takes you to a section called "What the Slave Movement Site Can and Cannot Do for You." There's also helpful instruction on how to cite the resources found at this site and links to other related Web sites.

Ahlul Bayt Digital Islamic Library Project
http://www.al-islam.org/organizations/dilp/

The Digital Islamic Library Project is an effort to digitize important Islamic resources and make them available to the masses through the Internet. Its ultimate goal is the creation of an Islamic Study Database. You'll find an extensive section of full-length texts and journal articles, as well as a section of links to multimedia sites, including such things as "Translations Corner," where you'll find information on planned translations of Islamic texts, and "Online Islamic Courses," in case you're looking to sign up for a class.

Speeches
http://www.historychannel.com/speeches/index.html

Here's a great place to hear some of the most important broadcasts and recordings in twentieth-century history. Although there is a definite emphasis on American history, you can hear plenty of international folks here, too. There is Yasir Arafat signing the historic peace accord with Yitzhak Rabin; Neville Chamberlain, the British Prime Minister, signing the Munich Pact with Adolf Hitler; and King Edward VIII speaking about his decision to abdicate the throne in order to marry American divorcee Wallis Simpson.

From the home page you can access speeches through the search function at the left or by browsing the categories: Politics and Government; Sciences and Technology; Arts, Entertainment, and Culture; and War and Diplomacy. Don't try to access material through "Speech Archives." You'll get a message asking you to use the search function.

READY TO RESEARCH

Evaluating Web Material

For excellent subject guides specific to the field of world history, check out the following:

Historical Documents on the Internet
http://www.cssjournal.com/hisdoc.htm

Magellan Education: Arts and Humanities: History
http://magellan.excite.com/education/arts_and_humanities/history/

Horus's Web Links to History Resources
http://www.ucr.edu/h-gig/horuslinks/

HyperHistory
http://www.hyperhistory.com/

World Wide Web Virtual Library: History
http://history.cc.ukans.edu/history/VL/index.html

Format for Electronic Source Citations for History Papers

This site is especially for history papers. See "The Basics" section in Volume 1 of this set for general sites.

Citing Electronic Information in History Papers
http://www.people.memphis.edu/~mcrouse/elcite.html

This site focuses specifically on citation in academic history papers. It includes recommendations for an electronic source citation style that is derived from the traditional Chicago (Turabian) style.

2

❧

Researching Individual World History Topics on the Internet

Researching a specific topic on the Internet can be overwhelming. Type a topic such as "Atomic Age" into a search engine, and you'll pull up hundreds—if not thousands—of Web pages, some of which are only remotely connected to your subject.

This section of the book is designed to help you over this major hurdle to online research. In it, you'll find a list of roughly 60 broad topics in world history, such as the "Holy Roman Empire," the "Spanish Civil War," and "Capitalism." For each of these topics, you'll see several key terms listed that will make searching the Internet a little easier. For instance, under the "Spanish Civil War," you'll learn that it might be helpful to search by keywords like "anarchy," "fascism," and "international brigade." The best search engine to use will also be listed.

Below these recommendations on how to search, you'll see the names and descriptions of several Web sites that best cover the topic. Some of the Web sites give basic overviews, some are multimedia extravaganzas, and some make primary source material available to you. Because each main topic is so broad, some of these Web sites will only look at a particular facet of the topic. Use these tried-and-true sites as a jumping-off point, and then follow the links until your heart's content . . . and your paper topic has come into crystal-clear focus.

ABASSID AND ALMORAVID EMPIRES

Best Search Engine:	http://www.google.com/
Key Search Terms:	Abassid empire + history
	Almoravid empire + history
	Islamic history + Abassid
	African history + Almoravid

The Abassid Dynasty
http://www.wsu.edu/~dee/ISLAM/ABASSID.HTM
middle school and up

This Web site is one of the best you'll find if you're trying to review the basic history of the Abassid Empire. Although *The Abassid Dynasty* contains the kinds of features that make Internet resources special—interactive maps, galleries of illustrations, and links for more information—it does lay out the history of the period with precise detail. This site, which is part of Washington State University's *World Civilizations*, is an excellent place to begin your research on the Abassid dynasty.

The page on the Abassids is constructed like a long essay. To get the information you need, simply scroll down the screen. The piece provides a thorough review of the Abassid. You'll find sections on the background of the empire and its rise to power, the Abassids' conflict with the Umayyads, the key Abassid rulers and their innovations, the intellectual climate of the empire, and its ultimate decline.

The essay on the Abassids is part of *World Civilizations'* unit on Islam. So, if you are trying to place the events of the Abassid empire into the broader context of Islamic history, you might want to check out the pages in the rest of the section on Islam. To do so, scroll to the bottom of the page on the Abassids and select "World Civilizations," which will take you to the site's home page. Then click on "Contents" from the browse menu on the left-hand side of the screen. Select "Tradition and Memory: World Civilizations to 1500" and then scroll down the page to "Unit 11: Islam." Select the "On-line Text" heading from Unit 11 and then click on "Contents" from the browse menu. You'll find the index of the essays in the sections on Islam: "Islam"; "Pre-Islamic Arabic Culture"; "Muhammad"; "The Qur'an"; "The Caliphate"; "Civil War and the Umayyad Dynasty"; "Shi'a"; and "The Abassid Dynasty" Below this index, you'll find other resources, including an essay on the Arabic language, a glossary of Islamic terms and concepts, and a section on Internet resources on Islam.

Virtual Baghdad
http://www.nv.cc.va.us/home/nvbrada/braddog/Index.htm
middle school and up

If you explored *The Abassid Dynasty* to get a sense of the history of this Islamic era, you'll want to check out *Virtual Baghdad* to learn about the culture of the Abassid Empire. This site, created at Northern Virginia Community College, provides a view into the literature of the Abassid empire. Eventually, this site will have sections on the art, history, music, philosophy, theology, and literature that emerged from Baghdad during the Abassid Caliphate. Unfortunately, only the section on literature is up and running. Nevertheless, it's well worth a visit to this site to learn about the poetry and prose of this era.

To access the information, select "Literature" from the "Topics" menu on the home page. The "Literature" section has two parts—one on poetry, the other on prose. You can either scroll down the screen to find both parts, or use the menu at the top of the "Literature" screen to select "Poetry" or "Prose." There's an informative essay about literature in the Abassid empire that discusses major authors and their impact on Arabic literature. Within the essay you'll see links to follow if you want more information on a topic. The material on poetry genres is especially helpful. You'll also find links to the major Abassid poets (Abu Nuwas, Ibn al-Mu'tazz, al-Mutanabbi, and al-Ma'arri). Click on each to read biographical information as well as a cogent discussion of the author's work. There's similar information about the post-Abassid poets.

Another great feature of *Virtual Baghdad* is its extensive section on Internet resources. From the site's home page, select "Links" from the "Resources" menu. You'll find dozens of links to recommended Web sites. Better yet, each site is reviewed so that you won't waste time exploring sites that aren't related to your research needs.

Don't expect to use *Virtual Baghdad* by itself to learn about the Abassid empire. The site's strength is that it illuminates one aspect of the empire's history and makes it come alive. Be sure to use other material for your more factual historical research.

Almoravids and Almohads Itinerary
http://www.legadoandalusi.es/itinerarios/eng/historia.htm
middle school and up

There's a dearth of good sites covering the history of the Almoravid empire. Most of the material on the Almoravids is a snippet in a site dealing with the broader history of North Africa. Although *Almoravids and Almohads Itinerary* has some drawbacks, it does provide an overview of this historical period. It contains a detailed chronology of the empire, a list of Almoravid and Almohad rulers, maps of the empires, and material about the culture of the period.

Perhaps the site's most useful feature is its chronology. To view this, simply scroll down the home page. The Almoravid chronology is first, followed by the time line of Almohad dynasty. After each empire's chronology, you'll see a link to follow for a list of rulers. The links to the maps of each empire are also on the home page. Click on the ones that interest you for a full view. Don't overlook the section on "Hispano-Moorish Art." Click on the link at the top right-hand corner of the home page. It charts the impact of the Amoravid and Almohad empires on art and architecture, especially on the development of a unique architectural style. On the other hand, do feel free to skip "Circuits of the Almoravid and Almohad Itinerary," which will connect you to a Spanish-language site that recommends travel itineraries in Spain and North Africa.

A-BOMB AND HIROSHIMA

Best Search Engine: http://www.google.com/
Key Search Terms: Hiroshima + history
                         Hiroshima + atomic bomb
                         World War II + history + atomic bomb

A-Bomb WWW Museum
http://www.csi.ad.jp/ABOMB/index.html
high school and up

Type in "Hiroshima" or "atomic bomb" into a search engine, and you'll be confronted with a list of hundreds of sites that deal with the topic. The problem is that many of these sites are either narrowly focused or are blatantly political (trying to either condemn or justify the United States' decision to use the atomic bomb against Japan). Luckily, there are some excellent Internet resources that don't fall into this trap. *A-Bomb WWW Museum* is a great place to start your research on the topic. The site is comprehensive and thorough. It focuses less on the political decision to drop the bomb and more on the implications of that decision. The site weaves together firsthand accounts of the bombings, photographs, and contemporary responses to the event to provide a unique historical perspective on the bombings. It manages to convey the horrors of the bombing of Hiroshima and Nagasaki without bogging down in debates about whether or not the weapon should have been used.

The site is easy to navigate. Scroll down the home page to the heading "Welcome to the A-Bomb WWW Museum" under which you'll find a short but detailed description of the bombing of Hiroshima and Nagasaki. Keep scrolling to reach the table of contents. Select the links in this index that apply to your research. The "Introduction" is useful if you want statistics about the effects of the atomic bomb on Hiroshima and Nagasaki, ranging from the precise amount of heat emitted from each weapon to the number of deaths. To view the reality behind these numbers, check out "From the Exhibit at the Peace Memorial Museum," "Things That Tell the Story," and "Record of the A-Bomb Disaster." Each of these sections contains photographs from the bombings. These images record the physical damage that occurred: melted glass bottles, thermal radiation burns on children, and a bent steel building frame, among others. Because these sections are graphic, they are *not* appropriate for younger children.

If you want to learn what it was like to live through the terror of the bombings, read "Voices of A-Bomb Survivors," "A Child's Experience," and "Children of Hiroshima," each of which provides firsthand accounts of the events. For a sense of Hiroshima's and Nagasaki's legacy, check out "Hiroshima Today" and "The Second Generation," which deal with the reality of growing up in Japan after the bombings. Those of you with literary inclinations will like the short fiction about Hiroshima. Simply select "Short Story" from the table of contents. If you want to gauge the response of others who visited this site, check out "Contributions from Readers." There's even a link to a virtual tour of Hiroshima's Peace Park from the table of contents. Don't overlook the last entry in the index, "The Atomic Bombing of Nagasaki." This section describes the bombing of Nagasaki and also contains photographs.

The Decision to Drop the Atomic Bomb
http://www.whistlestop.org/study_collections/bomb/large/bomb.htm
high school and up

While *A-Bomb WWW Museum* does a great job of conveying the effects of atomic weapons on Hiroshima and Nagasaki, *The Decision to Drop the Atomic Bomb* approaches the topic of the bombings from an entirely different perspective. As part of Project WhistleStop's *Harry Truman Digital Archive*, the site concentrates on President Truman's decision to use the atomic bomb against Japan. *The Decision to Drop the Atomic Bomb* uses primary documents to explain how the events of World War II culminated in the bombing of Hiroshima and Nagasaki.

The site is divided into two main sections, "During the War" and "After the War," which you'll find on the home page. Under each section are folders of primary documents that deal with Truman's momentous decision. The major downside to this site is that it doesn't give you much background material to understand the documents. The major exception to this shortcoming is the online book *Truman and the Bomb, a Documentary History* that you'll find in "During the War." This terrific resource explains the history of the atomic bomb in an easy-to-follow chapter format. Each chapter gives you the background to understand the documents it includes. You'll be able to browse a dizzying array of documents, such as several reports sent to Truman from his generals about the war in the Pacific; Einstein's famous letter to Roosevelt urging the president not to use atomic weapons; the report issued by the Truman administration on the effects of the atomic bomb on Hiroshima and Nagasaki; excerpts from Truman's diary; and the letter from the Hiroshima city council president to Truman after the bombing of Hiroshima. Another helpful section is the "Chronology" folder, which contains time lines of the events leading up to the bombing.

The rest of the site has some excellent material, as well, although it's not annotated for your benefit. Be sure not to overlook the folder that contains the minutes of the meeting held at the White House on June 18, 1945 (*Evaluation of Current Situation Regarding the War in the Pacific against Japan*), when Truman's administration weighed the pros and cons of using the ultimate weapon against Japan. The reports from the United States Strategic Bombing Survey, especially the July 1, 1946, study on *Japan's Struggle to End the War*, are also informative. There is a folder that contains the official version of the story—the press releases from the White House and the War Department that were issued after the bombings—as well as one all about the testing of the bomb. If you want to read documents about the creation of the weapon, check out the "Groves Project" folder.

ABSOLUTISM

Best Search Engine:	http://www.northernlight.com/
Key Search Terms:	Europe + monarchy + absolute
	Absolutism + Europe + history
	Age of Absolutism + history
	Early modern + Europe + history
	Louis XIV + absolute + history
	Peter the Great + absolute + history

Pre-Enlightenment Europe
http://www.wsu.edu/~dee/ENLIGHT/PRE.HTM
middle school and up

This Web page, which is part of Washington State University's *World Civilizations* site, is an excellent place to start your study of absolutism. Written by Professor Richard Hooker, *Pre-Enlightenment Europe* provides a sound overview of the Age of Absolutism. Although it doesn't go into a lot of detail, *Pre-Enlightenment Europe* does a great job of explaining the rise of absolute monarchies across Europe. It also looks at the different absolute rulers in Europe.

To navigate the page, simply scroll down the screen. The essay is well organized and easy to follow. Hooker starts off by defining absolutism and explaining the events that led up to the implementation of absolute monarchies in Europe. Make sure you don't overlook the links on the left-hand side of the page that you can follow for more information about some of the causes of absolutism. Once you've gotten a sense of why absolutism took hold, you can read about the philosophy of absolutism. Select the "Divine Right of Kings" from the left-hand side of the screen to learn how absolutism was justified. The rest of the essay examines individual nations and their rulers: France and Louis XIV, Prussia and Frederick William, Austria and the Hapsburgs, and Russia and Peter the Great.

Pre-Enlightenment Europe doesn't offer enough information to write a term paper or to delve into a specific topic. What the Web site does provide is the framework for understanding absolutism. You'll be able to compare and contrast different regimes and get a sense of why they emerged. Use this site as a starting point for more research.

Absolutism
http://www.fordham.edu/halsall/mod/modsbook05.html
middle school and up

If you're in the market for primary documents about absolutism, you will love this Web site. Part of Fordham University's *Internet Modern History Sourcebook*, this site contains links to dozens of documents pertaining to absolutism. Like other sites that concentrate on primary material, *Absolutism* doesn't give much explanatory information about the original documents. So you'll want to use *Absolutism* in conjunction with more basic sites such as *Pre-Enlightenment Europe* or *Louis XIV.*

This Web site is divided into three main sections: "Absolutism," "France and the Ancien Regime," and "French Culture in the 16th and 17th Centuries." You can either select a section from the menu at the top of the home page, or simply scroll down the page until you find the appropriate heading.

The section on "Absolutism" has links to documents relating to the monarchies in Spain and England, including some of Phillip II's letters, James I's *True Law of Free Monarchies*, and excerpts from *The Leviathan*, Thomas Hobbes's philosophical treatise on absolutism. Those of you focusing on French absolutism will want to check out the section on "France and the Ancien Regime," where you'll find documents that explain the causes of absolutism as well as those from the creation of the French absolutist regime. You'll find eyewitness accounts of the St. Bartholomew's Day Massacre, Cardinal Richelieu's *Political Testament*, and the *Edict of 1626 Ordering Demolition of French Feudal Castles*. There's also an array of documents relating to Louis XIV, such as Bishop Jacques Bossuet's *Political Treatise on Kingship* and Louis XIV's *Letter to the Town Officers and People of Marseilles*. The section on "French Culture" has some interesting material as well, including excerpts from Blaise Pascal and François Rabelais, among others.

Louis XIV
http://www.louis-xiv.de/
middle school and up

If you want to learn about the most famous of the absolute monarchs, this site is for you! Created by Elena Steingrad, *Louis XIV* is chock-full of information about the Sun King and his court. It also contains more than two hundred pictures and is a snap to navigate. Although you'll learn everything there is to know about Louis XIV, the site doesn't contain many primary documents. No worries, though; you can always supplement with documents from *Absolutism*.

Once you've entered *Louis XIV*, use the menu at the top of the screen to select the sections that interest you. The "Biography" section is stellar, as is the one on "Wars." Use the menu at the bottom of the screen once you've entered a section. In "Wars," for instance, you can read about "Wars in General," "Wars in Detail," or "The Command." The section on "Religion" lets you examine "Louis and the Papacy," "Louis and the Heresies," and "The Edict of Nantes." Don't pass by the sections on the "Court" or on Louis's "Family," both of which contain excellent historical information about the key players of the period. You can skip over "Castles," "Afterlife," and "Women," unless you want to learn about Louis's palaces, the cemetery where he's buried, or his mistresses. If you have questions or comments, you'll want to join the site's "Forum."

ATOMIC AGE

Best Search Engine:	http://www.google.com/
Key Search Terms:	Atomic age
	Nuclear disarmament + atom bomb
	Nuclear disarmament + international politics

Atomic Archive
http://www.atomicarchive.com/main.shtml
middle school and up

Although designed as a companion to a CD-ROM of the same name, this site contains stellar information in an easy-to-follow format. Explore the complicated history of the atom bomb's invention, read biographies of key scientists from the atomic age, or follow a chronology of our nuclear past, from the 1920s to the present. If you're interested in the disarmament movement, you won't want to miss the summaries of arms-control treaties found here.

Other sections include "Reflections," which contains thoughts on the dropping of the bombs by key players in the atomic age, most of them scientists or military officers; "Nuclear Fission and Nuclear Fusion," which provides simple but thorough explanations of these processes; "Photographs"; "Videos"; "Maps"; and "Glossary." A teacher's guide offers exercises on such topics as arms control, nuclear fission and nuclear fusion, and several lesson plans, including one that involves a mock trial. The usual "Links" page brings up the rear end.

The High Energy Weapons Archive
http://www.fas.org/nuke/hew/index.html
high school and up

An extensive site with historical information on the atomic age, including pages on the discovery of the atom bomb, Little Boy and Fat Man, the Manhattan Project, and other core topics, as well as up-to-date technical information on the nuclear arsenals of all the declared nuclear states and the shadow states of Israel and South Africa. A nuclear weapons "Frequently Asked Questions" page and a collection of major reference articles and links cover lots of ground.

This site will be especially helpful if you're interested in detailed or technical information about weapons and the ongoing arms race. There's even an article on suitcase bombs and terrorism, with quite a bit of speculation about Osama bin Laden and his interest in obtaining nuclear weapons.

AFRICA—EXPLORATION

Best Search Engine: http://www.google.com/
Key Search Terms: Africa + history

Africa + Europe + history

Africa + European exploration

David Livingstone + Africa

Slave trade + history + Africa

The European Voyages of Exploration: The Fifteenth and Sixteenth Centuries
http://hist.ucalgary.ca/tutor/index.html
middle school and up

This excellent Web site from the University of Calgary will introduce you to the topic of the earliest European exploration of Africa. The site focuses on the two countries that led the way in European expansion— Spain and Portugal. Because the site is broad (discussing the countries' exploration of Asia, Brazil, the Caribbean, the Americas, and Africa), it allows you to place the voyages to Africa in their historical context. You'll learn *why* Spain and Portugal were drawn to Africa's shore, what they hoped to accomplish, and what the consequences of their actions were.

Since the site is structured as an online tutorial, you can either choose the topics from the menu on the home page or follow the entire narrative by clicking on "Proceed with the Tutorial" at the bottom of each screen. If you want to skip over the history of Spain and Portugal in Asia and the Americas, you won't miss too much material that's relevant to Africa. You probably won't want to miss the "Introduction," which provides good background material on Spain and Portugal's motivations in exploring the rest of the world. Also don't overlook the sections "Iberian Pioneers," "Spain," "Portugal," and "Knowledge and Power." These sections explain the history of Spain and Portugal (which again will help you make sense of what prompted these countries to explore), as well as the political, economic, and social conditions in Spain and Portugal at the time they launched voyages to Africa.

Once you've gotten a sense of the factors that propelled Spain and Portugal to take to the high seas, select "Africa" from the menu on the home page to learn about the countries' actions in Africa. The section begins in 1415 with the Portuguese assault on the Moorish port of Ceuta in North Africa, and covers the search for gold and slaves, and the establishment of trading routes. The section on Africa also contains helpful maps.

Exploring Africa: An Exhibit of Maps and Travel Narratives
http://www.sc.edu/library/spcoll/sccoll/africa/africa.html
middle school and up

If you want the chance to examine primary documents related to the European exploration of Africa, hurry over to this fascinating Web site. The site contains digitized excerpts of rare documents from the Thomas Cooper Library's Special Collections at the University of South Carolina. You'll find copies of fifteenth-century maps and the travel logs of nineteenth-century explorers in Africa's interior. You can view the sketches of African plants and people that explorers included in their books and portraits of the explorers themselves.

The site is easy to navigate. Use the menu on the home page to examine the documents that interest you. "Island One (Africa before European Exploration)" contains a series of Renaissance maps and early accounts of Africa, such as Arab scholar Leo Africanus's description. "Island Two (Portuguese Discoveries and Dutch Map Makers)" offers additional maps. Check out "Island Three (Exploration from the Cape to the Nile)" for a look at Anders Sparrman's description of his journey to the Cape of Good Hope, Sir John Barrow's account of his travels, and much more. "Island Four (West Africa, Niger, and the Quest for Timbuktu)" houses material such as Robert Adams's account of his shipwreck in Africa—and the subsequent three years he spent as a slave to African Arabs. There are also some interesting descriptions from explorers who attempted to find the mythic Timbuktu. Finally, "Island Five (Central and East Africa and the Legacy of Exploration)" contains documents related to David Livingstone, the most famous nineteenth-century explorer of Africa, as well as those pertaining to Henry Morton Stanley, Sir Samuel White Baker, and Cameron Chesterfield Alleyne. If you want to view the bibliography of the document included, simply select "References" from the main menu.

One of the best features of this Web site is that it provides a short summary of each document. This capsule history allows you to place the document in its broader historical context. To view the excerpted portion of the document more closely, simply click on its image. Despite its many positive features, the site does have one major drawback. It doesn't allow you to view complete documents—only the limited excerpts it makes available. Nevertheless, *Exploring Africa* is a gem of a site because it gives you access to rare manuscripts that reveal a great deal about the European exploration of Africa. The site is also a great source to launch further research, since the names of the explorers included virtually provide a history of European exploration. It's a snap to conduct searches using the names contained in *Exploring Africa*.

The Slave Kingdoms
http://www.pbs.org/wonders/Episodes/Epi3/slave.htm
middle school and up

It's nearly impossible to research the history of the European exploration of Africa without also studying the history of slavery. Not long after charting Africa's shores, Europeans began to trade with West African tribes—the Europeans traded guns and gold for human slaves. This Web site, which is part of the larger PBS site that is a companion to the television show *The Wonders of the African World*, is one of the few top-notch sites that gives the history of the slave trade from the perspective of African history. *The Slave Kingdoms* focuses on the western African kingdoms that flourished because of their role in the slave trade. There is almost no direct material about European exploration available at this site, so make sure to supplement your research here with other resources.

The site combines essays, interviews, photographs, maps, and video clips to tell its story. For an excellent overview of the slave trade, select "Continue" at the end of the paragraph under "Confronting the Legacy of the African Slave Trade." Return to the home page when you're ready for the site's in-depth features: "Wonders," "Retelling," "Gates' Diary," and "Cultural Close-Up." Select the topics that interest you from the menu at the bottom of the home page. "Wonders" contains a history of two West African tribes that grew rich and powerful from the slave trade—the Ashanti and the Dahomey. "Retelling" has a wealth of fascinating material. You can watch an interview of a current Ashanti leader explaining the Ashanti role in the slave trade, as well as an interview of Martine de Souza, a descendant of one of the most infamous slave traders. There's also a written firsthand account of growing up in Ghana with the legacy of the slave trade, and the perspectives of African Americans who visit Africa and must confront the history of the slave trade. "Gates' Diary" is less helpful. It contains the written reflections of the show's narrator, Henry Louis Gates, on how the slave trade has affected African Americans. "Cultural Close-Up" has a short profile on the Gbeto warriors of western Africa.

AFRICA—COLONIZATION

Best Search Engine: http://www.northernlight.com/
Key Search Terms: Africa + history
                        Colonial Africa + history
                        Europe + imperialism + Africa + history

African Timelines
http://www.cocc.edu/cagatucci/classes/hum211/timelines/htimelinetoc.
   htm
middle school and up

It's pretty tough to find a Web site that provides a comprehensive history of the colonization of Africa. It's a daunting topic, and most of the Internet resources you'll find will deal with one nation or some unique aspect of colonial Africa. So if you do need some help grasping the history of *all* of colonial Africa, you'll definitely want to check out this site from Central Oregon Community College. It's in time line format, so don't expect detailed discussions of events; nevertheless, it does a good job of covering key events, movements, and people. Another bonus is that the chronology contains dozens of links (right in the time line) to other Web sites. Follow these for more information on specific topics.

African Timelines is divided into four main sections: "Ancient Africa," "African Empires," "African Slave Trade and European Imperialism," and "Anti-Colonialism and Reconstruction." Unless you need background material on other periods of African history, you can skip Parts I, II, and IV, and simply use the time line on the "African Slave Trade and European Imperialism" (Part III). You'll see the link to Part III in the main menu on the home page.

The "African Slave Trade and European Imperialism" chronology covers the late fifteenth century to 1855. In between these dates are individual entries that relate the important events in the history of the European colonization of Africa. In addition to these entries, the time line also includes brief summaries of certain topics, such as "The Holocaust" (about the slave trade), "The Resistance" (to the slave trade), and "African Cultural and Oral Traditions." The internal links to other Web sites are incredibly handy. For instance, the 1818 entry refers to the Zulu chief Shaka unifying the Nguni people to resist white Europeans. Right below this are links to several Web sites, including *Zulu History and Culture* and *Anglo-Zulu Tours: Battlefields of the Anglo-Zulu War*.

Africa Texts
http://www.historywiz.com/africasources.htm
middle school and up

If you're in the market for a manageable collection of documents related to the European colonization of Africa, you'll definitely want to visit this site, which is part of the broader *HistoryWiz* project. Like its name suggests, *Africa Texts* contains primary documents about Africa. The site is in no way comprehensive, but it does make available an assortment of documents that illuminate different aspects of the history of European meddling in Africa. Because *Africa Texts* doesn't include any explanatory information about the documents it contains, you'll want to turn to other Web sites, such as *Africa Timelines*, or interpret the primary source material.

To navigate this site, simply scroll down the home page, and select the texts you want to read. The documents are arranged into four categories: "The African Kingdoms," "Slavery," "Imperialism," and "Colonial Africa." Scroll down the home page to find the two sections that are directly pertinent to the topic of European colonization of Africa—"Imperialism" and "Colonial Africa." The "Imperialism" section contains documents (or excerpts from documents) such as *Confession of Faith* by Cecil Rhodes, *The White Man's Burden* by Rudyard Kipling, *The Black Man's Burden* by Edward Morel, and *The Economic Bases of Imperialism* by John Hobson. In the "Colonial Africa" section you can view cartoons of Cecil Rhodes straddling the Continent and gruesome photographs of the effects of the forced labor system on the Congolese. You can also read excerpts of *How I Found Dr. Livingstone* by Henry Stanley, *On Empire and Education* by Thomas Babington Macauley, and *Heart of Darkness* by Joseph Conrad.

At the bottom of the home page there are links to two excellent online exhibits that focus on specific aspects of European colonization. "That Magnificent African Cake" details the Belgian Congo and "Bitter Union" provides a history of South Africa.

AFRICA—INDEPENDENCE MOVEMENTS

Best Search Engine: http://www.google.com/
Key Search Terms: Africa + history
                       Africa + colonialism + history
                       Africa + independence movements

A Review of the Twentieth Century in Africa
http://www.channelafrica.org/english/2000/introduction.html
middle school and up

The history of African independence movements is just as complicated as the history of the European colonization of Africa. This site,
produced by Channel Africa, does a great job of explaining African
independence. Think of it as an annotated time line. It gives you the
important events in different nations' struggles for independence, as well
as a quick summary that explains the significance of these events. Of
course, *A Review of the Twentieth Century in Africa* won't provide the
level of detail necessary, say, to write a research paper. What it does give
you is an easily digestible history of African independence movements.
Armed with this framework of the key events, you'll be able to make
sense of this complex period of history.

To navigate this site, use the menu on the left-hand side of the home
page. Although the site is divided into five sections—"Introduction,"
"1945–1959," "1960–1989," "1990–2000," and "Conclusion"—only the
first three are directly relevant to the topic of African independence
movements.

One of this site's best features is the "Introduction," which provides
a thorough review of African history immediately *before* independence
movements gained force in Africa. In other words, the "Introduction"
will familiarize you with the political situation in Africa at the time that
anticolonial movements took hold. There's an excellent map (click on
the small image for a larger view) that shows African colonial possession
by country, as well as armed resistance to colonial rule in 1930. Once
you've checked out the map, scroll down the screen to read a quick
history of colonial Africa.

The other sections you'll want to browse are "1945–1959" and "1960–
1989," which consist of time lines of the key events during these periods.
Click on the years listed for a more full description of the events that
took place. There are also photographs in the summaries. If you have
the time, read the "Conclusion," which discusses the legacy of colonialism, as well as the challenges facing postcolonial Africa.

The Story of Africa
http://www.bbc.co.uk/worldservice/africa/features/storyofafrica/
middle school and up

This Web site from the British Broadcasting Service (BBC) is one of
the best resources on the history of Africa that you'll find on the Inter-

net. It does a terrific job of covering African independence movements, just as it does explaining all other periods of African history. What makes this site so special is that it tells the history of Africa from an African perspective. The site relies on African historians to examine the key events of their continent's history. It also includes an array of materials to help make your learning process fun. There are numerous radio clips, photographs, and time lines to supplement the site's essays.

Although the entire site is engaging and informative, most of it is not directly related to the topic of African independence movements. If you want to stick to this narrow area of African history, you'll mainly want to rely on two sections—"Between World Wars" and "Independence"—which you'll find in the menu on the left-hand side of the home page.

"Between World Wars" deals with the impact of World War I and World War II on African independence movements. Use the index on the right-hand side of the screen to navigate this section. You'll probably find the material on "Early Nationalism," "The Pan-African Vision," and "Socialism" (all listed in the index) especially helpful to your research on African independence movements.

"Towards Independence" is chock-full of useful and fascinating material. Like the section on "Between World Wars," this one has an index on the right-hand side of the screen. You might want to start with the "Timeline," which is near the bottom of this list. This chronology, which gives the dates that African nations achieved independence, is a helpful framework for your research. Once you've grasped the basic chronology, dive into the rest of this section. "Towards Independence" covers the events of the 1950s; "French and British Colonial Styles" explains the differences in the ways that those two nations dealt with African demands for independence; "From Gold Coast to Ghana" reviews the demise of the British colonial empire in Africa; and "The Nation State" discusses the difficulty that African leaders faced because of the arbitrary borders that Europeans imposed upon Africans. In each of these essays, you can follow the links to listen to radio broadcasts of key events, such as Patrice Lumumba's proclamation of Congo's independence.

The "Towards Independence" section has some other gems for you to discover. Make sure to check out the four case studies (also in the index at the right-hand side). You can read a detailed report of the events that took place in Guinea Conakry, Algeria, Congo, and Kenya. There are also essays on "Post Independence," which explores the coups and border disputes that erupted in many African countries after independence was won, "One Party States," and "Forces for Change."

AGE OF DISCOVERY

Best Search Engine: http://www.google.com/
Key Search Terms: Age of discovery + history
                        European explorers + New World
                        Christopher Columbus + history
                        Henry the Navigator + history

Discoverers Web
http://www.win.tue.nl/cs/fm/engels/discovery/#age
middle school and up

This rambling meta-site is a great place to begin researching the European age of discovery. *Discoverers Web* allows you to access loads of useful information—time lines of voyages, biographies of key explorers, and links to dozens of Web sites. Although this Web site doesn't just cover the history of exploration during the vaunted age of discovery (1400–1520), the bulk of the material is related to this topic. Because it is so vast and contains so many links, it might take a little time to find what you need at this site. But this extra effort will pay off. You can expect *Discoverers Web* to point you in the right direction to find information about a specific topic related to the age of discovery. If you haven't yet settled on a topic, don't worry. *Discoverers Web* will help you navigate your way to a topic that interests you.

To find your way around this site, scroll down the home page, and select the links that you need. The first set of links are listed under the heading, "Apart from this page on this site there are." Beneath this wordy header, you'll find a number of useful links, such as one to a "special page for multi-page sites on voyages of discovery." In other words, follow this link if you want to view an index of other big sites related to the topic of exploration. Keep in mind that these links are *not* just to other sites about the Age of Discovery. You'll find an array of Web sites listed here—from the "Polynesian Voyaging Society" to the "Columbus Navigation Homepage" to the "History of Cartography Gateway." If you're looking for print sources to use in your research, select "a list of primary and secondary sources" from the home page. Also in this section are a substantial number of links to biographies of key explorers, many of whom sailed the high seas during the age of discovery. Keep scrolling through the list, and chances are you'll find the name you need.

You can navigate the remainder of the site by either scrolling down the screen or by using the topical index you'll find right below the links to the biographies. Simply click on "Age of Discovery" in this index, and you'll be able to scan through a list of links that is impressively comprehensive. You can access a paper about the spice trade, dozens of additional biographical sites about explorers, charts and maps, and much more. All you have to do is point and click.

Unfortunately, there is other material from the period of the age of discovery scattered throughout some of the other sections on this site. So, if you don't find what you need under "Age of Discovery" scroll through the other sections, as well. Although it's disorganized, you'll appreciate the site's breadth.

1492: An Ongoing Voyage
http://www.loc.gov/exhibits/1492/
middle school and up

Christopher Columbus is one of the most familiar names from the age of discovery. This site—one of the Library of Congress's many excellent online exhibits—uses Columbus's famed voyage to America as the starting point for further discussion. *1492: An Ongoing Voyage* examines the world that existed before European explorers arrived. You can examine the age of discovery from the perspective of the native peoples whose lives were irrevocably changed when the Europeans reached their shores. The site also provides an overview of the Mediterranean world and the worldview from which Columbus and other explorers emerged. There's detailed information about Columbus, as well as a look at how explorers invented America.

One of the coolest features of this site is that you can view objects and manuscripts from the Library of Congress's holdings. As you read through the different sections, you'll be able to examine maps from medieval Spain, a digitized copy of Columbus's *Book of Privileges*, sketches of native communities made by fifteenth-century explorers, and much more. Simply click on the small pictures to get a larger view.

Like other Library of Congress sites, *1492: An Ongoing Voyage* is well organized, clearly written, and a snap to navigate. The main menu, which you'll find at the top of the home page, directs you to the site's different sections. The first section, "What Came to be Called America," discusses the native peoples (and their communities) as they existed before Columbus showed up. "Mediterranean World," the second main section, provides a background for understanding why Columbus and others of his ilk began to venture beyond the narrow confines of their known world. This section has some especially useful material on the European worldview of the time. "Christopher Columbus: Man and Myth" covers the biography of Columbus. The last two sections—"Inventing America" and "Europe Claims America"—deal with the imposition of European policies and philosophies on the New World. Check out the "Epilogue" for some final thoughts on these subjects.

ANTI-SEMITISM

Best Search Engine: http://www.northernlight.com/
Key Search Terms: Anti-Semitism + history

Anti-Semitism + Holocaust + history

Anti-Semitism + Europe + history

Dreyfus + anti-Semitism + history

Middle Ages + anti-Semitism

Beyond the Pale: A History of the Jews in Russia: The Development of Anti-Semitism
http://www.friends-partners.org/partners/beyond-the-pale/
middle school and up

This exhibit is an online version of an original exhibit that has toured Russia since 1995. It includes text on the "Middle Ages," the "Development of Modern Anti-Semitism," "Jews in the Russian Empire," "Jews in the Soviet Union," "Nazism and the Holocaust," and "Jews in the Soviet Union, 1941–present." Click on "Middle Ages," for example, and you'll find sections on "Christian Images of Jews," "Anti-Jewish Myths," and "Patterns of Discrimination."

Under the "Development of Modern Anti-Semitism," the section on "The Dreyfuss Affair" is an excellent introduction to one of the most famous cases of anti-Semitism in nineteenth-century Europe. The text will help you understand the historical context in which the incident occurred, as well as something about the impact of the incident on future relations.

The site is easy to use and nicely illustrated with images from the original exhibition. It's available in Russian, too. If you want to further explore some topic of Russian-Jewish culture, check out the links at the bottom of the page.

Anti-Semitism: What Is It?
http://www.cdn-friends-icej.ca/antiholo/summanti.html
middle school and up

This highly personal site, written by a Christian woman from Canada as a form of witness, takes on a thorough examination of anti-Semitism, beginning with the literal meaning of the word and then tracing the history of anti-Semitism from 175 B.C. to the present. A time line of events, starting with the desecration of a Jewish temple in 135 B.C., spans a tremendous amount of history. If you keep in mind that this is not an objective, scholarly work, you'll be able to appreciate the scope of what it does have to offer.

APARTHEID

Best Search Engine: http://www.northernlight.com/
Key Search Terms: Apartheid + history
                        South Africa + history
                        Apartheid + South Africa + history
                        Apartheid + Nelson Mandela + history

The History of Apartheid in South Africa
http://www-cs-students.stanford.edu/~cale/cs201/apartheid.hist.html
high school and up

This Stanford University student site opens with a page on the history of apartheid and continues with a page that explores the ethical question posed to the international community and another page that lists the tallies of votes, broken down by state, in the 1994 democratic elections. Charts and photographs throughout the site graphically illustrate the brutality of apartheid.

You'll also find current information at this site on the criminal justice system, policing and security, crime and crime prevention, and the Truth and Reconciliation Commission, among other topics.

Crime, Justice, and Race in South Africa
http://www.uaa.alaska.edu/just/just490/
middle school and up

Click on "History" midway down the page to explore South Africa's history of apartheid policies under the Nationalist government from 1948 to 1993. You'll find links to recent history topics first, followed by older historical topics and a section on Nelson Mandela. At the bottom of the page you'll find "Other Resources," which includes a link on "Computers and Apartheid" that explores the enabling technology of computers and how they were used to support the oppression. Two other links take you to award-winning photographs of South Africa's first democratic elections in 1994.

ARAB-ISRAELI WARS

Best Search Engine: http://www.google.com/
Key Search Terms: Arab-Israeli Wars + history
                      Israel + War of Independence
                      Israel + Sinai Campaign
                      Israel + Arabs + Six-Day War

The Arab-Israeli Wars
http://www.israel.org/mfa/go.asp?MFAH00us0
middle school and up

Although this is an official state of Israel site, its aim is to provide the facts about the Arab-Israeli wars since 1948. The text is well written, the site easy to navigate, and it's all available in Spanish. Links to related resources are provided within the text, and the site also contains pages on Israel's government, judiciary, Jerusalem, and other topics if you want to acquaint yourself better with Israel before delving into research on its wars.

The URL listed above takes you directly to the page on the wars. Other information is accessed through links in the menu at the left.

Arab-Israeli Wars and Conflicts
http://www.historyguy.com/arab_israeli_wars.html
middle school and up

You'll like the History Guy's handy dandy chart if you have a hard time keeping all these wars straight. The chart lists each conflict, with a description and its chronological order among all the conflicts since 1948, when the first Israeli War of Independence began. You'll find the Sinai War (also known as the Suez War), the Six-Day War, the Yom Kippur War, and others. There's not a lot of detail, so you won't be able to rely on this site alone if you're researching these wars, but you can use it to get an overview, and to read brief descriptions of each war, before proceeding to the following site that delves into each war more deeply.

JCRC: History of Israel Timeline
http://www.minndakjcrc.org/educatorsResearchIsrael.htm
middle school and up

Use this site instead of the History Guy's site listed above if you're looking for in-depth information about any one of the Arab-Israeli Wars. The time line at this site begins in 2000 B.C. and ends in February 2001 with the election of Ariel Sharon as prime minister of Israel. It's a wonderful time line that contains many quality links, but you don't have to read the time line to find the links to the wars. They are all pulled out for you at the top of the page, so that you can go straight to the article of your choice. There are links to articles on each of the wars, as well as information about the Partition Plan, Camp David Accords, and other key events in twentieth-century Israel's history.

Arab-Israeli Wars
http://www.palestinehistory.com/war.htm
middle school and up

This site is the Palestinian counterpart to the state of Israel site offered above and makes an interesting comparison. Look at both sites and notice the differences in names of wars (Yom Kippur War vs. the October War), as well as the differences in how each conflict is described. This site includes several colorful maps with descriptions of each of the conflicts.

The Arab-Israeli Conflict: Basic Facts
http://www.science.co.il/Arab-Israeli-conflict.asp
middle school and up

Reading this won't necessarily give you the basic facts, but it will help you understand the complexity of the relations between Israel and the Arab states. This is another state of Israel page, but it's worth looking at despite its bias. It compares Arab nations to Israel, in terms of land mass, population, and wealth and contains a brief page on four of the Arab-Israeli Wars, as well as pages on "Nationhood," "Jerusalem," "Arab and Jewish Refugees," "Holy Places," "The Peace Process," and several other topics. Links at the bottom of the page address "Arab Anti-Semitism," "Myths about Arab-Israeli Conflicts," "The U.S. as Israel's Ally," and other provocative subjects. There's also a link to pictures of Arab terrorism.

ARCHITECTURE

Best Search Engine: http://www.google.com/
Key Search Terms: Architecture + history
                       Pyramids + history
                       Ancient history + architecture
                       Cathedrals + history + architecture

Architecture through the Ages
http://library.thinkquest.org/10098/mayan.htm
middle school and up

You'll love this one if touring the world to see famous monuments, pyramids, and castles strikes your fancy. Begin this student-written exploration of architecture in the land of the Maya, where you can learn about basic structures, architectural styles, artistic elements, beam roofs, and temples. Each section is nicely illustrated with recent photographs of Mayan ruins. From here the journey continues with pages on Chinese, classical, Egyptian, Greek, Roman, and Aztec architecture. There's also a page devoted solely to cathedrals.

If you want to test your knowledge of the world's architecture, take the multiple-choice test, which is a series of pictures with four different civilizations written beside each one. Choose the civilization that matches the building in the picture, and rack up your brownie points. Finally, if your modem can handle the download of many large files, there's a wonderful virtual tour of these sites around the world.

The Great Buildings Collection
http://www.greatbuildings.com/
middle school and up

Those of you who are truly serious about architecture probably already know of this site, which touts itself as the leading architecture site on the Web. Access a thousand buildings and hundreds of leading architects with 3-D models, photographic images, and architectural drawings, including commentary. You'll also find bibliographies, Web links, and more.

The site is searchable by building, architect, or name of place, so if you know what you're looking for, you're likely to find it here. If you'd like to explore the architecture of a specific country, for example, just click on "Places" and you'll be given a list of countries, and even states within countries, to explore. We searched for "Taj Mahal" under building names and found a page with all the pertinent data on the building, as well as four photos, a 3-D model, and several pages of commentary on the building's architectural style. Links to other Web resources on the Taj Mahal are provided at the bottom of the page and include an online virtual tour.

English Architecture
http://www.britainexpress.com/architecture/
middle school and up

This nicely organized site provides a rough time line of periods and styles of building in England, beginning with prehistoric monuments and ending with Victorian architecture. In between you'll find more than 20 other periods/styles, including Roman villas, medieval architecture,

Eleanor crosses, medieval manor houses, and Georgian classical, to name just a few. There are also lists of architects, landscape architects, and great buildings in England, with pages devoted to each entry on the list. Links to photographs that illustrate the building style are situated within the text for easy reference and additional Web resources are abundant.

The Byzantine Monuments: Hagia Sophia
http://www.patriarchate.org/ecumenical_patriarchate/chapter_4/html/
    hagia_sophia.html
middle school and up

Part of a larger site that showcases pictures of dozens of churches and monuments, this page on the Hagia Sophia contains over 30 high-quality photographs on the Church of Hagia Sophia and its famous mosaics. It's actually organized as four separate pages, so that folks with slow modems won't have to sit through the loading of all 30 photographs.

The photos and lithographs reproduced on this site are annotated with lots of historical information about the church, architectural trivia, and excerpts from older texts that refer to the church, so in addition to learning about the church, you'll absorb some general Byzantine history as well.

Don't forget to take a look at some of the other impressive structures represented on this site. The Hagia Sophia is probably one of the most famous, but just a glance at the menu of churches, monasteries, and other buildings on the left-hand side of the page might tell you that there's much to be learned here about the architecture of the Byzantine Empire. If you're looking for something in particular, try the search function, which has a link of its own at the top of the menu.

The Forbidden City
http://www.chinavista.com/beijing/gugong/!start.html
middle school and up

Take a virtual tour of the Forbidden City in Beijing, China, which includes the palaces of 24 former Chinese emperors during the Ming and Qing dynasties (1368–1911). This site takes you to recent photographs of nine important structures, including the Meridian Gate, the Watch Tower, and the Hall of Union and Peace. Brief captions accompany each photograph with information about the location, construction, and overall purpose of the structure.

ARMS AND ARMOR

Best Search Engine: http://www.google.com/

Key Search Terms: Armor + history

Weapons + history

Arms + war + history

Modern weapons + history

Ancient weapons + history

Swords + history + Japan

Maille + warfare + history

Arsenal of Dictatorship
http://home.inreach.com/rickylaw/dictatorship/
high school and up

Created to describe and examine the many weapons produced and/or designed by Nazi Germany to use against the Allies during World War II, this site is a virtual encyclopedia of German weaponry. It chronicles the transformation of world warfare from, in the Webmaster's own words, "two dimensions to three dimensions, from propeller age to jet age, from using tanks as infantry-supporters to using infantry to support tanks, from battleship power to carrier power, from dynamite age to nuclear age, and from soldiers' war to total war."

The site is neatly organized for searching by type of weapon—"Heer," "Luftwaffe," "Kriegsmarine," (air, land, sea) and "Wonder Weapons." Each weapon is first classified by the branch of the armed forces (Heer, Luftwaffe, or Kriegsmarine) to which it belonged, then it is classified by its function (fighter, bomber, battleship, cruiser, tank, machine gun, etc.). The "Wonder Weapons" page presents weapons from all branches of service that were of extraordinary or unconventional design.

Nihonto: A Japanese Sword Site
http://www.nihonto.com/
middle school and up

Everything you want to know about Japanese swords—a gallery of images, a glossary of terms, articles about swords and the different schools of sword making, and lists of sword shows and clubs, to name just a few of the offerings. This basic site would benefit from a search function, but otherwise it's well organized and easy to use. If you're browsing for information on Japanese swords, this is a great place to look.

The Arador Armour Library
http://www.arador.com/
middle school and up

If you're interested in armor, you won't want to miss this one. There's a page devoted to the construction of armor, articles and essays such as "Maille for Beginners" and "The Essence of Stage Combat," a "Discussion Forum," "Classified Ads," a "Gallery of Armour," and a "Glossary of Armour Terms." While you'll definitely find historical information here, this site is aimed at the contemporary devotee and will give you a good glimpse into that world, while introducing you to some basic armor concepts.

ASSYRIA (SEE MESOPOTAMIA)

BABYLON (SEE MESOPOTAMIA)

BALKANS AND BALKAN WARS

Best Search Engine:	http://www.google.com/
Key Search Terms:	Balkan Wars + history
	Ottoman empire + history
	Yugoslavia + history
	Bosnia + history

Russia and Eastern Europe Chronology: The Balkans
http://campus.northpark.edu/history//WebChron/EastEurope/Balkans.
   html
middle school and up

Part of a larger chronology site addressing all of Russia and Eastern Europe, this page devoted to the Balkans begins with the breakup of the Ottoman empire (1907–14) and ends with the Siege of Sarajevo (1992–96). In between you'll find entries for all the Balkan wars, some with links to Web sites on the topic.

This is an excellent site for getting an overview of twentieth-century events in this region, as well as a place you can go to delve deeper into topics related to the Balkans, such as the "Breakup of Yugoslavia" or the "First Balkan War." Although not every entry in the time line has a corresponding article, most of the entries on wars do.

CBS News: The Lessons of Balkan History
http://www.cbsnews.com/now/story/0,1597,279827–412,00.shtml
high school and up

If your main interest in Balkan history is understanding current conflicts in the region, and you're not completely new to the topic, then you'll want to check out this slick CBS News site, which contains a sophisticated essay on the region by a veteran news correspondent, as well as an interactive video called *Eye on Yugoslavia* and related stories and links.

CNN: The Balkan Tragedy
http://www.cnn.com/WORLD/Bosnia/history/
middle school and up

We're including CNN's page on the Balkans for a lesson in comparison and contrast with the CBS page. Both are excellent sources of recent and historical information on the region, but each is suited to a slightly different audience. This CNN site is for the total neophyte, starting with the basics and explaining the current Balkan conflict in straightforward, easy-to-understand prose. Links within the page take you to dictionary-type pages that define the people and events in concise, simple paragraphs.

You'll also want to scroll down to the bottom of this article and click on the link for "Main Balkan Tragedy Page." Here you'll find a variety of information, including the "Bosnia Archive," which contains articles on "The Balkan Players" and "Recent Events in the Balkans."

BARBARIAN INVASIONS AND KINGDOMS

Best Search Engine: http://www.google.com/
Key Search Terms: Barbarians + history
                              Attila the Hun + history
                              Barbarian invasions + history

History of the Barbarians
http://www.wizardrealm.com/barbarians/history.html
middle school and up

You'll love the flaming torches on the opening page, but there's nothing barbaric about this comprehensive Web site. In addition to a good general history of the Barbarians that covers their origins as well as their conquests, this Web site will let you get up close and personal with the barbarians of more than a thousand years ago. Go to "Lifestyles of the

Wild and Barbaric," where you can explore "Families," "Daily Living," "Philosophies and Beliefs," and "Society and Government." Or you can click on "Famous Barbarians" to meet Attila the Hun or Boadicea, Queen of the Celts, for example.

There are also pages on "Barbarian Contributions to Modern Society" and the "Vikings." Lots of good links throughout this site will help you explore specific topics in more depth.

Barbarian Invasions
http://www.lukemastin.com/history/barbarian_invasions.html
middle school and up

This is a better chronology than the one listed below if you want to read about invasions. Here you'll find stated in clear terms which barbarians—Goths, Huns, Visigoths, Vandals, or some other group—invaded whom, and when, but the site doesn't contain links to in-depth articles, so you should only use it as a quick reference.

Barbarian Invasions and Internal Turmoil
http://campus.northpark.edu/history/WebChron/World/Barbarian.html
middle school and up

This brief chronology covers the period from 200 to 1000. Although it does not contain many entries, most events listed in this time line are actually links to sites that explore the event in some depth. Click on "768–814 Reign of Charlemagne," for example, and you'll find a nice biographical essay on Charlemagne, complete with bibliography.

BERLIN—BLOCKADE

Best Search Engine:	http://www.google.com/
Key Search Terms:	Berlin Blockade + history
	World War II + Berlin Blockade
	Cold war + Berlin Blockade
	Berlin airlift + history

The History Channel—Berlin Blockade
http://www.historychannel.com/
middle school and up

For an excellent but concise description of this post–World War II conflict, go to *The History Channel* home page and do a keyword search on "Berlin Blockade." The paragraphs here will give you excellent background information on the disputes that led to the blockade of Berlin and the yearlong Berlin airlift, when Western pilots flew in thousands of tons of supplies everyday to West Berlin. Links at the bottom of the page on the cold war and German-U.S. relations provide more in-depth information on those topics if you want to keep exploring.

U.S. Airforces in Europe Berlin Airlift Web Site
http://www.usafe.af.mil/berlin/berlin.htm
middle school and up

Check out the "Photo Gallery" first to get acquainted with the different types of planes and the excitement associated with the airlift, then go to "Facts and Figures" to explore a wide range of topics related to the airlift. You'll find exciting video clips of aircraft, air corridors, Berlin sectors, and key players in the airlift, as well as some interesting contemporary information, comparing the capacity of today's aircraft with those used in the airlift. Among the links, you'll find the Berlin Airlift Historical Association and the Berlin Airlift Veterans Association.

This site is easy to navigate and quite comprehensive especially if you're more interested in the military and humanitarian side of the topic than in the political.

BERLIN—THE BERLIN WALL

Best Search Engine: http://www.google.com/
Key Search Terms: Berlin Wall + history
                         Berlin Wall + cold war
                         Germany + history

A Concrete Curtain: The Life and Death of the Berlin Wall
http://www.wall-berlin.org/gb/berlin.htm
middle school and up

Explore the history of the Berlin Wall's creation and destruction, including detailed sections on security at the wall and statistics about victims, escapes, and espionage. The text is informative and thorough and includes the following sections: "The Shared Sky," "Operation 'Wall of China,'" "The 'Wall' System," "In the Shadow of the Wall," "The Fall," and "What Is Left of the Wall." Appendixes to the site include a highly detailed chronology. You'll also find online exhibits of paintings and photographs.

Berlin Wall Online
http://www.dailysoft.com/berlinwall/
middle school and up

This Berlin-based Web site will take you inside lots of the personal history behind the wall. You'll find pages at this site devoted to Checkpoint Charlie, the wall's construction in 1961, maps, photographs, and more.

Click on "Memories" to read the personal recollections of those who experienced the wall firsthand. You'll also find a historical summary, links to related sites, a time line, a FAQs section, and an archive that contains historical documents about the Berlin Wall, the German-German border, Germany, and the cold war. Lots of links within the text let you explore the Berlin Wall and the cold war beyond the boundaries of this site.

BLACK DEATH AND PLAGUES

Best Search Engine:	http://www.google.com/
Key Search Terms:	Black Death + history
	Bubonic Plague + history
	Great Plague + London
	Boccaccio + plague
	Medieval medicine + history

The Black Death
http://history.idbsu.edu/westciv/plague/
middle school and up

Dr. Ellis Knox from Boise State University created this Web site that covers the causes and consequences of the Black Death. *The Black Death* is an excellent place to start your research on this topic. The site is clearly written and is organized into easily digestible sections. There aren't many Web sites that are nearly as comprehensive as this one. The only downside is that *The Black Death* doesn't incorporate any visual aids or interactive features to make learning about the plague more interesting.

To navigate the site, use the table of contents on the home page. You can either go through the entire site or choose the sections that are relevant to your research. Since the entries in the table of contents are straightforward, you shouldn't have any problems picking the sections you need. Each of the sections is fairly short, so don't expect a lot of detailed information. You'll probably need to supplement the broad brushstrokes outlined at this site with more specific information from other resources.

The best part about *The Black Death* is that it covers the topic from many different angles. It has sections with all the obvious information, such as "Origins," "Forms of Plague," and "Medical Measures," as well as ones that give you another perspective on the Black Death, including material on "Official Reactions," "Avoidance," and "The Flagellants." The site also examines the impact of the Black Death on different aspects of life. There are sections that address population loss, and the impact of the plague on the economy, culture, art, and politics of Europe. You'll also find that *The Black Death* has plenty of primary source material to round out your research. To access these firsthand accounts, check out the sections "A Description," "Another Description," and "Description of the Flagellants."

The Black Death
http://www.rbls.lib.il.us/dpl/HIDblackd.htm
middle school and up

This Discovery Channel site is a tribute to what an educational Web site can be like. *The Black Death* takes you on an interactive journey back in time, in which you follow the plague across Europe. You'll listen to firsthand accounts of the plague, view illustrations of the plague's ravages, and make choices about where to go next. In the process, you'll be learning about the causes of the plague, what it was like to have the disease, and how people responded to the threat of the disease.

Navigating *The Black Death* is a snap. You start your journey in Caffa, Crimea, in 1346, just as the plague took hold there. Click on the rat icon to move from one city to the next. At critical junctures, you'll have to choose which rat to follow. Do you go from Avignon to London or to Germany? At each city, you can read an overview of the events that took place. You'll also be able to listen to firsthand accounts of the plague in that city. (If you'd rather read the transcript and skip the audio clip, you can do that too). These are genuine primary documents read by actors. In Florence, you can listen to Boccaccio describing people fleeing the city for the countryside in hopes of avoiding the disease. In Germany, you'll hear Henry of Herford blaming Jewish townspeople for poisoning the village's well and causing the plague. In Ireland, Brother Clyn relates how his entire monastery was killed by the plague. A couple of your stops aren't at cities, but at explanatory pages that relate the plague's origins and manifestations.

If you want to backtrack along the way and visit a city that you bypassed, click on "Map" and then choose the city. Once you've reached the end of this intense journey, you'll have the option to listen to a plague specialist at the *Science Live* Web site.

BOER WAR

Best Search Engine: http://www.northernlight.com/
Key Search Terms: Boer War + history
                        Transvaal War + history
                        Alfred Milner + Boer War
                        Afrikaner + history
                        Peace of Vereeniging + Boer War

The Boer Wars
http://british-forces.com/fkac/conflicts/1800–1914/boer_wars.html
middle school and up

This site is one of the most detailed sources of information about the Boer War, especially from a military perspective, that you will find. It's also well written, clearly organized, and packed with maps. It contains overviews of important Boer War battles, biographies of key figures in the Boer War, and a substantial number of links to other sites about the Boer War. Since the site is actually part of the broader site *British-Forces.com: A History of the British Armed Forces*, it focuses on military history. While some of you might enjoy the blow-by-blow accounts of battles and regiment movements, it might be a bit too much for others who want a more general history of the Boer War. Don't worry, though. It's fairly easy to skim the detailed descriptions of battles to get the fundamental information you need.

The Boer Wars is organized into five main sections, which you'll find in the index on the home page. The first section, "Brief History," provides a succinct overview of European activities in South Africa from 1652 to 1879 and gives a framework for understanding the outbreak of the Boer War. The second section, "Transvaal (or the First Boer) War," covers the hostilities between the British and the Boers from 1880 to 1881. You'll notice that in the index there are pages devoted to the battles of Laing's Nek, Ingogo, and Majuba Hill, as well as to biographies of people who played a role in this stage of the conflict (such as George Pomeroy and Evelyn Wood). The material contains a lot of photographs taken during battles. Look for links to follow to view excellent maps. "Interlude," the third section, describes the events that took place between 1883 and 1899.

The most substantial part of this site is the fourth section, "The Second Boer War." There are multiple pages in this section, each of which covers a different aspect of the Anglo-Boer War from 1899 to 1902. These pages that are part of this section are listed in the index under the heading "The Second Boer War," so you can pick the ones that apply to your research or read them all. You'll find pages on "Opposing Forces," "Black Week," and the "Fall of the Free Orange State." There are also accounts of individual battles, many photographs, additional maps, and another section of biographies. Don't overlook "Relevant Links" if you're in the market for more online resources about the Boer War.

The "Conclusion and Effects," the fifth and final section, is disappointing. It mainly notes the impact that the Boer War had on the British army. This shortcoming points to a broader flaw in this Web site—its pro-British stance. The site gives short shrift to the perspective of the Boers. It glosses over the concentration camps where nearly 20 thousand Boers died, and does little to explain the Boers' outrage at the British. Despite this large gap, *The Boer Wars* is worth a visit. It'll be hard to surpass the history of the war itself that this site provides.

South African War Virtual Library
http://british-forces.com/fkac/conflicts/1800–1914/boer_wars.html
high school and up

This Web site is a tremendous resource for students researching the Boer War. It contains a wealth of information—ranging from time lines of the war's key events to photo galleries to firsthand accounts of the Boer War—that will suit the needs of those looking for a general overview of the war and those in search of specific material. Unlike *The Boer Wars'* site, the *South African War Virtual Library* reviews the Boer War from multiple perspectives, not just from that of military history. It contains sections on the concentration camps and prisoner-of-war camps that housed thousands of Boers, as well as ones on women in the Boer War. If you do want to focus on military history, don't worry, because this site has that too. You'll find a section on the weaponry of the war, reviews of major battles (though not as detailed as in *The Boer Wars*), and descriptions of the different forces. There's also a ton of logistical data.

To access these resources, select "Contents" from the menu at the top of the home page. This will bring you to an index that is divided into 12 main sections: "Overviews"; "Galleries"; "British/Commonwealth Forces"; "Boer Forces"; "Biographies"; "Tributes"; "The Camps"; "Logistical Data"; "General"; "Bibliographica"; "Links"; and "Battles/Engagements." Each of these sections contains an index of the pages contained in it, which makes it easy to focus your research on this site.

For those of you who want to start with the background of the Boer War, make sure to look at the "Overview" section, where you'll find a detailed time line of the events leading up to and during the Boer War ("Chronology"). The page on "The Short History of the War" is also excellent, covering the events that preceded and cause the war along with a short but thorough description of the war.

If you're searching for more specific information, the site is a snap to use because it is so well indexed. Let's say you want biographical information about selected people involved in the war. All you have to do is look at the index of the "Biography" section. You can pick from "British Political Figures," "Boer Political Figures," "South African Political Figures," "British Military Figures (A–J)," "British Military Figures (K–Z)," "Boer Military Figures (A–J)." "Boer Military Figures (K–Z)," "South African Military Figures," "Foreign Volunteers," "African Figures," "Female Figures," "Media Figures," "Randlords and Financiers," and "Children." Or perhaps you want to learn more about the camps that interned Boers. Go to "The Camps" section, and select either "Concentration Camps" or "POW Camps" from that index.

One section that is easy to overlook—but tremendously interesting—is "The Tributes" section, where you'll find essays on "Women in the War" and "Africans in the War." These informative pieces will give you a fresh angle on the Boer War. Also in "The Tributes" section are pages on two military figures: General C. R. De Wet and Mechiel du Toit. From the De Wet section you can access a digitized copy of the general's memoir on the Boer War, *Three Years War*.

BRITISH EMPIRE

Best Search Engine:	http://www.google.com/
Key Search Terms:	British empire + history
	Britain + possessions + history
	British Raj + India + history
	Queen Elizabeth + British possessions

The Sun Never Set on the British Empire, Circa 1937
http://www.friesian.com/british.htm
middle school and up

Here's the most comprehensive site we can recommend on the British empire, nearly as daunting in its wealth of resources as the empire once was. The site contains an excellent article on the empire that gives a very useful historical overview and is chock-full of graphs and charts, detailing the empire's possessions and relevant dates, as well as specific demographic information.

Following the list of possessions is an extensive bibliography, then another article on the prime ministers of the dominions, which included Canada, New Zealand, Australia, Ireland, India, and Pakistan. Nice charts accompany this article too. Links to other useful Internet resources are listed at the bottom of the site.

British Empire
http://www.infoplease.com/ce6/history/A0808983.html
middle school and up

Don't expect to use this site as your only reference, but if all you need is a brief overview of the first and second British empires, as well as Britain's change from empire to commonwealth, try reading this little article. You'll get your bearings with the topic and find links to key terms, such as "chartered companies," "Navigation Acts," and "mercantilism."

Another cool feature at this Infoplease site is the "Hotwords" button. Highlight any word within the text on the site, and click the "Hotwords" button to find dictionary, almanac, and encyclopedia entries about the word, as well as articles that contain references to the word.

The British Empire
http://pages.britishlibrary.net/empirehist/
middle school and up

For general reference value, this academic site can't be beaten. Among its offerings are EmpireHist, the premiere academic mailing list for the history of the British empire, as well as an international research directory of scholars in this field, a collection of links to relevant archives, libraries, museums, journals, a recommended reading list, and an overview of British empire history. Read the overview to get a feel for the topic and then refer to the other main sections for reference information to continue your search. The mailing list could be very helpful if you have specific research questions you want to explore with specialists in the field.

The British Raj (1858 A.D.–1947 A.D.)
http://www.historyofindia.com/britrule.html
middle school and up

If you're interested in Britain's presence in India, look here to read brief but informative mini essays on British policy, the development of transport, trade, and industry, and the economic impact of the Raj. The page is part of a larger site on the history of India, so you might use it as a jumping-off point to explore other British empire–related Indian topics, such as the East India Company or the independence movement that eventually ended the British empire's reign in India.

BUDDHISM (INCLUDING LAM-BUDDHISM)

Best Search Engine: http://www.google.com/
Key Search Terms: Buddhism + history

> Buddha + religion + history
>
> Buddhism + China + history
>
> Buddhism + Japan + history
>
> Buddhism + India + history

The History, Philosophy, and Practice of Buddhism
http://www.acay.com.au/~silkroad/buddha/index.htm
middle school and up

This simple but thorough site received a Study Web award for academic excellence. Divided into three sections—history, philosophy, and practice—it contains numerous topics to explore. Click on "History" on the home page, then choose from the following: "The Life of Buddha," "Early Buddhism and the Development of Theravada and Mahayana Buddhism," "The Spread of Buddhism along the Silk Road," "Tantric Buddhism including Tibetan Buddhism," "Buddhism in Japan including Zen," "Western Buddhism," and "Maps Showing the Spread of Buddhism." The pages for each topic offer historical accounts of the development of the particular practice, as well as photographs and quotes from relevant texts.

Under the "Philosophy" section of the site, explore "The Four Noble Truths," "The Eightfold Path," "The Karma and Intention," and other aspects of Buddhist philosophy. If you're more interested in the practice than in the philosophy, skip the above and go straight to "Practice," where you'll find information on "The Mandala," "The Stupa," "Meditation," "Vegetarianism," and other topics.

The Online Buddhist Center
http://www.idsl.net/heather/onlinebuddhistcenter/
middle school and up

This is a gorgeous site, all bright orange and yellow, with prayer flags blowing in the imaginary winds on the home page. Come here to bask in Buddhism. There's a kitchen, where you can find veggie recipes, a prayer to say before dinner, and an article on mindful eating. In the

"Meditation Hall," you can create a collage of an altar and experience a guided meditation. In the "Counseling Center," you can join a support group, and in the "Lounge" you can relax and listen to online Buddhist radio.

Oh, but you say you have to study? Well in that case, just enter "The Study," where you'll find original essays and links to other Buddhism articles and Web sites. Although you might come across some helpful information here, this is not the best place to come for a concise historical overview. *The Online Buddhist Center* is the place to come once you've read your history and decided that you'd like to practice a little Buddhism yourself. Have fun!

Bodh Gaya, The Sacred Buddhist Village
http://www.otterbein.edu/dept/RELG/BodhGayaPage.htm
middle school and up

Although slow to load, this photographic essay on Bodh Gaya, site of the sacred Mahabodhi temple, is well worth the visit. Each photograph is accompanied by an explanatory caption with historical information woven in when relevant. You'll see not only the temple but also photos of monks and laypeople worshipping and scenes from the grounds surrounding the temple. You'll learn the significance of this particular site, one of Buddhism's most sacred, while experiencing the personal journey of a western Buddhist traveling in India. You'll even find tips for making your own travel arrangements to Bodh Gaya, in case a personal pilgrimage is part of your research.

BYZANTINE EMPIRE

Best Search Engine:	http://www.altavista.com/
Key Search Terms:	Byzantine Empire + history
	Constantine the Great + history
	East Roman empire + history
	Hagia Sophia + history

Byzantium
http://www.fordham.edu/halsall/byzantium/
high school and up

Here's a good first stop for Byzantine studies on the Internet. It's an academic gateway site, and thus will link you to most other important

Byzantine sites, as well as provide you with an excellent introduction to the Byzantine Empire.

At the home page, acquaint yourself with the general history of the Byzantine Empire in the site's "Introduction" before perusing the contents for other offerings of interest. These include a link to the "Greek Orthodox Archdioceses: Byzantine Music Site," where you can listen to online music and liturgy. There's also a section called "Basic Reference Documents," where you'll find chronologies, bibliographies, lists of Byzantine patriarchs, and other helpful resources. "Information on Byzantine Saints" warrants its own page at this site, and there are also reviews of books, and an annotated guide to Byzantine mailing lists on the Internet.

The Byzantine Monuments: Hagia Sophia
http://www.patriarchate.org/ecumenical_patriarchate/chapter_4/html/
      hagia_sophia.html
middle school and up

Part of a larger site that showcases pictures of dozens of churches and monuments, this page on the Hagia Sophia contains over 30 high quality photographs on the Church of Hagia Sophia and its famous mosaics. It's actually organized as four separate pages, so that folks with slow modems won't have to sit through the loading of all 30 photographs.

The photos and lithographs reproduced on this site are annotated with lots of historical information about the church, architectural trivia, and excerpts from older texts that refer to the church, so in addition to learning about the church, you'll absorb some general Byzantine history as well.

The Glory of Byzantium
http://www.metmuseum.org/explore/Byzantium/byzhome.html
middle school and up

If you fancy the study of Byzantine art, you'll love this Metropolitan Museum site, created in conjunction with an international exhibition that was at the museum in 1997. This online exploration of things Byzantine lets you explore a work of art, investigate a theme in Byzantine art, probe the history of Byzantium, see the works of art in a visual time line, check definitions in a special Byzantine glossary, or find educational resources if you're a teacher.

The images are of excellent quality, and the explanatory text is just right if you're coming to the subject for the first time.

CAPITALISM

Best Search Engine: http://www.google.com/
Key Search Terms: Capitalism + history
                        Adam Smith + history + economics

History and Theories of Capitalism
http://hsb.baylor.edu/html/gardner/CESCH03.HTM
middle school and up

This gateway site from Professor Stephen Gardner at Baylor University was designed as a companion to his book *Comparative Economic Systems,* but you don't need the book to make good use of the site.

The list of links is divided into four sections: "Precapitalist Economic Systems," "Early Views of Capitalism," "Contemporary Views of Capitalism," and "Global Capitalism." If you're researching the history of capitalism, you'll probably be most interested in the links that fall under the "Early Views" section. "Classics of Economics," for example, will take you to a McMaster University archive site that has collected a large number of significant texts in the history of economic thought. It's an ongoing project, but already you can find a wide array of primary source material here, all organized by the names of historical economists.

Great Economists and Their Times
http://www.frbsf.org/publications/education/unfrmd.great/greattimes.html
middle school and up

This educational Web site from the Federal Reserve Bank contains articles on each of 10 great economists (think Adam Smith, John Stuart Mill, Karl Marx, Thorstein Veblen, etc.) and articles that correspond to the major schools of economic theory promoted by these 10 economists. Articles cover mercantilists, physiocrats, the Institutionalist School, the Keynesian School, and others.

While you will find more than just capitalism discussed here, there's much that pertains to capitalism and its development. You'll read about the Classical School's beginnings with the publication of Adam Smith's famous *The Wealth of Nations,* a seminal book in the development of capitalism, and how the ideas put forth by Smith were later shaped by Thomas Robert Malthus, John Stuart Mill, and others.

Introduction—The Early History of Capitalism in England
http://www.history.rochester.edu/steam/lord/1–6.htm
high school and up

We take for granted the ability to save money and create wealth, but what did people do before there was money? Read this essay to learn about the impact of the money system replacing barter, the discovery of new trade routes, and the Church's decision to loosen restrictions upon usury. This site is nothing fancy, but it does provide a straightforward essay on the history of capitalism in England, up to the eighteenth century.

History of Capitalism
http://history.wisc.edu/dunlavy/
high school and up

If you're interested in researching the history of corporations, this site's for you. The page provides a gateway into the history of capitalism in the nineteenth and twentieth centuries, exploring the United States, Britain, France, and Germany with links provided to numerous types of resources, including "Research Tools," "Primary Sources Online," "Reading Lists," and more. But the link to "Corporations" is the one you won't want to miss.

The "Corporations" page is provided to encourage research on the history of the corporation. Its focus is a database of some 10,000 corporate charters granted by the United States, Britain, France, and the German states between 1825 and 1870. If you're fascinated by the growth of corporations and want to delve into this topic, you'll love the wealth of data collected here.

CAROLINGIAN EMPIRE

Best Search Engine:	http://www.google.com/
Key Search Terms:	Carolingian empire + history
	Charlemagne + history
	Franks + history

The Carolingian Empire
http://www.ukans.edu/kansas/medieval/108/lectures/carolingian_empire.
    html
high school and up

This helpful and amusing lecture by Dr. Lynn H. Nelson at the University of Kansas provides a good general overview. It's written as a dialogue between a student and teacher and presents plenty of heavy-duty history without the heavy-duty language and tone that so often accompany historical texts.

Don't be put off at first by the less-than-attractive presentation of the dialogue. Once you start reading and get used to her humor, the switching back and forth between speakers becomes easy to follow. Before you know it, you've absorbed quite a bit of Frankish history without falling asleep once.

Carolingians
http://www.geocities.com/EnchantedForest/Dell/1376/carol.htm
middle school and up

Here you'll find chronicled the history of the Frankish family's struggle for and maintenance of power. This is a basic site for biographical information on the key players of the Carolingian empire. In addition to Charlemagne the Great, you'll meet Pepin the Short, Louis the Debonair, and Charles II the Bald (notice any discrepancies here?), among others. The site provides brief but information-packed biographies (here called "Life Stories") of these rulers, as well as images when available, and an introduction at the beginning.

CHINA—GENERAL

Best Search Engine: http://www.google.com/
Key Search Terms: China + history

Ancient China + history

History of China
http://www-chaos.umd.edu/history/toc.html
middle school and up

If you're interested in looking at the whole scope of Chinese history, don't miss this Web site. This comprehensive but straightforward site covers prehistoric China up through the reforms of 1980–88. It's divided into the following broad time periods: "Ancient Dynasties," "The Imperial Era," "The Emergence of Modern China," "Republican China," and "The People's Republic of China." Within these pages, you'll find sections on the "Zhou Period," the "Rise of the Manchus," the "Opium War," the "1911 Republican Revolution," the "Communist Revolution," the "Cultural Revolution," and much, much more. If you're learning to read Chinese and want to test your familiarity with Chinese characters, you'll appreciate the inclusion of Chinese characters for many names and events.

In addition to the historical essays, there is a wonderful time line of the dynasties, with names given in both English and Chinese. Most of the dynasties also have a link that will take you to a list of emperors for that dynasty.

Secrets of the Great Wall
http://www.discovery.com/stories/history/greatwall/greatwall.html
middle school and up

Discovery.com presents this fascinating look at China's Great Wall from an engineering and cultural point of view. The site provides information about each dynasty's construction of a part of the wall, begun in 221 B.C. by the Qin dynasty. Visitors will also read about what each dynasty contributed to the world and what was happening in other parts of the world during that period. Also included on the site are IPIX panoramic views of the wall, radar images taken from space, and a great collection of fun facts in the "Random Factoid Generator."

CHINA—CULTURAL REVOLUTION

Best Search Engine: http://www.google.com/
Key Search Terms: China + Cultural Revolution + history
                        China + history
                        Mao + Cultural Revolution
                        Gang of Four + China + history
                        Red Guard + China + history

Discovering China: The Middle Kingdom
http://library.thinkquest.org/26469/
middle school and up

This ThinkQuest site explores China's history, particularly in the last two centuries, its noteworthy people ("Movers and Shakers"), and its cities. In addition, an entire section is devoted to the "Cultural Revolution," so if that's your area of interest, this site is highly recommended. Just choose "Cultural Revolution" from the main menu. You'll find detailed sections on "History," "Background," "Impact," and "The Aftermath." Since this is a Thinkquest site, created by high-school students, the writing can sometimes be a bit weak, but if you're looking for a general introduction to the Cultural Revolution, the students have done a good job of covering the most important material.

There's also an "Interactive" section, which provides multiple-choice quizzes and online polls that cover such timely questions as "Do you think China has problems with human rights?" The section also has a message board for interacting with others and a dozen short RealPlayer movies that provide glimpses of daily life in China. This is great material for high-school students studying current affairs in the Far East.

CHINA—DYNASTIES AND REVOLUTIONS

Best Search Engine: http://www.google.com/
Key Search Terms: China + dynasties + history
                       China + dynastic history
                       Shang + history
                       Tang + history
                       China + Communist Revolution + history
                       China + Cultural Revolution + history
                       China + 1911 Revolution + history

China
http://emuseum.mankato.msus.edu/prehistory/china/index.shtml
middle school and up

Although not especially attractive to look at, the pages at this University of Minnesota site contain some of the Web's best introductory information on China's dynasties. The site is divided into the following sections: "Ancient China," "Early Imperial China," "Classical Imperial China," "Later Imperial China," "Map," and "Timeline." Within these sections, you'll find brief histories of the Xia, Shang, Zhou, Qin, Han, Xin, Chin, Tang, Sung, Yuan, Ming, and Ch'ing (Qing) dynasties, among others.

CHINA—REVOLUTIONS

Best Search Engine: http://www.google.com/
Key Search Terms: China + revolutions + history
                       China + 1911 Revolution + history
                       China + Communist Revolution + history
                       Chairman Mao + revolution + history
                       China + Cultural Revolution + history

Washington State University: World Civilizations: China
http://www.wsu.edu:8080/~dee/WORLD.HTM
high school and up

From the opening page of this huge site, click on "Contents," then on "World Civilizations: The Learning Modules," then scroll down to "China," and choose from among "Ancient China," "The Chinese Empire: From Ch'in to the Yuan," "Ming China," "Ch'ing China," "Modern China," and the "Chinese Philosophical Traditions."

If you're researching particular dynasties, just click on the link that best covers the time period of your dynasty. You'll find varying amounts of information on the dynasties, but they are all covered here. If you don't know the time period of the dynasty you want to find, check the University of Minnesota site previously mentioned. You can read a brief history there and find the time period of the dynasty, then locate that dynasty at this site. One downfall of this wonderful University of Washington site is that it has no search function.

If you want to study either the 1911 Revolution or the Communist Revolution, click on "Modern China." For information about the Cultural Revolution, follow the link for the "Chinese Communist Party" and then scroll down to the section on the "Great Proletariat Cultural Revolution." However, if you have time, we recommend reading the entire section on the Chinese Communist Party. It's not terribly long, and it will provide you with a contextual understanding of the political and social environment in which the Cultural Revolution took place.

CHINA—TIANANMEN SQUARE

Best Search Engine: http://www.google.com/

Key Search Terms: China + democracy movement

        Tiananmen Square + history

        China + protests + history

The Gate of Heavenly Peace
http://www.pbs.org/wgbh/pages/frontline/gate/
middle school and up

If you're looking for a multimedia experience of the Tiananmen Square protests of 1989, look no further. At this user-friendly PBS site, you can watch clips from a PBS documentary about the event; probe themes from the film, such as democracy, human rights, and the role of the media; take a virtual tour of the Square; learn about the Democracy Wall, where Chinese people posted their complaints and protests in 1978–79; and trace key events in twentieth-century China using the site's own chronology. The inclusion of Chinese perspectives is an added bonus here.

Tiananmen Square, 1989: The Declassified History
http://www.gwu.edu/~nsarchiv/NSAEBB/NSAEBB16/
high school and up

This Electronic Briefing Book from the National Security Archive offers the American perspective on the events in Tiananmen Square and includes documents from the microfiche collection entitled *China and the United States: From Hostility to Engagement, 1960–1998.* Of primary interest are the U.S. government accounts of the military assault by the Chinese government, as well as descriptions of the student demonstrations in late 1985 and 1986 that, in hindsight, predicted the events to come.

CHRISTIANITY

Best Search Engine: http://www.google.com/
Key Search Terms: Christianity + history
                            Religion + history
                            Church + history

The Ecole Initiative: Creating a Hypertext Encyclopedia of Early Church History on the World Wide Web
http://cedar.evansville.edu/~ecoleweb/
high school and up

Wow. The scope of this site is, well, encyclopedic to say the least. Five sections—"Documents," "Glossary," "Articles," "Images," and "Chronology"—contain thousands of in-depth reference entries on major and minor topics and figures in the history of Christianity, as well as information on Judeo-Christian iconography and art and translations of primary sources up to the year 1500.

Check out "Glossary" if you want an extensive definition (100 to 200 words) of some person or event. You'll find several hundred subjects. Look under "Articles" for longer essays on significant topics, such as "Early Christian/Jewish Relations," "Pontius Pilate," and "Stoicism." The "Documents" section contains hundreds of texts and includes numerous histories (of both the Church and specific people in the Church), a section on "Lives of the Saints," and a section on "Church Councils." The Chronology comes with a geographical cross-index, and the "Images" section consists of links to images stored at various places on the World Wide Web.

The depth and breadth of this collection is magnificent. The site comes equipped with an alphabetical index, so if you know the name of something you would like to find, just click on the first letter of the name, and let the exploration begin.

Christianity
http://campus.northpark.edu/history/WebChron/Christianity/Christianity.
   html
middle school and up

Get more than just your dates straight at this excellent Christianity time line. The chronology of events begins with the birth of Christ and continues through the nineteenth century, ending with an entry on missionaries in Alaska. Almost every entry is a link to an essay on the topic, and these are concise and introductory in nature. What better place to begin! Once you peruse this time line and read some of the linked essays, you'll probably have a better idea of what you would like to explore further.

Internet Ancient History Sourcebook: Christian Origins
http://www.fordham.edu/halsall/ancient/asbook11.html
middle school and up

This comprehensive site is an archive of primary source material on Christianity. The URL listed here will take you up to about the fourth century. From there, you'll need to access the *Medieval History Sourcebook* (link at top of home page) to continue.

So, if you're looking for the history of early Christianity, this is the place to start. You'll find sections on "Christian Origins," "Jesus of Nazareth," "Source Problems" (the New Testament, the Dead Sea Scrolls, etc.), "Early Church," "Emergence of Theologies," "Early Christian Art," "Triumph of the Church," and "Modern Perspectives on Early Christianity." Under each of these headings, you'll find numerous topics, each of which is a link to a primary text or other resource.

CLOTHING AND FASHION

Best Search Engine: http://www.google.com/
Key Search Terms: Clothing + history

                      Fashion + history

The Costume Page: Costuming Resources Online
http://members.aol.com/nebula5/tcpinfo2.html#history
middle school and up

Researching the toga? Or perhaps you have questions about the Viking apron-dress. If it's about clothing, you're sure to find it at this giant gateway to clothing and fashion on the Web. Although the site contains links to ethnic clothing sites, Halloween clothing sites, and other such topics, you'll want to go straight to "History," where you'll find links organized under the following useful headings: "Ancient," "Medieval Era," "Renaissance," "Elizabethan/Shakespearean," "17th and 18th Centuries," "19th Century—Regency and Victorian Era," and "20th Century."

If you want to research a certain type of clothing across different time periods, you'll need to continue on to "Historical Topics (Multiple Eras)." (There's a link for this at the bottom of the "History" page.) Here you'll find links organized by subject instead of time period. "Accessories," "Arms, Armour, and Uniforms," "Male Attire," and "Underpinnings" are just a few of the offerings.

Costumes and Clothing
http://www.geocities.com/Heartland/Acres/7631/costume.html
middle school and up

This site boasts its own original historical essays on clothing throughout history. Starting with ancient clothing, the site index progresses through classical, medieval, renaissance, and the seventeenth, eighteenth, nineteenth, and twentieth-century clothing. It also contains a section on non-Western clothing, where you can read brief summaries of the clothing history of Africa, India, Southeast Asia, China, Japan, and Korea, among other places. The graphics are fairly basic, but there's good information to be found.

COLD WAR

Best Search Engine: http://www.google.com/
Key Search Terms: Cold war + history
    Soviet Union + cold war
    Yalta Conference + history

CNN Interactive: Cold War
http://www.cnn.com/SPECIALS/cold.war/
middle school and up

If you're looking for a spiffy site with all the bells and whistles, look no further. This documentary series from news giant CNN will take you, in its own words, "From Yalta to Malta." You can navigate interactive maps, view rare archival footage, study recently declassified documents, take a tour of cold war capitals with CNN's own 3-D images, and learn more about the key players.

Want to get off the beaten track a bit? How about an article on the space race and its contribution to the cold war? Or maybe you'd rather visit a gallery of espionage tools—all the weapons and gadgets of the trade.

Tired of sitting at your keyboard alone? Try one of the many ways to interact with this site. You can take tests on cold war material, debate and discuss the topic with other students, or track key events on the interactive maps.

The East-West Divide
http://www.usnews.com/usnews/news/991018/timeline.htm
middle school and up

This *U.S. News* Online site provides a brief time line of the 45 years of the cold war—from March 1946, when Winston Churchill used the term "Iron Curtain" in reference to communism, to December 1991, when Gorbachev resigned from office and the Soviet Union collapsed. In addition to the time line, there are the following sections: "Quizzes," "Cold War Resources," "Cold War Declassified" (selected documents from the Cold War), and "Cold War Revisited" (selected *U.S. News* archive articles) to round out your research.

The Cold War Guide: People of the Cold War
http://www.geocities.com/CapitolHill/Lobby/4907/People.htm
middle school and up

Here are biographies of 157 key players in the cold war. Use the alphabetical index to look up specific people by name, or browse by simply scrolling from the home page. Bold entries are links to other people found on the site.

COLOMBIAN EXCHANGE

Best Search Engine: http://www.google.com/
Key Search Terms: Colombian exchange + history
                        Columbus + Americas + history
                        New World + history

Colombian Exchange
http://www.bbc.co.uk/history/discovery/exploration/conq_2.shtml
middle school and up

Look here for an introductory overview to the Colombian exchange. Part of a larger BBC site on science and discovery, this section, called the "Story of the Conquistadors," provides a concise history of the conquest of the Americas by the Europeans, including an overview of the significance of this period in history, both to the European explorers and to the native societies they displaced.

If you're interested in the topic and want more information, just click "Next" at the bottom of the page, and go on to the following sections, which include "The Aztecs," "Conquistador Regret," "New Identities," and "Go Further."

You'll see a menu at the left-hand side of the page. Under "Discovery" there are four sections: "By People," "Exploration," "Revolutions," and "Medicine." These links will take you to information in other parts of the site, so you can research other explorers and places, if you're hooked on the history of exploration.

1492: An Ongoing Voyage
http://www.loc.gov/exhibits/1492/about.html
high school and up

This Library of Congress site, designed in conjunction with an original exhibit by the same name, describes both pre- and post-contact America, as well as the Mediterranean world at the same time. It's a comprehensive look at a complex period in European and American history.

The exhibit is divided into six sections: "What Came To Be Called 'America,'" "The Mediterranean World," "Christopher Columbus: Man and Myth," "Inventing America," "Europe Claims America," and the "Epilogue." The original exhibit included over 300 objects: manuscripts, books, maps, and artifacts such as globes, jewelry, and musical instruments. The online exhibit includes images of 22 objects from the original exhibit, representing each of the six sections.

COMMUNISM

Best Search Engine: http://www.google.com/
Key Search Terms: Communism + history
                       Soviet Union + Communism
                       Karl Marx + history
                       Lenin + Soviet Union + history

The History of Communism
http://www.gmu.edu/departments/economics/bcaplan/museum/history.htm
high school and up

Although this George Mason University Web site is still under construction, it contains an excellent article on communism. The article is broken down into 17 sections, and some of these sections have not yet been loaded on to the Web page, but you'll find "The Czarist Origins of Communism," "The Marxist Origins of Communism," and "Lenin and the First Communist Revolutions," which give you an excellent foundation in the early history of communism.

Communism: Development and Duration
http://users.erols.com/mwhite28/communis.htm
middle school and up

For a really cool visual on the spread of communism in the twentieth century, check out this colorful, interactive atlas. There's no text to give you background information, so you'll want to familiarize yourself with the topic before popping in.

CONFUCIANISM

Best Search Engine: http://www.google.com/
Key Search Terms: Confucianism + history
                       China + religion + history
                       Confucius + history

Confucianism
http://www.thespiritualsanctuary.org/Confucianism/Confucianism.html
middle school and up

This basic introduction to Confucianism contains excerpts from several books about the faith, and an outline of key concepts, people, and events in the history of Confucianism. There is a list of primary beliefs and practices, a short list of important works and important dates, and a very brief history. A list of links at the bottom of the page contains "A Lexicon of Confucianism" and several sites that contain Confucian primary source documents.

Although this is a simplistic site, it provides good information in a concise and easy-to-use format. For more in-depth research, try the following site, which contains an excellent article on Confucianism.

Confucianism
http://www.askasia.org/frclasrm/readings/r000004.htm
high school and up

Although just straightforward text, this site is worth visiting for an introduction to Confucianism. It's fairly long and dry, but it will provide the foundation you need to explore this Chinese religion in more depth. The article, written by Judith Berling, begins with a definition, and then summarizes the history of Confucianism from its beginnings in the sixth century B.C. up to the twentieth century.

CRIMEAN WAR

Best Search Engine: http://www.google.com/

Key Search Terms: Crimean War + history

                            Florence Nightingale + war + history

The Crimean War, 1854–1856
http://www.geocities.com/Broadway/Alley/5443/crimopen.htm
high school and up

This boldly illustrated site contains an excellent overview of the war, as well as sections on the main battles—"The Battle of the Alma," "The Battle of Balaclava"—and one on the "Kerry Recruit," a name given to Irish soldiers who joined the army.

Read the overview first to get all the main facts straight. You'll learn that this was Britain's only war between the Napoleonic conflict in 1815 and the beginning of World War I in 1914. Although they eventually won the war, the British military was not highly regarded, and the name of the war itself became a byword for poor leadership. The overview discusses the origins of the conflict and the main battles fought in some detail.

In addition to maps and images of artifacts from the war, you'll find excerpts of songs and quotes about the war from people like Florence Nightingale and Queen Victoria.

The Crimean War
http://www.hillsdale.edu/dept/History/Documents/War/19Crim.htm

For primary source material on the Crimean War, this is your best bet. There are general accounts of the war, accounts of the Battle of Inkerman, and accounts of the Battle of Balaclava. You'll find *New York Times* articles, reports from army officers, and poems, for example.

CRUSADES

Best Search Engine: http://www.google.com/

Key Search Terms: Crusades + history

                            Middle Ages + church + history

Crusades
http://www.newadvent.org/cathen/04543c.htm
middle school and up

This thorough Catholic Encyclopedia article by Louis Bréhier defines the crusade movement and covers the origins and progress of the Crusades through the fifteenth century and beyond. You'll find each paragraph is chock-full of links to sites where you can further explore such terms as "Mohammedans," "cross," "excommunication," "Middle Ages," "Frederick II," "Christendom," "Richard Coeur-de-Lion," and hundreds more.

If you want a brief definition of the Crusades, you can read the first three paragraphs of this article and peruse the bulleted chart that lists the eight different crusades along with who conducted them, then call it quits. But if you're looking for more in-depth information about any one of the eight Crusades, you'll also find that here. Just keep reading. The article contains 10 sections with titles like "Origin of the Crusades," "First Destruction of the Christian States (1144—87)" and "The Crusade in the Fifteenth Century."

Chronology of the Crusades
http://www.people.wcslc.edu/faculty/m-markow/sscle/ssclechr.html
middle school and up

This useful time line lists the most significant events from the first call to crusade in 1095 to the fall of the Hospitallers in Malta. It does not claim to be all-inclusive, but for those just becoming acquainted with the Crusades, this list should suffice.

Internet Medieval Sourcebook: The Crusades
http://www.fordham.edu/halsall/sbook1k.html
high school and up

If you've read a good general introduction to the Crusades and are searching for more in-depth information on a particular topic, try browsing this stellar list of primary source sites at the *Medieval Sourcebook*. Links are divided into the following categories: "General," "Background," "The First Crusade," "The Kingdom of Jerusalem," "The Crusade Orders," "The Second Crusade and Aftermath," "The Third Crusade," "The Fourth Crusade," "The Fifth and Later Crusades," and "The Effects of the Crusade Ideal in the West." Under each section, you'll find numerous links to all kinds of helpful documents.

CUBAN REVOLUTION

Best Search Engine: http://www.google.com/
Key Search Terms: Cuban Revolution + history
                       Castro + revolution
                       Socialism + Cuba + history

¡Cuba Va!
http://www2.truman.edu/~x526/#history
middle school and up

This site was written by students at Truman State University for a class on twentieth-century Latin American revolutions. Its simple, no-nonsense approach includes a general overview of the events of the Cuban Revolution, beginning with the attack on Moncada Barracks and ending with Castro's occupation of Havana.

Following this overview is a list of amply annotated links, divided into the following categories: "Cuban Revolution: General History"; "Socialism or Death!" "Fidel Castro's Speeches"; "Favorable Socialist Responses to the Revolution"; "Unfavorable Socialist Responses to the Revolution"; and "Cuba after the Revolution," which includes pro-revolution and anti-revolution Web sites.

Modern History Sourcebook: Fidel Castro: Second Declaration of Havana, 1962
http://www.fordham.edu/halsall/mod/1962castro.html
middle school and up

For a look inside the ideology of the Cuban Revolution, read this speech given by the leader of the revolution, Fidel Castro, just two years after the revolution first began. The Second Declaration of Havana was delivered on February 4, 1962, and it clearly demonstrates Castro's adoption of Marxism-Leninism as the ideology of the Cuban Revolution.

DAOISM

Best Search Engine: http://www.google.com/
Key Search Terms: Taoism + history
                       China + Tao + history
                       Yin Yang + religion + history
                       Tao Te Ching + history

Daoism Depot
http://www.edepot.com/taoism.shtml
middle school and up

At the rotating yin-yang symbol, you'll find the contents of this Web site listed under the following categories: "Communicate," "Contemplate," and "Related Subjects." For an excellent overview of Daoism, you'll want to follow the link to "Contemplate," where there's an introduction that includes information on the "Main Figures in Philosophical Daoism," "Daoist Deities in Religious Daoism," "Philosophical History and Religious History of Lao Tzi," the "Major Sects," "The Dao," "Yin and Yang," "Wu Wei," "Governing," and the "Three Jewels."

After you've read the introduction, you can contemplate more with the pages on "Daoist Scriptures," "Daoist Characters," "Daoist Cosmology," "Daoist Alchemy," "Daoist Art," "Daoist Humor," and more.

When you've contemplated enough, go to "Communicate," where you can join a live chat or participate in a discussion forum.

History of Taoism
http://www.nauticom.net/www/asti/history.htm
high school and up

This site offers a collection of links on the history of Daoism. You'll find links to an essay on the origins of classical Daoist philosophy, an essay on the development of Daoist philosophy and religion, and one on classical Daoism in historical context, among others. The site is part of a larger site on Daoism, where you'll find translations of the Tao Te Ching, chat rooms, newsgroups, and mailing lists, and Daoism Web sites, as well as many other diverse resources.

DUTCH REPUBLIC

Best Search Engine:	http://www.google.com/
Key Search Terms:	Dutch Republic + history
	Holland + history
	Netherlands + history

The Holland Ring
http://www.thehollandring.com/toen-nu.htm
middle school and up

Although this is a general history of The Netherlands, the section on the history of the Dutch Republic is useful and concise. And reading the overall history, of which the Dutch Republic is just a part, only helps you to better understand the significance of this period in The Netherlands's history.

The article, which appears when you arrive at the home page, begins in the first century B.C. and continues up to 1995. The section on the Dutch Republic is just a few paragraphs in the middle of the article, in the sixteenth and seventeenth centuries. Following this historical overview, there are sections on "Geography," "Climate," "Landscape," "Water Control and Land Reclamation," "Population," "Immigration," the "Dutch Language," "Religion," and "Compartmentalization."

EGYPT, ANCIENT

Best Search Engine:	http://www.northernlight.com/
Key Search Terms:	Ancient Egypt + history
	Pharaohs + history
	Hieroglyphs + ancient Egypt
	Pyramids + ancient Egypt

Ancient/Classical History
http://ancienthistory.miningco.com/cs/
middle school and up

Here you can look into any part of the ancient world that interests you. From the home page, just click on "Egypt" to enter a kingdom of resources on ancient Egypt's pharaohs, hieroglyphs, pyramids, gods and goddesses, art, and archaeology.

If you're interested in the Rosetta Stone, the basalt stone found in Egypt that provided the key to understanding hieroglyphics, just follow the link for "Egypt-Archaeology," then click on "Rosetta Stone." You'll be given nine different sites all focused on the Rosetta Stone. Some provide images; others describe the process of translating and deciphering the three languages found on the stone—Greek, demotic, and hieroglyphic. The Oberlin College site describes in layman's terms the fascinating process used to decipher the hieroglyphic code.

History of Egypt
http://interoz.com/egypt/ehistory.htm
middle school and up

This straightforward page offers you a chronology of Egyptian history, starting with the Lower Paleolithic (c. 2 million–100,000 B.C.), moving through all the dynasties, and ending with the British Occupation Period. Brief articles provide narrative histories to accompany the dates.

Visit *History of Egypt* if you need a basic, thorough summary of any period in ancient Egyptian history. The site touts the fact that the history articles are written using many different sources and thus reflect a wide variety of theories on Egypt's past.

Duke Papyrus Archive
http://odyssey.lib.duke.edu/papyrus/
high school and up

This Duke University archive is a must-see if you're researching the texts, languages, or scripts of ancient Egypt. It provides electronic access to nearly 1,400 papyrus images and texts, and it allows you to search by topic, such as "slavery," "women and children," or "religious aspects" or by language, such as Hieratic, Demotic, Coptic, and Latin. Students can find basic introductions to the world of the papyri, the history of ancient Egypt, and Egyptian papyrus writing under Greek and Roman rule. A search engine for keywords will be useful if you already know of a specific text or topic you want to research.

1848 REVOLUTIONS

Best Search Engine: http://www.google.com/
Key Search Terms: 1848 revolutions
                              Italian revolutions + 1848
                              Austria + revolution + 1848
                              Eastern Europe + revolutions + 1848

Encyclopedia of 1848 Revolutions
http://www.ohiou.edu/~Chastain/
high school and up

This gem of a site provides an in-depth look at the 1848 revolutions. While most Web sites give you the history of one country's revolutionary events during this period, the *Encyclopedia of 1848 Revolutions* covers all the revolutions of this era. The result is that you can compare events, look for broader themes, and conduct more comprehensive research. You can investigate the first of the 1848 revolutions in Sicily, read about the struggles in Austria, Hungary, and France, and take an in-depth look at the often-overlooked revolutions in Eastern and Central Europe.

The *Encyclopedia of 1848 Revolutions* is also unique in that it brings together the work of dozens of scholars who are experts in their fields. You'll find essays written by historians from the United States, Canada, and Europe (each piece is in English). The site is also a snap to navigate.

From the home page, select "Table of Contents," and then simply scroll down the extensive index to find the topics that interest you. The index contains links to essays that explain concepts that are important to understanding the 1848 revolutions, such as absolutism and liberalism. You'll also find entries to essays about specific events, such as the March Revolutions in Germany, as well as those about key people. Don't over-look the essays that deal with broader themes and topics, such as "Russia in 1848," "Women's Rights in France," and "Students of Paris." The site also does an excellent job of examining women's roles in the various revolutions.

Although this site is a terrific resource, it does have a few drawbacks. You won't want to turn to the *Encyclopedia of 1848 Revolutions* if you don't already have a basic grasp of the subject matter. The site doesn't outline events that took place in each country, and the index isn't ar-ranged according to nation or year. It is simply alphabetical. So unless you want to spend a lot of time clicking on each index topic, you'll want to approach this site with an understanding of the revolution you're studying. In other words, this site will not spoon-feed you the material. Brush up on your basics at *Encyclopedia Britannica* before you dive into *Encyclopedia of 1848 Revolutions*. Also, keep in mind that *En-cyclopedia of 1848 Revolutions* doesn't have any photographs, illustrations, or time lines. It is a perfect resource for college students and more ad-vanced high school students. It is likely too advanced for younger students.

1848: Year of Revolutions
http://idcs0100.lib.iup.edu/modernera/newpage4.htm
middle school and up

Those of you looking for a more basic review of the 1848 revolutions will probably find this site a lot more helpful than the more advanced *Encyclopedia of 1848 Revolutions*. Because *1848: Year of Revolutions* is organized according to the nation in which a revolution took place, it's also easier to access. As an added bonus, *1848: Year of Revolutions* con-tains a number of excellent primary documents that are easy to find.

If you want to limit your research to the events that took place in one country, check out the menu that runs down the left-hand side of the home page. You can select "France," "Italy," "Austria," or "Prussia" to access a lot of helpful information. Each of these nation sections contains an overview of the political events that took place before and after the revolution. Within each overview you'll also find subsections that further break down the key events and people of this period. Select "Personalities" to learn about the people who shaped revolutionary events in each country. "Timeline" lays out each country's history in an outline format. Take the quiz to test how well you've absorbed the material. In addition to the overviews (and the "Personalities," "Timeline," and "Quiz" subsections), each nation section has links to scholarly essays (some within *Encyclopedia*) and primary documents.

For those of you who aren't trying to stick to the events of one nation, explore the menu in the center of the home page. Here you'll find some good material that examines the 1848 revolutions as a whole. For a short essay on the broad causes of the various revolutions, select "Overview" from this menu. If you want a more detailed perspective on the events (as well as the causes and outcomes) of the revolutions, select "The Revolution of 1848," which will take you to a thorough history written in outline form by Professor Gerhard Rempel of Western New England College. Maybe you just want to learn about the people involved in the different revolutions. If so, simply click on "The Personalities of 1848," which contains brief biographies of the key figures (along with some famous quotations). For a firsthand account of the events, follow the link to "Carl Schurz," a recollection of the revolutions written in 1907.

One of the best features of *1848: Year of the Revolutions* is its comprehensive time line. This valuable tool allows you to examine *all* the revolutionary events taking place across Europe. It's easy to read, fairly detailed, and a great way to review material. All you need to do is scroll down the home page to the "1848 Revolutions Timetable."

ENGLAND—GENERAL

Best Search Engine: http://www.google.com/
Key Search Terms: Britain + history
                                England + history

Britannia
http://britannia.com/history/
middle school and up

Britannia is an enormous commercial site covering British history, culture, and current events. Although you have to skirt the flashing advertisements, it's worth the effort.

This URL takes you directly to the "History" page, where you'll find just about anything you can think of. The table of contents page is divided into many sections, including "Timelines of History," "Narratives of History," "Historic Documents," "Time Periods," and much more.

If you're interested in the Anglo-Saxon period, for example, you won't be disappointed. Under "Timelines," you'll want to try "Anglo Saxon England." You also may want to access "The Anglo Saxon Chronicle" under "Historic Documents" and the "Saxon Shore c. 370" under "Historic Maps." And this is only an inkling of what you can find at this site on the Anglo-Saxon period.

The same wealth of information can be found on numerous other British topics, including "The Reformation and Restoration," "The Age of Empire," and "Arthurian History," for example. There are also links to histories of London, church histories, original sources and texts, biographies of key people, maps, mailing lists, and much more.

ENGLAND—TUDOR/ELIZABETHAN

Best Search Engine: http://www.google.com/
Key Search Terms: England + history + Tudors
                     Elizabethan + history
                     Henry VIII + history

Elizabethan England: A Compendium of Common Knowledge, 1558–1603
http://renaissance.dm.net/compendium/home.html
middle school and up

Written for writers, actors, and reenactors, this site explores the daily life of Elizabethans in all its nitty-gritty detail. The table of contents includes such topics as "Money: The Basics," "Marriage and Family," "Domestic Details," "Honor and Dueling," "Shopping in London," "Wedding Customs," and many other topics, including a short history of the era. You'll also find maps and plans, a bibliography, and links to related sites.

Click on "Marriage and Family," for example, and you'll learn that girls could legally marry at 12, boys at 14, although this was not recommended. You can read what was usually included in the marriage contract, how people felt about love before marriage, and lists of successful and unsuccessful marriages of the time.

The Tudors
http://hiwaay.net/~crispen/tudor/index.html
middle school and up

With information on "The Tudor Family Tree," "Tudor Chronology," "The Arts in Tudor England," "The Six Wives of Henry VIII," "Tudor Heraldry," "Cause of Death of Henry VIII," and "The Music of Henry VIII," this site covers lots of ground.

If you're interested in Henry VIII's six wives, for example, follow this link and you'll find complete genealogical information for each of them, including previous marriages. You'll find a very interesting discussion of heraldry, peerage, and royal arms under "Tudor Heraldry." The origins of heraldry are discussed, definitions are given for the various titles, and an assortment of historical figures are discussed.

Helpful links, quotes from Queen Elizabeth, and pretty illustrations make this a user-friendly site.

ENGLAND—NORMAN AND 1066

Best Search Engine: http://www.google.com/
Key Search Terms: England + history
                                    Norman conquest + history
                                    William the Conqueror + England
                                    Battle of Hastings + history

EyeWitness: Invasion of England, 1066
http://www.ibiscom.com/bayeux.htm
middle school and up

This attractive EyeWitness Web site details the events of William the Conqueror's invasion of Britain in 1066, including the events that preceded the invasion. Images from the Bayeux Tapestry, which describes the invasion, illustrate the site.

Invasion of England, 1066 begins with an excellent overview of the Battle of Hastings and then continues with a fascinating section on the Bayeux tapestry, which tells the story of the conquest of England from the Norman perspective. The text describing the tapestry is broken into segments that correspond to the scenes of the tapestry. There's a piece called "King Edward Sends Harold on a Mission," "Harold Swears an Oath to William," "The Death and Burial of Edward the Confessor," and more.

This page is part of a larger *EyeWitness History* site, with sections on various time periods. *Invasion of England, 1066* is part of the "Middle Ages/Renaissance" section, and within this section are seven other pages, which may be of interest to you if you're researching the Norman invasion within the broader context of the Middle Ages. Some of the other pages listed in the menu are "The Crusaders Capture Jerusalem, 1099" and "Richard the Lionheart, 1191." The complete menu of "Middle Ages/Renaissance" pages runs down the left-hand side of this page.

ORB: The Online Reference Book for Medieval Studies
http://orb.rhodes.edu/

This ambitious site serves as an online textbook for medieval studies. The site contains an encyclopedia with essays, bibliographies, images, documents, and links to other sources; a list of essential medieval topics; a textbook library; a collection of resources for the nonspecialist; and a list of external links.

The Normans
http://www.schoolshistory.org.uk/Normans.htm
middle school

This is a true middle school site, complete with lesson plans for grades seven, eight, and nine, but if you're just doing some research on the Norman invasion, you'll probably be more interested in reading the text than in looking at the lesson plans. Start on the home page with the overview of the Normans, then proceed through the menu of Norman conquest topics at the bottom of the page, or pick and choose the ones you're most interested in. Choices include pages on "Edward the Confessor," "William the Conqueror," "The Battle of Hastings," "Castles," and more. The site is searchable by keyword and contains interactive resources, such as quizzes, as well as an excellent page of links.

ENGLAND—VICTORIAN

Best Search Engine: http://www.google.com/
Key Search Terms: Victorian + England
                              Victorian + history
                              Queen Victoria + history

Queen Victoria's Empire
http://www.pbs.org/empires/victoria/
middle school and up

This attractive PBS site, based on the PBS series of the same name, features the following sections: "History of a Reign," "Her Majesty," "The Changing Empire" (which focuses on the people, places, and events of Victoria's reign) and "Secrets of the Empire" (an interactive game). In addition to these historical sections, there's a list of Web resources on the topic and a section devoted to educational resources. Look under "History of a Reign" for the most information about Victorian England.

The Victorian Web (1837–1901)
http://65.107.211.206/victorian/victov.html
middle school and up

For all things Victorian, this is your site. The wealth of historical information is a little mind-boggling, but the site is extremely well organized and easy to navigate, so you shouldn't have a hard time making your way through the pages. The site is divided into 20 sections—everything from "The Victorians," "Political History," and "Gender Matters" to "Genre and Technique" and "Economic Contexts." There are several sections that offer additional resources, a search function, a bibliography, and other related aids.

Choose any one of the main sections, and you'll be presented with a long list of topics, each of which is a link to an essay of substantial depth. Choose "Political History" for example, and your essay topics will be arranged under the following headings: "Corn Laws," "Reform Acts," "Women's Suffrage," "Prime Ministers," "Other Figures," "Miscellaneous," "The British Empire and International Relations," "Economic History," "Related Topics," and "Pre-Nineteenth Century Political History." In addition, there's a time line of British history at the top of this page.

ENLIGHTENMENT

Best Search Engine: http://www.google.com/

Key Search Terms: Enlightenment + history

European Enlightenment + history

Age of Reason + history

Scientific revolution + history

The European Enlightenment
http://www.wsu.edu/%7Edee/ENLIGHT/ENLIGHT.HTM
middle school and up

This extensive and attractive overview of seventeenth- and eighteenth-century Europe makes considerable use of frames, which will give some browsers trouble, but otherwise it's a very useful site. You'll find 12 topics in the table of contents, each of which links you to academic essays that are quite captivating. You'll find topics such as "The Case of England," "Blaise Pascal," "The Scientific Revolution," and "Women: Communities, Economies, and Opportunities." Try the two general links on the seventeenth and eighteenth century for an introduction, then proceed from there to the more specific topics.

Internet Modern History Sourcebook: The Enlightenment
http://www.fordham.edu/halsall/mod/modsbook10.html
middle school and up

For primary sources on the Enlightenment, there's a wealth of material at the *Internet Modern History Sourcebook,* and as always it's organized in a very useful and readable way. You'll find the page divided into two major parts—"The Enlightenment" and "Religion in an Age of Reason"—both of which are subdivided into numerous specific sections. You'll find texts here from Voltaire, Adam Smith, and Lady Mary Wortley Montagu to name just a sampling of the authors represented.

The European Enlightenment Glossary
http://www.wsu.edu:8080/~dee/WORLD.HTM
middle school and up

Stop wandering around in the dark of your modern vocabulary. Define the Enlightenment and its heavy-duty intellectual movements with the help of this helpful glossary.

ETHIOPIA

Best Search Engine: http://www.google.com/
Key Search Terms: Ethiopia + history
                     Africa + history

History of Ethiopia
http://www.emulateme.com/history/ethiophist.htm
high school and up

This comprehensive history site begins with a section called "Origins and the Early Periods," which covers such topics as the "Aksumite State" and the "Zagwe Dynasty" and ends with "Ethiopia in Crisis: Famine and Its Aftermath, 1984–88." In between, you'll find seven other sections, covering all of Ethiopia's history. "The Making of Modern Ethiopia" will be of particular interest if you want to research Menelek II or the beginnings of Haile Selassie's reign.

Links within the site take you to an Ethiopian glossary, where you'll find some unusual terms, as well as others you've probably heard before, defined in significant detail.

"Ethiopia: Land of Plenty," One World Magazine
http://www.oneworldmagazine.org/focus/etiopia/index.html
high school and up

Here you'll get a sort of patchwork history of Ethiopia as well as some insight into contemporary issues. This site is a 1996 production of an online environmental publication focused on Ethiopia. Gorgeous photographs illustrate the text, which is divided into sections written by scholars.

"The Past" contains three articles—"The Sign and the Seal," "Sellassie vs. Mussolini," and "Lost Cities of Africa." These three articles will probably help you most if you're studying Ethiopia's history. But there's lots to learn from the other articles, too.

"The Land" contains "Africa High and Wild," "Ethiopian River Adventures," and "Gelada Baboons." The final section, "The People," has "Surviving Salvation," "Women in Power," and "The Bobo Dread."

EUROPEAN UNION

Best Search Engine: http://www.google.com/

Key Search Terms: European Union + history

Europa: The European Union On-line
http://europa.eu.int/index_en.htm
middle school and up

News, activities, institutions, ABC, official documents—these are some of the sections you'll find at this online headquarters for the European Union. Look under the section called "ABC" for an excellent history of the European Union, as well as for copies of treaties, a glossary, and other useful materials.

If there's a specific body of the Union you'd like to research, try clicking on "Institutions," where you'll find the "European Investment Bank," "The European Ombudsman," and the "Court of Justice," for example.

While this site offers good historical information, it's also quite up-to-date and contains a news section where you can research recent European Union news, as well. This section is nicely organized into about 20 different topic areas, so if you're interested in the debate on Europe's future, for example, or in the euro, you'll find news stories and more collected under each of these topics.

EUROPE—POST-NAPOLEONIC

Best Search Engine: http://www.google.com/

Key Search Terms: Europe + nineteenth century + history

Europe + post + Napoleon

Encyclopedia of Revolutions of 1848
http://cscwww.cats.ohiou.edu/~Chastain/contents.htm
middle school and up

More than 170 historians from around the world have contributed articles on the experience of the revolutions throughout Europe, from Ireland in the west to Russia in the east, and all points between. You'll find articles on the Austrian Reichstag, the Bulgarian Uprising, the October Revolution in Vienna, and Polish women, to name just a few of the topics listed in the table of contents.

The Internet Modern History Sourcebook: The Long Nineteenth Century: The Hegemony of the West
http://www.fordham.edu/halsall/mod/modsbook3.
    html#Council%20of%20Vienna
middle school and up

This collection of primary source documents is one of the first and most extensive on the World Wide Web. Most of the included documents are in English, but there are texts available in Latin, French, and Spanish as well. *The Modern History Sourcebook* is divided into convenient categories, one of them being "The Long 19th Century: The Hegemony of the West," the URL for which is provided at the top of this entry. Just scroll down a bit from the top of the page to find "The Long 19th Century." The site is searchable by author, title, or keyword.

EUROPE—POST WORLD WAR I

Best Search Engine: http://www.google.com/
Key Search Terms: Europe + post + World War I
                       Europe + history + twentieth century
                       Russian Revolution + history

Modern World History
http://www.bbc.co.uk/education/modern/
middle school and up

Put together by the BBC, this site offers extensive coverage of European politics and events from the end of World War I through World War II. It is expansive in its coverage of the era, with such sections as the "Treaty of Versailles," "Russia in Revolution," "The Wall Street Crash," "Propaganda," and "Allied Victory." No other site comes close in combining Web technologies, historical research, and a storehouse of images to bring to life the condition of Europe in the middle of the last century.

*The Internet Modern History Sourcebook: War, Conflict, and Progress: The
    Emerging World*
http://www.fordham.edu/halsall/mod/modsbook4.html
middle school and up

This collection of primary source documents is one of the first and
most extensive on the World Wide Web. Most of the included documents are in English, but there are texts available in Latin, French, and
Spanish as well. This section covers the period from World War I
through the end of the twentieth century.

EUROPE—POST WORLD WAR II

Best Search Engine: http://www.google.com/

Key Search Terms: Europe + post + World War II

                      Europe + twentieth century + history

AllExperts: European History
http://www.allexperts.com/getExpert.asp?Category=670
middle school and up

This great site offers experts on many different topics, but the URL
provided here is just for European history. Each visiting scholar is listed
with a brief description of his or her special areas of interest. One historian lists his focus as Nazi Germany, fascist Italy, and World War II.
Another says he is an expert on the Nuremberg Trials and the foreign
policy of European powers since Napoleon. Quite a few scholars are
available to answer your questions, and links are provided for submitting
your question right on the site. You can also read rankings of these
experts in categories such as "timeliness of response," "knowledge," "clar-
ity," and "politeness."

*The Internet Modern History Sourcebook: War, Conflict, and Progress: The
    Emerging World*
http://www.fordham.edu/halsall/mod/modsbook4.html

This collection of primary source documents is one of the first and
most extensive on the World Wide Web. Most of the included documents are in English, but there are texts available in Latin, French, and
Spanish as well. This section covers the period from World War II
through the end of the twentieth century.

FASCISM

Best Search Engine: http://www.google.com/
Key Search Terms: Fascism + history

Mussolini + history

Fact Monster: History of Fascism
http://www.factmonster.com/ce6/history/A0858080.html
middle school and up

Fact Monster has an excellent article that addresses the history of fascism. It's part of a larger fascism article, which has sections on "Characteristics of Fascist Philosophy" and "The Fascist State," as well as a "Bibliography," all of which might interest you, too, depending on your particular area of research. See the links at the bottom of "History" if you'd like to read more.

In any case, start with the "History" section, which contains the following: "Origins of Fascism," "Emergence after World War I," and "Fascism since World War II." This overview will go a long way toward helping you understand the rise of fascism in Europe, how it managed to win followers, and how its popularity was shaped by other events and movements of the time.

Modern World History: Fascism in Italy
http://www.bbc.co.uk/education/modern/
middle school and up

Part of a larger BBC site, reviewed under "**Europe—Post World War II,**" this page on fascism in Italy gives excellent background information on the origins of the movement after World War I, the ways in which Mussolini changed Italy, and why Mussolini became so unpopular.

If you're researching the spread of fascism throughout Europe, you'll want to pay special attention to the first section of this article, which explains numerous reasons for the popularity of Italy's fascist party following World War I. In addition, the final part of the third section sheds some light on Mussolini's relationship with Hitler and how this led to his own demise.

FEUDALISM AND FEUDAL LIFE

Best Search Engine: http://www.google.com/
Key Search Terms: Feudalism + history

Middle Ages + history

ORB: The Online Reference Book for Medieval Studies
http://orb.rhodes.edu/
high school and up

This ambitious site serves as an online textbook for medieval studies. It contains an encyclopedia with essays, bibliographies, images, documents, and links to other sources; a list of essential medieval topics; a textbook library; a collection of resources for the nonspecialist; and a list of external links.

The site itself recommends starting with the encyclopedia. You won't find any resources listed under "feudalism," but you will find much that relates to the topic, so use this to supplement your research if you're looking into a particular aspect of feudalism.

Click on "What Every Medievalist Should Know" for an alphabetical list of topics that the site manager says is "meant for the beginning to semi-advanced graduate student." Under "F," you'll find "Feudalism and Knighthood." These are by and large print resources, so if you want to do your research online, don't bother with this section as it will refer you to books and articles. However, if you're ready to be referred to essential texts on this topic, the list you'll find here is top-notch.

For strictly online resources, try "Medieval Studies for the Non-specialist," which contains sites that offer FAQs and bibliography sections, sites that specialize in living history, and articles that address misconceptions about the Middle Ages.

Feudal Terms of England (and Other Places)
http://www.geocities.com/abrigon/terms.html
middle school and up

You'll find terms like "adulterine castle" and "moneyer" at this extensive site. Terms are listed alphabetically and are accompanied by a brief (one to three sentence) definition. This is a handy reference if you're researching any topic from the Middle Ages, but especially if the topic is related to feudal life.

Exploring Japanese Feudalism
http://www.variable.net/hidden/jap/introduction.html
middle school and up

This is an academic course, designed as a showcase for RealPlayer which is no longer enabled, but the vivid graphics and helpful text make it worth your visit. There are sections on "Japan's Founding Myth," "Japan's Feudalist Society," and "Militarism in the Feudalist Society," which addresses the warrior ethic and the establishment of the Shogunate.

From the home page, click on "Begin the Regular Course," then just choose the section that interests you most, or start at the beginning and read all the way through for a thorough introduction to the topic. The text is quite accessible for the beginning student, the articles are fairly brief, and the illustrations bring the text alive. A quiz and glossary complete the offerings at this site.

Tales of the Middle Ages: Daily Life
http://www.godecookery.com/mtales/mtales08.htm
middle school and up

If you're researching feudal life, you may use this site to get a broader understanding of day-to-day life in the Middle Ages. Here you'll find true stories, fables, and legends about daily life in the Middle Ages. The URL listed will take you directly to the page on "Daily Life," which is just one section of a larger site called *Tales of the Middle Ages*. The brief essays in "Daily Life" deal with an eclectic array of topics that includes hygiene, cosmetics, and medicine, but at the bottom of the page, you'll find links to other sections on subjects as diverse as "Cats," "Christmas," "Clergy," "Food and Drink," "Miracles," "Religious Art," "Gardens," and "Riddles."

FOOD AND DOMESTIC LIFE

Best Search Engine: http://www.google.com/
Key Search Terms: Food + history

Domestic life + history

Home arts + history

Culinary History Timeline
http://www.gti.net/mocolib1/kid/food1.html
middle school and up

This gateway site lists links that deal with social history, manners, and menus, which should just about cover it if you're interested in domestic life. After an initial section that provides links to sites on American culinary traditions and surveys, world surveys, and social and culinary surveys, you'll find the actual time line, which begins with a link for prehistory and moves gradually forward from there.

Although the list is focused more on North American sites, it does list sites that deal with medieval Europe, the Middle East, Africa, and Central America, for example.

Following is a sample of the survey topics: *An American Feast: Food,*

Dining, and Entertainment in the United States (1776–1931), *Eating in the 20ᵗʰ Century*, and *Religious Food Practices*. Individual topics include *Prehistoric Puzzle: Diet and Subsistence in Africa*, *Fooles and Fricassees: Food in Shakespeare's England*, and *Rice Planter Lifestyle*, which should give you a feel for the diversity of subjects found here.

Medieval/Renaissance Food Home Page
http://www.pbm.com/~lindahl/food.html
middle school and up

For a manageable gateway site on the topic of food and beverage in the Middle Ages, this little site can't be beat. The list of links is organized by the following topics: "Primary Sources, Reference, Bibliography"; "Articles/Publications"; "Individual Recipes"; and "Other Information that Might Be of Interest."

You'll find original thirteenth-century cookbooks, an article on Viking foods, and recipes for making a fourteenth-century English feast, among the offerings. There's also a mailing list associated with this page, in case you want to stay in regular contact with other folks interested in the topic.

Tales of the Middle Ages: Food and Drink
http://www.godecookery.com/mtales/mtales14.htm
middle school and up

Here you'll find true stories, fables, and legends about daily life in the Middle Ages. The URL listed here takes you directly to the page on "Food and Drink," which is one section of a larger site called *Tales of the Middle Ages*. It's also one of the best sections on the site. You'll find information on an eclectic array of topics that includes meat preservation, eating during Lent, table settings, table etiquette, seating arrangements, recipes, holidays, and more. There's quite a bit of information on the drinking and brewing of ales.

FRANCE—GENERAL

Best Search Engine: http://www.google.com/
Key Search Terms: France + history

Histoire de France
http://instruct1.cit.cornell.edu/Courses/french_history/
high school and up

Following these general sites, you'll find quite a few specific topics in French history, with suggested Web sites for researching those topics, but this gateway site is a good place to search for any subject within French history. Though its title is French, this site from Cornell University is all in English, except for occasional links to French resources.

Check out the menu on the home page—"Generalities," "Cinema," "Middle Ages," "Renaissance," "17th Century," "18th Century," "Revolution," "First Empire," "1814–1914," and "1914–." If you can't find it here, it's probably not on the Web. Click on any one of these sections, and you'll be treated with oodles of links, most of them annotated to make it easier for you to pick the one you need.

French History Introduction
http://www.france.com/culture/history/
middle school and up

Although this site is oriented toward tourists planning a visit to France, it provides a nicely organized and comprehensive introduction to all the periods in French history. Once you read the introduction, you can check the menu on the left for the time period that interests you, or you can begin reading at the beginning with "Pre-History" (2 million B.C.–200 B.C.). Other sections include "Antiquity," "Middle Ages," "Renaissance," "Grand Siècle," "Revolution," "Napoleon," "19th Century," and "20th Century."

Each section contains a fairly brief article on the period, a chronology, and links to sites that address important people and events. Click on "Grand Siècle," for example, to get an excellent introduction to the age of Louis XIV, with all its grandeur and power. You'll see a picture of Versailles, and one of the Sun King himself, and there's a link you can follow that will give you a brief description of Versailles.

Timeline of French History
http://www.info-france-usa.org/profil/glance/history.htm
middle school and up

This time line of France's history begins with prehistory, cave art, and stone monuments and proceeds to 1997, when Lionel Jospin was named prime minister. An excellent resource if you're looking to place something chronologically in France's past.

FRANCE—AGE OF CHARLES V

Best Search Engine: http://www.google.com/
Key Search Terms: Charles V + history
                      Hundred Years' War + history

The Age of King Charles V
http://www.bnf.fr/enluminures/aaccueil.htm
middle school and up

This site from the Bibliothèque Nationale features 1,000 images of illuminated text in addition to its excellent content on the age of Charles V. Delve in by looking at the table of contents, which you can access by clicking on "Introductory Text" on the home page. Choose either "Themes" or "Manuscripts" to browse a list of those. In the table of contents, you'll find basic topics such as "Hundred Years' War," "History of France and Dynastic History," and "Charles V, King of France."

If you'd rather search by themes, you can choose from this list of five links: "History," "Religion," "Science and Technology," "Sports and Entertainment," and "Miscellaneous."

The manuscripts accessible on this page include the *Breviary of Martin of Aragon* and *The Catalan Atlas*.

FRANCE—FIRST EMPIRE

Best Search Engine: http://www.google.com/
Key Search Terms: Napoleon + history
                       France + Napoleon

The PBS Empire Series: Napoleon
http://www.pbs.org/empires/napoleon/home.html
middle school and up

"To Destiny," "Mastering Luck," "The Summit of Ambition," and "The End" are the names of the four PBS episodes around which this site is organized. You can read an overview of Napoleon I's life, organized around these episodes, by clicking on "About Napoleon." Under "Special Features," you can look at a battlefield simulator, send a Napoleon e-postcard, or download the Napoleon screensaver. There's also a time line and a section on classroom resources. This is a pretty multimedia site, available in Flash 4 as well as in HTML for those who prefer the simpler version.

FRANCE—SECOND EMPIRE

Best Search Engine: http://www.google.com/
Key Search Terms: France + history
                       Napoleon Bonaparte + history
                       Second Empire + France

Chronology, The Second Empire, 1852–1870
http://www.france.diplomatie.fr/archives/dossiers/140ministres.gb/empire2/
  chrono.html
high school and up

Part of the *French Diplomatic Archives* site, this thorough chronology of the Second Empire begins with Napoleon Bonaparte being declared emperor and ends with the capitulation of Napoleon III and the proclamation of France as a republic. It's just dates and brief descriptions of corresponding events, but it will help you keep track of what can be a confusing period in French history.

FRANCE—THIRD REPUBLIC

Best Search Engine: http://www.google.com/
Key Search Terms: France + history
                  Third Republic + France

1870–1914: France as a Republic: Crises and Consolidation
http://www.france.diplomatie.fr/france/gb/histoire/histoire03.html
middle school and up

This is an excellent brief overview of the Third Republic, from its origins in the Paris Commune uprising to its final days before World War I.

The Siege and Commune of Paris, 1870–1871
http://www.library.northwestern.edu/spec/siege/
middle school and up

Hosted by Northwestern University Library, this site contains more than 1,000 digitized photographs relating to the siege and commune of Paris. People, buildings, and events are organized in several indices, which include portraits, handwritten documentation on the backs of photos, and a master list. This site is fully searchable, or you can browse from the table of contents.

FRANCO-PRUSSIAN WAR

Best Search Engine: http://www.google.com/
Key Search Terms: Franco-Prussian War + history
                  Otto von Bismarck + history
                  Franco-German War + history

Franco-Prussian War
http://www.encyclopedia.com/articles/04695.html
middle school and up

For a basic overview of this war, try this article at *Encyclopedia.com*. Three sections—"Causes," "The Course of the War," and "Results"— give you a general history, complete with links to related articles in the encyclopedia.

This site is best used as a starting point, to help you get your facts straight. For more in-depth information on the war, you'll want to use the following sites.

The Siege and Commune of Paris, 1870–1871
http://www.library.northwestern.edu/spec/siege/
middle school and up

Hosted by Northwestern University Library, this site contains more than 1,000 digitized photographs relating to the siege and commune of Paris during the Franco-Prussian War. People, buildings, and events are organized in several indices, which include portraits, handwritten documentation on the backs of photos, and a master list. This site is fully searchable, or you can browse from the table of contents.

Modern History Sourcebook: A War Correspondent in the Franco-Prussian War, 1870
http://school.discovery.com/homeworkhelp/worldbook/atozhistory/f/209000.html
middle school and up

Here's a captivating look at an English war correspondent's experience covering the Franco-Prussian War. From his dispatch in London to his arrest by the French, who suspected him of being a Prussian spy, this story reveals both the history of the war, as well as some of the history of journalism. If you're interested in wartime reporting, you won't want to miss this little gem from the *Modern History Sourcebook*.

FRENCH REVOLUTION

Best Search Engine:	http://www.google.com/
Key Search Terms:	French Revolution + history
	Napoleon + history

Links on the French Revolution
http://userwww.port.ac.uk/andressd/frlinks.htm#Intro
middle school and up

At this index site, you'll find a wide variety of annotated links to specialized sites on the French Revolution. Most are in English. The site is organized into the following sections: "Introductory Material," "Deeper Exploration," "If You Read French," "Further Reference," and "Assorted Materials."

The French Revolution
http://www.geocities.com/Paris/Arc/8639/revolution.html
middle school and up

In addition to an excellent overview of the "French Revolution and the Reign of Terror," you'll find "Before 1789," which explores the Royal and Louis XVI era, and "After 1789," which explores Napoleon Bonaparte and the New France.

You can also research specific characters or events in the Revolution by following the links to those sections of the site. Click on "Character" for a list of links to biographies of key historical figures in the Revolution. You'll find Robespierre, Marie Antoinette, Louis XVI, Rosalie, Elisabeth de Bourbon, and Comte Mercy, to name just a few. While written for beginning students of the French Revolution, the biographies don't skimp on information.

If you're interested in reading more about a specific event, such as the "Death of the Dauphin" or the "March of Women," click on "Events." The list of events is arranged in chronological sequence for your convenience.

"Scripts from Hans Axel von Fersen" is a fascinating section. It contains excerpts of letters written between 1789 and 1793 either to or from Hans Axel von Fersen. The excerpts provided reflect on the relationship between him and Marie Antoinette, especially during the time that the royal family was captured.

GENOCIDES

Best Search Engine: http://www.google.com/
Key Search Terms: Genocide + history
                        Holocaust + history

Horus Links: Western History by Periods: Twentieth Century
http://www.ucr.edu/h-gig/hist-periods/twent.html
middle school and up

This index site deals solely with the twentieth century. In the table of contents, you'll see links for the "Holocaust," the "Korean War," "Mass Murders and Genocides," "World War I," "World War II," the "Vietnam War," and "Post–World War II." These are fairly self-explanatory categories, and each one contains dozens of links.

"Mass Murders and Genocides" is the largest category and is broken down into a collection of links that includes the Armenian, Cambodian, general, Muslim, Nanjing, and Rwandan genocides. There's also a link for "Genocide Studies." Under each of these categories, you'll find several links to sites that cover the specific subject. The Rwandan links were not working when we visited the site, but the rest were, so we include it here since it covers such valuable information.

There's also a "Miscellaneous" section at the bottom of the page, which contains a few very interesting links, one on the Kent State University 1970 attack on four students, another on President McKinley's assassination, and several others.

The Wolf Lewkowicz Collection (1922–1939)
http://web.mit.edu/maz/wolf/
middle school and up

If you're looking for a personal resource on the Holocaust, you'll want to take a look at this online collection of letters between Wolf Lewkowicz of Poland and Sol J. Zissman, his deceased sister's son, who was living in America. The letters reflect many of the difficulties that faced Jews in Poland during a terrible time of persecution. The letters end several years before Wolf and his wife were transported to the Treblinka concentration camp, where they died.

The Nanjing Massacre, 1937
http://www.princeton.edu/~nanking/
middle school and up

Commemorating the 60th anniversary of the holocaust, this Princeton University Web site offers a brief history of the massacre, a gallery of photographs, and links to other useful sites. Follow the links in the menu at the left once you've entered the main site.

Pre- and Post-Holocaust Genocides
http://www.fordham.edu/halsall/mod/modsbook44.html
middle school and up

For primary source material on genocides, look at this page in the *Modern History Sourcebook*. You'll find quite a few useful links to Web sites on the Armenian, Rwandan, Cambodian, and other genocides.

There's also a link to a copy of "UN Resolution 260—On Genocide, 1948."

GERMANY—GENERAL

Best Search Engine: http://www.google.com/
Key Search Terms: Germany + history

German History WWW Links
http://www.tau.ac.il/GermanHistory/links.html
middle school and up

This is a personal selection of German history links by Ruti Ungar at the Institute for German History. According to him, it contains links appropriate for both beginning and more advanced students.

The directory of history resources is arranged by time period. A handful of other sections includes "German Literature," "German Philosophy," "Libraries," "German Studies," and "Museums," for example. Although some sections contain much more information than other sections, this is a helpful place to begin your explorations. Beware that some links take you to German-language sites, but most of the listings are in English.

History of Germany: Primary Documents
http://library.byu.edu/~rdh/eurodocs/germany.html
middle school and up

This Eurodocs page offers the most extensive selection of primary sources in German and Austrian history. Some are in German, and the collection begins with the classical period and continues up to the present. You'll find the complete works of Marx and Engels, as well as an excellent World War I document archive.

GERMANY—UNIFICATION

Best Search Engine: http://www.google.com/
Key Search Terms: Germany + unification
                              German unification + history
                              Unification era + Germany

The German Unification Era
http://www.geocities.com/Athens/Rhodes/6916/unification.htm
middle school and up

Part of a larger history of Germany site, this page covers the pre-unification and unification eras. The home page listed here presents a menu of topics under "The Pre-Unification Era (1790s–1867)" that begins with "The Congress of Vienna," "Conservatism and the Revolution of 1848," and "Germany before Bismarck" and ends, finally, with the "Franco-Prussian War." "The Unification Era (1870s–1880s)" covers "Unification Achieved," "Bismarckian Unity—The Constitutional Order," "Life in Bismarck's Germany," and other topics before ending with "The New King of Prussia and the End of Bismarck."

This is an excellent academic site. If you're writing a research paper on the unification era, you should be able to use these articles as much as you would an encyclopedia. You'll get a thorough overview without loads of detail on any one particular subject.

The essays are arranged so that you can read them from beginning to end, like a book, or click on links at the top of the page that let you skip over sections you don't want to read and go straight to what you do want.

If you find, after reading about this era, that you need more background on the period before pre-unification, or the period after for that matter, just click on the "Back to Main Page" link near the top of the page to see everything this site has to offer.

GERMANY—WEIMAR REPUBLIC

Best Search Engine: http://www.google.com/

Key Search Terms: Germany + Weimar Republic + history

                         Weimar Republic + Streeseman era

                         Treaty of Versailles + Weimar Republic

The Weimar Republic
http://home.carolina.rr.com/wormold/germany/history-12.htm
high school and up

This brief history of the Weimar Republic comes from the *Area Handbook of the U.S. Library of Congress*. It's a no-frills, evenhanded account of the German government between 1918 and 1933. You'll find sections on the constitution, the problems of parliamentary politics, and the Streeseman era. Follow the link at the bottom of the page back to the table of contents to find other German topics of interest.

Weimar and Nazi Germany
http://www.schoolshistory.org.uk/weimar.htm
middle school

Here you'll find covered the impact of the Treaty of Versailles, Gustav Streeseman, the Wall Street crash, and Hitler's rise to power in an attractive page with interactive capabilities. There's a quiz you can take to test your knowledge of this complex subject, and you might enjoy browsing the "Links" page and the "Backgrounds" page for other related topics of interest.

GERMANY—NAZISM

Best Search Engine:	http://www.google.com/
Key Search Terms:	Germany + Nazism + history
	Hitler + Nazism + history
	Nazi Party + Germany + history
	World War II + Nazism

Third Reich Pages Online
http://www.thirdreichpages.com/
middle school and up

This basic site offers educational articles that are easily accessible to students just beginning to study German history, as well as links to related resources. Articles are divided into two sections. "Behind the Third Reich" offers three articles on Hitler's family background and personality traits. "Hitler's Path to Power" traces his steps between 1914 and 1934 as he made his way to becoming Germany's dictator.

There's also a "Current News" section, which contains an article that compares the New Nazis to the Al-Qaeda Network responsible for the September 11, 2001, terrorist attacks in the United States. "Men of the Third Reich" contains useful biographies of key figures.

The Third Reich, 1933–45
http://home.carolina.rr.com/wormold/germany/history-13.htm

For a simple, concise account of the rise of Nazism under Adolf Hitler, the *Area Handbook for Germany* is great. The essay begins with a biographical section on Hitler, then continues with sections on the "Consolidation of Power," "Foreign Policy," "The Outbreak of World War II," "Total Mobilization and the Holocaust," and "Defeat."

GERMANY—POST WORLD WAR II

Best Search Engine: http://www.google.com/

Key Search Terms: Germany + post World War II + history

Germany + twentieth century + history

Germany + cold war + history

Historical Setting: 1945–1990
http://home.carolina.rr.com/wormold/germany/history-14.htm
high school and up

This page from the *Area Handbook for Germany* provides the best overview available on the immense changes that have taken place in Germany since World War II. From postwar occupation and division up through the opening of the Berlin Wall and unification, this essay concisely covers all the milestones of the second half of the twentieth century in text that is accessible to nonscholars.

GERMANY—RE-UNIFICATION

Best Search Engine: http://www.google.com/

Key Search Terms: Germany + re-unification + history

East Germany + West Germany + unification

Germany + Soviet bloc + 1989

Berlin Wall + Germany + 1989

Beyond the Fall: The Former Soviet Bloc in Transition, 1989–1999
http://www.time.com/time/btf/home.html
middle school and up

If you'd like a visual experience of German re-unification, try this photographic essay. For 10 years following the collapse of the Berlin Wall, *Time* contract photographer Anthony Suau traveled the lands of the former Soviet bloc. In hundreds of powerful images and audio commentaries, he documents the region's people as they leave behind their old lives and look toward an uncertain future.

Read the introduction for an essay that gives some background history on the Cold War and its eventual demise, while also weaving in the personal perspective of Suau. Then just follow the arrows at the bottom of each page for a tour of the exhibit.

GHANA, ANCIENT (SEE SONGHAY)

GREAT DEPRESSION

Best Search Engine: http://www.google.com/
Key Search Terms: Great Depression + history

Economic depression + U.S. history

Wall Street Crash + history

The New Deal Network
http://newdeal.feri.org/
middle school and up

The New Deal Network is an educational guide to the Great Depression of the 1930s. The site is divided into two sections, one for "Research and Study" and one for "Featured Exhibits." Under "Research and Study," you'll find a document library, a photo gallery, classroom resources, and an H-Net discussion group for teachers and historians. The really good stuff is listed under "Features." "The Magpie Sings the Great Depression" is a collection of stories, poems, songs, and graphics created during the 1930s by students at the Bronx's DeWitt Clinton High School to document their life and times. There's also a collection of 24 oral histories about the Depression from people living in Sevier, Utah.

*America from the Great Depression to World War II, Photographs from the
   FSA-OWI, 1935–1945*
http://memory.loc.gov/ammem/fsowhome.html
middle school and up

Among the most famous documentary photographs ever produced, these images show Americans in every part of the nation. During the first years of the project, photographers focused on rural life and the negative impact of the Great Depression, farm mechanization, and the Dust Bowl. Later photographs emphasize the country's mobilization for World War II.

GREAT ZIMBABWE

Best Search Engine: http://www.google.com/
Key Search Terms: Great Zimbabwe + history

                                Africa + ancient history

                                Africa + ancient empire

Washington State University: World Civilizations: Africa
http://www.wsu.edu/~dee/CIVAFRCA/CIVAFRCA.HTM
high school and up

This excellent history site is quite comprehensive and written for an academic audience, meaning it should cover the same ground you're trying to cover in that research paper for Ancient Civ. After a section on Egypt, the site moves through essays on Kush, Axum, the Iron Age south of the Sahara, Ghana, the Islamic invasions, the Aloravids, Mail, Songhay, the Hausa Kingdoms, Kanem Bornu, and Great Zimbabwe, among others.

In addition to the essays on these topics, you'll find a "Glossary of African Terms and Concepts," as well as a list of links.

Great Zimbabwe
http://www.bbc.co.uk/worldservice/africa/features/storyofafrica/10chapter1.
    shtml
middle school and up

This page from the BBC's *Story of Africa* site offers a wonderful multimedia introduction to the kingdom in Central Africa that flourished between 1200 and 1450 A.D. Read the text on this page, which includes sections on "Enduring Legacy," "Who Were They?", "Scope," "Building," "Wealth," and "Decline." Several inset boxes offer excerpts from other texts, and one includes an audio option, so that you can listen to the historian reading from his book.

At the right-hand side of the page is the menu for the entire Central Africa section of this site. The "Timeline" and "Useful Links" might also be of interest.

Great Zimbabwe Slide Show
http://www2.mc.maricopa.edu/anthro/lost_tribes/zimbabwe/index.html
middle school and up

Want a multimedia experience of this ancient walled city? Here's your chance. Some folks at Maricopa Community College have put together a slide show that includes 23 photographs of the ruins and text prepared by two professors in the Cultural Science Department of the college. The picture files are large, so be prepared to spend a little time waiting for these to load, but otherwise the site is user-friendly.

GREECE, ANCIENT: GENERAL

Best Search Engine: http://www.altavista.com/

Key Search Terms: Ancient Greece + history

Athens + history + culture

Ancient Greece + science

NM's Creative Impulse: The Development of Western Civilization: World History: Greece
http://history.evansville.net/greece.html
middle school and up

Here's a stellar index site on ancient Greece. The links are annotated to help you choose which ones are best for your interests, and the coverage is comprehensive. You'll find everything organized under "People," "Places," "Maps," "Events," "Timelines," "Resources," "Art," "Literature and Drama," "Music and Dance," "Religion," "Mythology and Philosophy," and "Daily Life and Culture." Unlike many index sites, this one feels personable and friendly, so don't fear getting lost in the maze of links. You're likely to find your way with ease at this gateway.

Washington State University: World Civilizations: Ancient Greece
http://www.wsu.edu:8080/~dee/GREECE/GREECE.HTM
high school and up

For an in-depth and comprehensive Greek history site, Washington State's online world civilizations course is the best. Sections include "Ancient Greece," "Sparta," "Athens," "The Delian League," "The Athenian Empire," "The Peloponnesian War," "The Spartan Hegemony," "The Theban Hegemony," and more.

GREECE, ANCIENT: CULTURE AND SCIENCE

Best Search Engine: http://www.altavista.com/

Key Search Terms: Ancient Greece + drama + history

Ancient Greece + culture

Ancient Greece + science

Ancient Theater
http://www.tlg.uci.edu/~tlg/index/resources.html
middle school and up

A concise but very helpful introduction to theater and stagecraft in ancient Greece, this page is part of a larger site on ancient drama, *Didaskalia*, which also publishes reviews of current and past productions of Greek and Roman dramas around the world. If you're writing a paper on Euripedes's famous drama *Medea*, for example, you can search here for current or past performances of the play around the world and read reviews. You can also find articles about ancient theater on the modern stage and a list of classical theater links.

Perseus Project
http://www.perseus.tufts.edu/
high school and up

Perseus, an undertaking of the Classics Department at Tufts University, is an evolving digital library for the study of the ancient Greek and Roman worlds. You'll find everything imaginable here, but its strength lies in its incredible collection of original texts, maps, diagrams, and images from ancient Greece. And just in case you'd like to search in Latin, for example, the site is fully searchable in multiple languages.

GREECE, ANCIENT: GOVERNMENT

Best Search Engine:	http://www.altavista.com/
Key Search Terms:	Ancient Greece + history + government
	Ancient Greece + politics
	Democracy + ancient Greece + history
	Athenian democracy + history
	Parthenon + ancient Greece + history

Introduction to Ancient Greece
http://www.greekspirit.com/
middle school

This basic history of ancient Greece covers land, people, Athens, government, jewelry, shopping, trade, education, writers and writing, entertainment, Olympic games, theater, art, and deities. Just click on "History" on the home page, and let the explorations begin.

You'll find sections on "The Dark Ages," "The Archaic Period," "The Classical Period," and "The Hellenistic Period."

If you're interested in government topics, click on "The Government" in the menu at the left. You'll read about how city-states came to be and the different types of government that existed in ancient Greece.

Bouleterion: Birthplace of Democracy
http://www.fhw.gr/projects/bouleuterion/en/
middle school and up

Travel to all areas of ancient Greece, using a clickable map, or simply choose from the list of places at the bottom of the home page. You can learn about the earliest forms of democracy . . . even watch a QuickTime video. To explore Athenian democracy, just choose "Hellas" and then "Athens" to begin your tour. Links within the text take you to more in-depth definitions of certain key terms.

GULF WAR

Best Search Engine: http://www.google.com/
Key Search Terms: Gulf War + history
                        Persian Gulf War + history
                        Desert Storm + history

The Gulf War
http://www.snowcrest.net/jmike/gulfwarmil.html
middle school and up

This is a dynamite list of links on everything from the cover-up of Gulf War Syndrome to UN resolutions on the Gulf. If you just want to browse Gulf War topics, this is a good place to start.

Don Mabry's Historical Text Archive
http://historicaltextarchive.com/
high school and up

Get the inside scoop. Don Mabry has collected historical documents on a number of different subjects, including the Persian Gulf War. If you're looking to read a personal account of the war, and maybe from a perspective that is not American, try one of the diaries found here. You can access the diary of an Israeli woman—"A Diary of the Gulf War: A View from Haifa" and the diary of an Iraqi soldier—"An Iraqi Lieutenant's Diary" (English translation).

Fog of War
http://www.washingtonpost.com/wp-srv/inatl/longterm/fogofwar/fogofwar.
   htm
high school and up

This extensive *Washington Post* site on the Gulf War contains many government documents, as well as interesting images and video clips. You'll find an article by analyst William Arkin, with counterpoints by General Charles Horner, on the role of the Baghdad bombing in the Iraqi defeat; you can read damage assessments of air strikes, listed by target and date, while viewing photographs of the damage in Baghdad. You can also review the U.S. military objectives for the war.

HAITIAN REVOLUTION

Best Search Engine: http://www.google.com/
Key Search Terms: Haiti + history
                        Haitian Revolution + history

Haiti Archive
http://www.hartford-hwp.com/archives/43a/102.html
high school and up

Here you'll find many wonderful resources, including a bibliography on the Haitian Revolution, an article that examines Poland's involvement in the revolution, and another that compares the revolutions in Jamaica and Haiti. There's also a link for *Heroes of Haiti* which examines the history of early Haiti with emphasis on the military perspective.

Haitian History
http://www.webster.edu/~corbetre/haiti/history/revolution/revolution.htm
high school and up

Bob Corbett's four-part essay, originally published in *Stretch* magazine in 1991 to honor the 200th anniversary of the beginning of the Haitian Revolution, is particularly good. It's a thorough and very readable historical account of the planters' move toward independence, the revolution of black people for full citizenship, and the slave uprising of 1791. The list of revolution-related links includes such things as Wordsworth's sonnet to Toussaint l'Ouverture and notes on the "Origin of the Term 'Maroon.'"

HAPSBURG EMPIRE (AUSTRO-HUNGARIAN EMPIRE)

Best Search Engine: http://www.google.com/
Key Search Terms: Hapsburg Empire + history
                        Hapsburg Empire + history

Holy Roman Empire + history

Austro-Hungarian Empire + history

Austro-German Empire + history

Austro-German Hapsburg Empire: 1438–1848
http://www.lukemastin.com/history/hapsburg_empire.html
middle school and up

A useful time line if you need to see the chronological relationship between the Protestant Reformation and the death of Johann Sebastian Bach, for example. This one includes a wide range of subjects, not just the political and military, and covers the dates and places commonly collected under the name "Holy Roman Empire."

Habsburg Biographies
http://www.antiquesatoz.com/
middle school and up

Need a little help navigating the family tree? Here's a fully alphabetized list of all the major Hapsburgs, with basic biographical detail (date of birth and death, title, names of parents) and some illustrations.

Habsburg: A H-Net Discussion Network
http://www2.h-net.msu.edu/~habsweb/
high school and up

Gathered here within H-Net are the folks who want to talk about the culture and history of the Hapsburg Monarchy, including its successor states in central Europe, from 1500 to the present. Does that description fit you?

There's a log of past discussions (searchable of course by topic), discussion threads, a book exchange, course syllabi, and a wonderful list of links geared toward academic research, as well as easy-to-follow instructions on joining a discussion group, if you're so inclined. If you can read German, you'll find access to an empire of information, although there's lots here in English too.

HAUSA, KANEM BORNU, AND YORUBA (ANCIENT NIGERIAN EMPIRES)

Best Search Engine: http://www.altavista.com/

Key Search Terms: Kanem Bornu + history

Hausa + history

Ancient Africa + history

Ancient Nigerian empires + history

Washington State University: World Civilizations: Africa
http://www.wsu.edu/~dee/CIVAFRCA/CIVAFRCA.HTM
high school and up

This excellent history site is quite comprehensive and written for an academic audience, meaning it should cover the same ground you're trying to cover in that research paper for Ancient Civ. After a section on Egypt, the site moves through essays on Kush, Axum, the Iron Age south of the Sahara, Ghana, the Islamic invasions, the Almoravids, Mali, Songhay, the Hausa Kingdoms, Kanem Bornu, and Great Zimbabwe, among others.

In addition to the essays on these topics, you'll find a "Glossary of African Terms and Concepts," as well as a list of links.

West African Kingdoms
http://www.bbc.co.uk/worldservice/africa/features/storyofafrica/
    index_section4.shtml
middle school and up

Part of the BBC's *Story of Africa* site, this section on the West African kingdoms contains pages on ancient Ghana, Kanem, Mali, Songhay, and the Hausa states, among other subjects. You'll love the multimedia presentations and the colorful illustrations.

Using the menu at the right, just pick the kingdom you want to explore, and click. You'll arrive at a separate page for each kingdom that explores, in a general overview, its complete history. Additional resources are woven into most pages. You'll find, for example, that within the "Ancient Ghana" page is a link to an audio recording of someone reading a quote from Al-Bakri, a tenth-century geographer, that describes the opulence surrounding the king of Ghana.

HEBREWS, ANCIENT

Best Search Engine: http://www.google.com/
Key Search Terms: Ancient Hebrews + history
                                    Diaspora + history

Washington State University: World Civilizations: The Hebrews
http://www.wsu.edu/~dee/HEBREWS/HEBREWS.HTM
high school and up

The Hebrews: A Learning Module is divided into two main sections—
"Hebrew History and Culture to the Diaspora" and "The Hebrew Reli-

gion." The first section contains pages on "The Land," "The Age of the Patriarchs," "The Occupation of Canaan," "The Two Kingdoms," "Exile," "The Diaspora," and other topics. The section on religion includes pages on "Pre-Mosaic Religion," "Monalatry and Monotheism," "The Prophetic Revolution," "Post-Exilic Religion," and "The Torah." Just follow the links to the sections that interest you and then click on "Continue" at the bottom of each page to read through the essays.

Under "Additional Resources," the "Glossary of Hebrew Terms and Concepts" will help you with unfamiliar terms, and the "Historical Atlas" may be of use for reference. There's also an anthology of Hebrew readings.

Virtual Museum Exhibits
http://rims.k12.ca.us/ancient_hebrews/
middle school and up

This exhibit on the ancient Hebrews has separate sections on "The Land," "The Common People," "The Exodus," "Beliefs," "Archaeology," "Artifacts," "Important People," and "Resources." The text is simple and straightforward but it's useful, and the site contains some nice graphics. Try this site if you're looking for a basic introduction.

HELLENISTIC EMPIRE (ALEXANDER THE GREAT) AND HELLENISM

Best Search Engine: http://www.google.com/
Key Search Terms: Alexander the Great + history
                        Hellenism + history
                        Hellenistic empire + Alexander

Alexander the Third (the Great)
http://www.hellenism.net/eng/alexander.htm
middle school and up

Hellenism is the focus of this site, and the URL above takes you directly to the page on Alexander the Great. You'll want to read this basic biography, which is broken down into the following four sections: "The First Years"; "Alexander Becomes King, the Campaign Begins"; "Alexander in Egypt, Guagamila, and India"; and "The End." You'll get the historical outline of his reign, as well as a bit of interpretation on his military and administrative prowess.

Ancient History Sourcebook: Hellenistic World
http://www.fordham.edu/halsall/ancient/asbook08.html
middle school and up

This URL takes you directly to the *Ancient History Sourcebook* page on the Hellenistic World. You'll find a table of contents brimming with topics of interest. Sections on "The Hellenistic World," "Alexander the Great," "The Hellenistic States," "Art and Architecture," "Literature," "Philosophy," "Religion," "Science and Medicine," and "Modern Perspectives" cover just about any subject you want to find. As always with the *Sourcebook,* you'll find many primary sources, as well as other Web sites with their own original material or lists of helpful links.

HINDUISM

Best Search Engine:	http://www.google.com/
Key Search Terms:	Hinduism + history
	Hinduism + religions
	India + Hinduism + history
	Hindu gods + history

Hinduism
http://www.bbc.co.uk/religion/religions/hinduism/history/index.shtml
middle school and up

This BBC site provides a stellar introduction to the long and complex history of Hinduism. The coverage is comprehensive, beginning with prehistoric religion in India—Hinduism dates back as far as 3,000 B.C.E. —and continuing through preclassical religion, when the Vedas were written, the rise of Jainism and Buddhism, the arrival of Islam, and more. There's even a section on the International Society of Krishna Consciousness. In addition to the history, you can read about Hindu beliefs, customs, worship, and holy days, too. If you just want a simple overview, go to "Features," where you'll find "The Bare Essentials of Hinduism."

History of India: Hinduism and Transition (600 B.C.–322 B.C.)
http://www.historyofindia.com/hinduism.html

This page on Hinduism is part of a larger *History of India* site, which means that you can easily expand your research by following links to other parts of the site. Click on the question, "What is Hinduism— Religion or Culture?" at the bottom of the page to explore this pervasive question.

HITTITES (SEE ALSO MESOPOTAMIA)

Best Search Engine: http://www.altavista.com/
Key Search Terms: Hittites + history

                        Mesopotamia + history

Ancient and Lost Civilizations: Hittites
http://www.crystalinks.com/hittites.html
middle school and up

Part of the *Ancient and Lost Civilizations* site, this page on the Hittites provides a good basic overview of the Hittites' empire, which dominated Mesopotamia from 1600 B.C. to 1200 B.C. A colorful graphic time line opens the page and is followed by an introduction and sections on "Homeland of the Hittites," "Language," "Legal System," and "Religion."

HOLOCAUST (SEE ALSO ANTI-SEMITISM)

Best Search Engine: http://www.google.com/
Key Search Terms: Holocaust + history

                        Death camps + history

                        World War II + Jews + history

Holocaust Survivors
http://www.holocaustsurvivors.org/
middle school and up

This Web site, which sets out to "present history with a human face," examines the tragedy of the Holocaust through the stories of Holocaust survivors. You can read personal accounts of survivors' experiences, listen to audio clips of them speaking and praying, and look at photographs. Through these firsthand accounts, you'll be able to learn about the Holocaust in an intense, personal, and moving way. In addition to giving you access to these primary documents, *Holocaust Survivors* also contains excellent interpretive material, including a historical introduction to the Holocaust, excerpts from scholarly texts, and an encyclopedia of Holocaust information.

To navigate this site, use the menu at the top right-hand side of the home page. Select "Survivor Stories" from this menu to listen to or to read Holocaust survivors' firsthand accounts of their experiences. You can choose to listen to specific sections of their stories or the entire narrative. If you'd rather read this material instead of listening to it, you can do that too. This section includes the narratives of people who experienced the Holocaust in different ways. Solomon Radasky's story is one of staying alive in a concentration camp. Eva Galler relates how she leapt from a "death train," while Jeannine Burk talks about being a "hidden child." Hearing these different perspectives will help you understand the differences—and underlying similarities—of Holocaust experiences.

Photographs accompany each of these narratives, but if you want to view an array of images (many of which are disturbing and not suitable for younger children), go to the "Photo Gallery" from the main menu You can then select the photographs you want to examine. There are dozens of pictures to choose from—photographs of Adolf Hitler, the inside of Auschwitz's gas chamber, the survivors of the Mauthausen concentration camp, and many more. Go to the "Audio Gallery" from the main menu to listen to survivors' accounts. Some of the audio clips in this section are related to those in "Survivor Stories," while others are totally different. For instance, you can hear survivors sing songs from their youth, say prayers for the families they lost in the Holocaust, and talk of their childhood. Listening to these records brings you intimately close to the history of the Holocaust.

Another great feature of this Web site is that it contains a lot of explanatory information to help you understand the primary source material. The "Survivor Stories" have links you can follow to the encyclopedia to learn more about specific people, places, or terms used by the survivors. Not sure what Shabbos is? Follow the link to find out what it means. If you want to go directly to the encyclopedia, just click on the heading from the main menu. For a general overview of the history of the Holocaust, you'll want to read "The Holocaust and History: An Introduction to the Survivors' Stories." To access this comprehensive essay, select "Texts" from the main menu. Then simply click on "The Holocaust and History." You'll find other interesting material in the "Texts" section, including "Documents from the Auschwitz Chronicle" and "The Death of Young Tzerna Morgenstern."

Holocaust Survivors has an online discussion group where you can post questions or engage in an ongoing dialogue with other visitors. Select "Discussion" from the main menu to reach it. If you are looking for additional resources to study the Holocaust, this site provides an extensive bibliography of the texts used to create *Holocaust Survivors* (choose "Bibliography" from the main menu) and of Internet material that might be of use (select "Links" from the main menu).

The Holocaust: A Learning Site for Students
http://www.ushmm.org/outreach/
middle school and up

If you are less interested in primary source material about the Holocaust and are instead looking for a site that provides the history of the Holocaust, you will definitely want to visit this excellent site from the United States Holocaust Memorial Museum. *The Holocaust: A Learning Site for Students* is thorough and engaging. It is packed full of information, but is well organized and easy to navigate. It contains time lines, artifacts, photographs, audio clips, and maps. While *Holocaust Survivors* brings you closer to the experience of the Holocaust, this Web site will allow you to better understand the history of the Holocaust and the events that came before and after it. *The Holocaust: A Learning Site for Students* is a gem of a site. It is one of those rare sites that are both educational and thoroughly engaging.

The Holocaust: A Learning Site for Students is arranged into five main sections: "Nazi Rule"; "Jews in Germany"; "The Final Solution"; "Nazi Camps"; and "Rescue and Resistance." Within each of these main topic headings, which you'll find across the top of the page (once you've clicked on "Enter the Learning Site" from the home page), there are several articles related to the main topic. In the "Nazi Rule" section, for instance, there are eight articles: "Hitler in 1993"; "Nazi Terror"; "SS Police State"; "Nazi Propaganda"; "Nazi Racism"; "World War II"; "Euthanasia"; and "Occupied Europe." Once you've selected a main topic, a menu of the specific articles will appear below the main topic menu.

The articles are fantastic. Each covers a discrete period of history and uses maps, photographs, and pictures to supplement the text. (Simply click on any photograph or map to view a larger version.) You'll also notice that there are links to follow to learn more about a person, place, or term used in the article. As an added bonus, *The Holocaust: A Learning Site for Students* also has a time line at the bottom of each page that allows you to place the events you are reading about in each article into a broader historical context. Scroll to the bottom of the screen to view it.

You'll also notice that there is a menu running down the right-hand side of the screen: "Key Dates"; "Artifacts"; "Biography"; and "Glossary." Select these after you've read each article to access even more information. "Key Dates" provides a detailed chronology for each article. "Artifacts" enables you to look at photographs of objects (from the United States Holocaust Memorial Museum's collection) that are related to the article. "Biography" contains eyewitness audio testimonies and written personal histories of people who experienced the Holocaust. Go to the "Glossary" if you want an explanation of a term used.

HOLY ROMAN EMPIRE

Best Search Engine: http://www.google.com/

Key Search Terms: Holy Roman Empire + history

Julius Caesar + history

Rome: Republic to Empire
http://www.vroma.org/~bmcmanus/romanpages.html
middle school and up

This page deals with more than just the Holy Roman Empire, but it's so well done and fun to use that we thought it should be included here. Historical topics include Julius Caesar and the Roman Republic as well as Augustus, Tiberius, and the beginnings of the Roman Empire. There's also a section on Caligula. The bonus at this site is that you can also find terrific resources on civilization and culture, everything from food to clothing to chariot racing.

The Roman Empire: The Basics of Our Culture
http://library.thinkquest.org/22866/English/FRAME.HTML
middle school and up

This Thinkquest site, although under construction when we visited, offers an impressive and comprehensive introduction to the Roman Empire that is especially well suited to high-school students. You'll find sections on "The Roman Empire," "Emperors," "Legend of Rome," "Daily Life," "Architecture," "Army," "Language," and a time line, just to name a few of the offerings. The site comes complete with maps and high-quality images, and is available in Dutch as well as English. Just chose your preferred language on the home page.

Maps and Codices of the Roman Empire
http://www.jmiller.demon.co.uk/
middle school and up

In addition to the maps you'll find at this pretty site—and those include maps of major buildings in Rome, as well as maps of the empire at large—there's an easy-to-read time line of the empire, too.

HUMANISM

Best Search Engine: http://www.google.com/
Key Search Terms: Humanism + history

                      Atheism + history

Humanism and the Humanist Manifestos
http://www.religioustolerance.org/humanism.htm
middle school and up

Here's a wonderful introduction to all the different types of humanism. Many humanist sites on the Web discuss one type of humanism, while neglecting all the others. I like this site because it provides a broad overview of humanist thoughts and practices.

Start with the definitions at the top of the page. You'll find all the different schools of humanism defined, from Christian humanism to literary humanism to secular humanism. A section on "Humanist Beliefs and Practices" follows this and provides lots of good information from the "Humanist Manifesto," which was prepared in 1933 (it's since been edited and updated) and endorsed by 30 some leading humanists of the day.

After these definitions, you're ready for the following essays: "Is Humanism a Religion?" "Conflicts over Secularism in Public Schools," "Ethical Behavior without a Belief in God," and other thought-provoking topics.

Humanism: Seeking the Wisdom of the Ancients
http://www.ibiblio.org/expo/vatican.exhibit/exhibit/c-humanism/
    Humanism.html
middle school and up

For a good brief overview of the philosophy of humanism and its origins in Renaissance Italy, try this essay. It focuses on the relationship between scholars and the church.

HUNDRED YEARS' WAR

Best Search Engine: http://www.google.com/
Key Search Terms: Hundred Years' War

                      Charles V + history

The Hundred Years' War
http://www.bnf.fr/enluminures/texte/atx2_02.htm
high school and up

This page is part of a larger Bibliothèque Nationale de France site on the era of Charles V. It's an excellent if somewhat complicated overview of the war and its significance in French history. It also contains a link to the *Chronicle* of Jean Froissart of Valenciennes, which is considered by many historians to be essential to an understanding of Europe in the fourteenth century and to the twists and turns taken by the Hundred Years' War. The four volumes of the *Chronicle* can be found here, complete with 112 miniatures painted by the best Brugeois artists of the day.

IMPERIALISM/COLONIALISM

Best Search Engine:	http://www.google.com/
Key Search Terms:	imperialism + history
	colonialism + history

History of Imperialism
http://members.aol.com/TeacherNet/World.html
middle school and up

This AOL gateway site on imperialism covers all parts of the world and spans all time periods. It's neatly organized, too, so that you don't spend all day trying to locate your specific topic. The table of contents at the top of the page contains hotlinks to all the entries, and these include sections on Africa, Asia, India, and Latin America, as well as sections on maps, cartoons, and other miscellaneous topics.

Encarta: Imperialism
http://encarta.msn.com/encyclopedia_76155831/imperialism.html
middle school and up

Want to read a general introduction to imperialism? This encyclopedia article is concise and to the point, but it covers everything you need for a good overview. Sections include an "Introduction," "History," "Explanations of Imperialism," and the "Effects of Imperialism."

INCAS

Best Search Engine:	http://www.google.com/
Key Search Terms:	Incas + history
	Incan empire + history
	Machu Picchu + history

Incan Indians
http://www.crystalinks.com/incan.html
middle school and up

This page offers a good history of the Incan people of Peru. It opens with a general overview, then continues with sections on the "First Known Incans," "Society," "Clothing," "Food," "Population," "Cities and Villages," "Incan Roads," "Crime," "Communication," and "Fall of the Incan Empire" among others. You'll find links at the bottom of the page to other Incan subjects of interest, including "Machu Picchu," "Pyramids in Peru," "Music Initiation," and other interesting topics.

INDIA—GENERAL

Best Search Engine: http://www.google.com/

Key Search Terms: India + history

History of India
http://www.historyofindia.com/
middle school and up

This comprehensive history of India site provides coverage from prehistory up through modern India. From the opening page, pick the version of the site you wish to use—high-tech with Flash, or low-tech, text only. The text-only version, which moves more quickly, opens to a page with quotes from several prominent Indians and the choice of the following sections—"Ancient India," "Medieval India," "British India," and "Modern India."

Each of these has a table of contents that pops up once you click on the section. Choose "Ancient India," and your table of contents will contain the following subsections, each with an outline beneath it so that you can determine the highlights of the section before actually reading it: "Prehistoric Period," "Indus Valley Civilization," "Vedic Age," "Epic Age," "Hinduism and Transition," "The Mauryan Age," "The Invasions," "Deccan and South India," "The Gupta Dynasty," "Age of Small Kingdoms," "Harshavardhana," "The Southern Kingdoms," "Chola Empire," and "Northern India." Each of the other sections is equally extensive in its coverage of topics.

This is a wonderful site—easy to use and detailed but straightforward enough that the beginning student will find it accessible.

INDIA—BRITISH RULE

Best Search Engine: http://www.google.com/
Key Search Terms: India + British empire + history
                        British India + history
                        Raj + India + history

History of India: British India
http://www.historyofindia.com/hist_text/eastind.html
middle school and up

(See complete review of the *History of India* site above.) This URL takes you directly to the *History of India*'s section on British India in the text-only version of the site. You'll find individual pages on "The East India Company," "The Independence Struggle of 1857," "The British Raj," "The Indian National Congress," "Indian National Movement," "The Gandhian Era," "The Government of India Act," "The Quit India Movement," and "Indian Independence."

If you read all these sections, from beginning to end, you'll have an excellent overview of the era of British rule in India. In addition, you can use the table at the top of the page to refer to other sections of the site if you want to better understand other time periods in Indian history.

INDIA—GUPTAS

Best Search Engine: http://www.google.com/
Key Search Terms: India + Gupta dynasty + history
                        India + ancient history
                        Chandragupta + India + history
                        Golden age + Indian history
                        Classical age + India

Washington State University: World Civilizations: The Age of the Guptas and After
http://www.wsu.edu:8080/~dee/ANCINDIA/GUPTA.HTM
high school and up

Part of the larger ancient India module at Washington State University's online world civilizations course, this page on the Gupta dynasty begins in 184 B.C. with the assassination of the last of the Mauryan kings, which opened the way for the Gupta dynasty to assert its dream of a unified empire. The text explains the flowering of Indian culture during the Gupta reign and ends with the beginning of Muslim rule in 1100 A.D.

For more context, read the sections in the table of contents that come just before and just after the "Gupta Dynasty" page. A link at the bottom of the page will take you to the table of contents.

History of India: The Gupta Dynasty
http://www.historyofindia.com/hist_text/gupta.html
middle school and up

(See complete review of the History of India site under *India—General*.) This URL takes you directly to the "Gupta Dynasty" page, where you'll get a thorough overview of what is referred to as the "Classical Age" in Indian history. The page covers key leaders in the dynasty, government, literature, architecture, and religion during the Guptas' reign.

INDIA—MAURYAS

Best Search Engine: http://www.google.com/
Key Search Terms: India + history + Mauryans
                       Mauryan empire + history

Washington State University: World Civilizations: Ancient India Module: Mauryan Empire
http://www.wsu.edu:8080/~dee/ANCINDIA/MAURYA.HTM
high school and up

This site goes into a little more depth than the *History of India* site, especially on the subject of religion during this period, so if you're looking for a detailed history of India's first empire, try this one first. You'll learn about the leaders, their conquests and expansion of the empire, and the religious reactions to their empire-building. The text will refer you to other sections of the *Ancient India Module*, namely the one on Buddhism, which is a fascinating read.

An "Anthology of Ancient Indian Readings," a "Glossary of Indian Terms and Concepts," a "Historical Atlas of Ancient India," and a "Gallery of Indian Images" round out the offerings at this excellent site.

History of India: The Mauryan Age
http://www.historyofindia.com/hist_text/maurya.html
middle school and up

(See complete review of the *History of India* site under *India—General*.) Here is where you'll learn about the Mauryans at the *History of*

India site. This ancient dynasty, which prospered for a mere 200 years, from 322 B.C. to 185 B.C., united all of northern India under its rule, a feat that would be attempted time and time again in the years that followed. Read about the Mauryans to understand the model that many subsequent Indian empires tried to emulate.

INDIA—MUGHAL EMPIRE

Best Search Engine: http://www.google.com/
Key Search Terms: Mughal empire + history + India
                        Mughal dynasty + Shah Jahan
                        Mughal architecture + history

History of India
http://www.historyofindia.com/hist_text/medieval.html
middle school and up

For this topic, we give you the home page for "Medieval India," one of the four sections of the *History of India* site, which is reviewed in full under **India—General.** The Mughal empire lasted from 1526 to 1857 and is covered by three separate pages, one for each Mughal dynasty.

If you're interested in the architecture of the Mughals, "Mughal Dynasty III" is where you'll want to begin. The Taj Mahal, Peacock Throne, and Red Fort were all built during this era, and Mughal art in general reached its height. Mughal Dynasty I was when the second classical age flourished in northern India, and the East India Company came into existence during the era of Mughal Dynasty II.

The Mughal Empire in Delhi
http://ourworld.compuserve.com/homepages/asimz/dmughal.htm

While this site won't add much to the history narrative that you can find at the *History of India* site, it does include some wonderful photographs of the Mughal-built Red Fort in Delhi, which was the royal residence built by Shah Jahan, the same emperor who constructed the Taj Mahal. Look here to supplement the text at the *History of India*.

INDIA—VEDIC AGE (SEE ALSO THE VEDAS)

Best Search Engine: http://www.google.com/
Key Search Terms: India + history + Vedic Age
                        Vedic Age + ancient India

History of India: The Vedic Age
http://www.historyofindia.com/hist_text/vedic.html
middle school and up

(See complete review of the *History of India* site under *India—General.*) This URL takes you directly to the page on the Vedic Age, which is found in the "Ancient India" section of this site. This is the age when the sacred hymns called the Vedas were written down by Aryans who had settled in what is now the Punjab and western Uttar Pradesh. Read about their way of life and their religious practices in this concise history.

INDIA—INDEPENDENCE

Best Search Engine: http://www.google.com/
Key Search Terms: Indian history + independence
                       India + history + British Raj
                       India + Pakistan + Partition

Chronology of Modern India (1757 A.D.–1947 A.D.)
http://www.itihaas.com/modern/index.html
middle school and up

This excellent time line of events in modern India provides a useful survey of the major events leading up to India's independence. Most entries are political in nature, although disasters such as plagues, earthquakes, and famines are listed as well.

Use this as you would any chronology—for reference to support your other research. Links at the bottom of the page take you to the chronologies for other time periods in Indian history.

History of India: Indian Independence
http://www.historyofindia.com/hist_text/independ.html
middle school and up

(See complete review of the *History of India* site under *India—General.*) This URL takes you directly to the "Indian Independence" page at the *History of India* site. The page is limited to the years 1945–47, the culmination of the independence movement and the actual declaration of India's sovereignty. For more background information, read the sections preceding this one in the "British India" section of this site. "The Government of India Act" and "The Quit India Movement" are especially important to understanding the origins of the independence movement and how it evolved over the course of the early twentieth century.

INDUSTRIAL REVOLUTION

Best Search Engine: http://www.google.com/
Key Search Terms: Industrial revolution + history
                        Industrialization + history
                        Child labor + industrialization + history

Victorian Social History: An Overview
http://65.107.211.206/victorian/history/sochistov.html
middle school and up

This link takes you directly to the "Social History" page of *The Victorian Web*, where you'll find numerous essays related to the topic of the industrial revolution. There's an entire section of links called "Conditions of Life and Labor" which might be of interest to you if you're researching the industrial revolution in England. Topics such as "Child Labor," "The Lack of Social Security in Victorian England," and "The Life of the Industrial Worker in Early Nineteenth-Century England" specifically address the impact of the industrial revolution.

Modern History Sourcebook: The Industrial Revolution
http://www.fordham.edu/halsall/mod/modsbook2.html#indrev
middle school and up

The *Modern History Sourcebook* has a particularly useful section on the industrial revolution. To find it, scroll down to Part V, near the bottom of the page.

The *Sourcebook's* specialty is its collection of original texts, and you'll find lots of interest on this topic, but it also contains references to Web sites, such as one called *The Steam Engine Library* that contains wonderful information on the revolution in power.

The primary source material collected here is helpfully organized by topic. There's a section on the agricultural revolution and one on the revolution in the manufacture of textiles, for example. There's also a section called "Literary Response," which contains poems, essays, and excerpts from books that address some aspect of the industrial revolution.

The Fabulous Ruins of Detroit
http://detroityes.com/home.htm
middle school and up

When we think of industrialization in the United States, the automobile quickly comes to mind, and no one place in this country had more to do with the automobile than Detroit. In the early twentieth century, the development of massive industrial structures changed the face of Detroit and heralded a second industrial revolution. This awesome site will take you on a tour of those abandoned automobile plants and company headquarters. Many of the pictures were taken during the destruction of the buildings, so you'll witness the detonation of the smokestacks above an electricity plant and the crumbling of bricks as a factory folds in on itself.

The text accompanying the photos illuminates not only the historical significance of the structures but also the current status of the buildings (some survive and are seeking supporters to keep them alive). In addition to the industrial ruins featured here, you can tour ruins of nineteenth-century residences, ruins of downtown Detroit, and neighborhood ruins. There's also a section called "The City Rises," where you can see images of a resurgent Detroit. Lauded as a Yahoo! Pick of the Year in 1998 and given four stars by *Encyclopedia Britannica*, this is a one-of-a-kind site.

INQUISITION

Best Search Engine: http://www.google.com/

Key Search Terms: Inquisition + history

Spanish Inquisition + history

Medieval Inquisition + history

Church history + inquisition

Historical Overview of the Inquisition
http://es.rice.edu/ES/humsoc/Galileo/Student_Work/Trial96/loftis/
    overview.html
middle school and up

This Rice University site offers an excellent introduction to the origins and evolution of the Inquisition. While the bulk of the essay addresses the Medieval Inquisition that originated in 1231, the Spanish Inquisition and the Roman Inquisition are also briefly outlined.

The Inquisition
http://net2.netacc.net/~mafg/jtchick/inquistn.htm
high school and up

This is also an historical overview, but it's more in-depth than the one listed above, and it's written almost solely about the Medieval Inquisition, with an emphasis on answering the question, "How could the Church, which for centuries was opposed to bloodshed, in the end permit and even command the secular princes to inflict the death penalty on obstinate heretics?"

The Inquisition Record of Jacques Fournier, Bishop of Pamiers 1318–1325
http://library.sjsu.edu/english/fournier/fournier.htm
middle school and up

For an inside look at those who were singled out for punishment during the Inquisition, read a few of these confessions. This site includes English translations of selected confessions by Cathar heretics and Jews as given to Bishop Jacques Fournier and the Inquisition at Pamiers, France. The confessors include several widows, a nobleman, a drunkard, and a Jew, among others.

IRELAND—GENERAL

Best Search Engine: http://www.google.com/
Key Search Terms: Ireland + history

                        Celtic + history

                        Irish Republic + history

The History of Ireland
http://www.emeraldgolf.com/music/history/
middle school and up

This comprehensive history site starts with ancient Ireland and moves forward to the present day. Section one is called "B.C. 1800," and you can choose from the following topics: "Ancient Ireland," "Saints and Scholars," "The Vikings in Ireland," "King Rivals," "The Normans in Ireland," "Plantations and Insurrections," "The Tudor Conquest," and "Two Nations." Section two is "The Struggle for Rights, 1801–1900." Sections here include "The Young Irelanders," "The 'Great' Famine," "The Fenians," and "Home Rule and the Land League." Section three is "The Growth of Nationalism," with a section on the "Labour Movement," "The Easter Uprising," and "The War for Independence," among others. The final section is "Independence (1921–2000)," with sections on "The Irish Free State," "The Fianna Fail Party," and "The Republic of Ireland."

IRELAND—FAMINE

Best Search Engine: http://www.google.com/

Key Search Terms: Irish famine + history

Potato famine + history

Ireland + great famine

Interpreting the Irish Famine, 1846–1850
http://www.people.virginia.edu/~eas5e/Irish/Famine.html
middle school and up

This attractive site begins with a brief overview of the famine, illustrated by drawings from the era, but the focus here is on collecting primary resources pertaining to the famine. You'll find a section for images of the famine, which includes photographs, drawings, and prints and a section for reporting and commentary on the famine, which includes "Voices from Ireland," "American and Irish-American Commentary," and "English Views of the Famine." The final section of the site is "Background Materials," which contains a glossary, a bibliography, and several other useful materials.

Irish Famine
http://www.local.ie/history/famine/
middle school and up

This is the best introductory site to the great famine. The text is informative and well written, and you'll also find some useful primary sources incorporated into the site. Some essays examine the community life, housing, and the general social order of the time. There's a chronology from 1845 to 1851, a unique glossary of terms, and a bibliography, as well as links to other sites.

ISLAM (SEE ALSO ISLAMIC EMPIRE)

Best Search Engine: http://www.google.com/

Key Search Terms: Islam + history

Muslim + religion + history

Sunni + Islam + history

Shi'i + Islam + history

Islamic Philosophy, Scientific Thought, and History
http://www.arches.uga.edu/~godlas/history.html
middle school and up

This gateway site on Islamic history will let you choose among many different topics. The site is divided into four sections, each of which contains numerous annotated links. The sections are "General Essays," "Islamic Philosophy," "Islam and Science," and "Islamic History."

Each section contains many different types of resources. You'll find maps, dictionary entries, personal memoir, historical essays, scholarly articles, brief biographies, and much more.

Washington State University: World Civilizations: Islam
http://www.wsu.edu/~dee/ISLAM/ISLAM.HTM
high school and up

For a scholarly but very enjoyable read, you'll love the history of Islam provided here. There are sections on "Islam," "Pre-Islamic Arabic Culture," "Muhammad," "The Qur'an," "The Caliphate," and more.

In addition, this Washington State University site, which is organized for a world civilizations online course, contains wonderful supporting material, such as a glossary, a gallery of images, and an Islam reader, as well as a list of other useful Internet resources.

Islam
http://www.cqpress.com/context/articles/epr_islam.html
high school and up

This article, which was originally published in the *Encyclopedia of Politics and Religion*, is an excellent, thorough introduction to the Islamic religion. It covers the origins of the religion, its core beliefs, and its spread throughout the world. It's fairly long, so don't look here for a brief introduction, but if you want an in-depth history of Islam, this is very readable and informative. There are sections on the "Sunni and Shi'i"; "Caliphs, Sultans, and the New Community"; "Spread of Islam"; "Early Modern Expansion and Transformation"; "Imperialism and Reform"; and "The New Islamists."

Islam: Empire of Faith
http://www.pbs.org/empires/islam/faithkoran.html
middle school and up

This interactive, multimedia PBS site deals more with Islam the religion, than it does with Islamic civilization. You'll find sections on "The

Koran and Tradition," "The Five Pillars," "People of the Book," and "Islam Today," for example. Click on any of these for superbly written introductions to the faith.

ISLAMIC EMPIRE

Best Search Engine: http://www.google.com/

Key Search Terms: Islamic empire + history

Internet Islamic History Sourcebook
http://www.fordham.edu/halsall/islam/islamsbook.html

Contents of this site cover the pre-Islamic Arab world up through the Islamic world since 1945. You'll also find sections on maps and additional resources. This *Sourcebook*, like the other *Sourcebooks*, is focused on primary resources—there are histories, political documents, stories, poems, music, letters, and more—but you'll also find links to some particularly useful Web sites. Use the *Sourcebook* table of contents in much the same way you would use a chronology, just to get your bearings straight, and then check out some of the diverse source material collected here.

See also **Islam.**

ISRAEL—ANCIENT

Best Search Engine: http://www.google.com/

Key Search Terms: Ancient Israel + history

                      Hebrews + history

Ancient Israel
http://campus.northpark.edu/history/WebChron/MiddleEast/
    AncientIsrael.html
middle school and up

This is a good concise chronology of ancient Israel, beginning with "The Hebrews as Pastoral Nomads (1950 B.C.)" and ending in 70 A.D. with the destruction of Herod's temple. Some chronologies of this period are much more detailed and cumbersome to read, but this one covers the most important events and people without getting bogged down in too many details. It also contains some links to short essays on key events.

ISRAEL—FORMATION OF MODERN STATE

Best Search Engine: http://www.google.com/
Key Search Terms: Israel + modern + history

Jewish + homeland + history

Israel at Fifty
http://www.israel.org/mfa/go.asp?MFAH00ul0
middle school and up

This site, established for Israel's 50th anniversary, has an excellent annotated time line of events from 1948 through 1997, with entries for every year. If you're looking for a brief introduction to the years of independence, this time line provides a concise and visual resource. There are also sections here on the Holocaust and anti-Semitism.

The Peace Encyclopedia: The War of Independence, 1948
http://www.yahoodi.com/peace/warindep.html
middle school and up

This interesting site is organized around a set of commonly asked questions about the establishment of the state of Israel. Under each question are numerous quotes addressing the question from people of different perspectives and backgrounds.

Within the article are many hotlinks to essays in other parts of the encyclopedia. These include "Refugees," "Zionism," and "Palestine."

Mr. Dowling's Electronic Passport: Conflicts in the Middle East: Israel
http://www.mrdowling.com/608-israel.html
middle school and up

Are you confused about the source of the conflict between Israel and the Palestinians? If so, let Mr. Dowling clear things up. This page provides a straightforward, evenhanded summary of the conflict, beginning with the declaration of Israel as an independent Jewish homeland in 1948. You won't find all the nuances and details here, but you will get the basic story straight.

ITALY—GENERAL

Best Search Engine: http://www.google.com/
Key Search Terms: Italy + history

The Italian Index
http://humanities.byu.edu/classes/ital420/index.html
middle school and up

At this Brigham Young University index site, you will find links to all areas of Italian history, including "Paleontology," "Etruscans," "Ancient Rome," "The Middle Ages," "Humanism," "The Renaissance," "Late Renaissance," "Baroque," "Romanticism," "The Risorgimento," and "Contemporary Themes." Subcategories include art, urbanism, history, philosophy, indexes, counties, kingdoms, republics, economics, and more.

If you're looking for information on the history of famous Italians, Italian cities, or Italian art and culture, you're sure to find it at this site. Begin your search on the home page by choosing from one of the time periods that make up the menu.

The History of Italy
http://www.arcaini.com/ITALY/ItalyHistory/ItalyHistory.html
middle school and up

If you want the entire history of Italy without going into much depth with any one period, this is a great site. From early Italy and the Bronze Age all the way up through postwar Italy, the site is really just one long article that has been divided into numerous sections, so that it does not take so long to load. An index to the sections is provided at the home page, and each section corresponds to a time period. Simply choose the time period you're looking for, or begin at the beginning.

Although the index of sections is long, each section by itself is quite short, so you could easily read the entire history without taking all day to do it.

ITALY—RENAISSANCE (SEE ALSO VIRTUAL RENAISSANCE UNDER THE RENAISSANCE)

Best Search Engine: http://www.google.com/
Key Search Terms: Renaissance + Italy + history
                    Italian + Renaissance + history
                    Florence + Renaissance
                    Renaissance + Medicis

Washington State University: World Civilizations: Italian Renaissance
http://www.wsu.edu/~dee/REN/REN.HTM
high school and up

You'll love this site. Although it's easy to stumble over the multitude of useless frames, the content is so terrific that you will soon forget the navigational shortcomings. If you're looking for a comprehensive history

of the Renaissance that's substantive but accessible to students just beginning their studies of the period, this is it.

The site is divided into two sections that will be of interest to you:
"The Thing Itself" and "Resources." Under "The Thing Itself," you'll find
historical essays on the following topics: "The Idea of the Renaissance,"
"The Background to the Italian Renaissance," "Humanism," "Renaissance
Neo-Platonism," "Pico della Mirandola," "Niccolo Machiavelli," "Leo-
nardo da Vinci," and "Architecture and Public Space."

"Resources" contains secondary material such as a "Glossary of Renaissance Terms and Concepts," "A Gallery of Renaissance Images," an
"Atlas," a "Timeline," and "Internet Resources."

History of Italy: Italian Renaissance and Foreign Domination
http://www.arcaini.com/ITALY/ItalyHistory/ItalianRenaissance.htm

(See **Italy—General** for a complete review of this site.) Read about
the origins of the Renaissance and its great families—the Viscontis,
Medicis, Sforzas, and Estes—as well as the French invasion of Italy and
the foreign domination that followed.

ITALY—UNIFICATION

Best Search Engine:	http://www.google.com/
Key Search Terms:	Italy + history + unification
	Italian + unification

The History of Italy: Italian Unification
http://www.arcaini.com/ITALY/ItalyHistory/ItalianUnification.htm

(See **Italy—General** for a complete review of this site.) This site
explores the impact of the French Revolution on Italians and the subsequent unification of Italy in 1861. The essay delves into the unification
struggle, examining numerous obstacles and the contribution of Giu-
seppe Garibaldi in particular.

ITALY—FASCIST

Best Search Engine:	http://www.google.com/
Key Search Terms:	Fascism + Italy + history
	Italy + Mussolini

History of Italy
http://www.arcaini.com/ITALY/ItalyHistory/FascistPeriod.html
middle school and up

(See **Italy—General** for a complete review of this site.) This URL takes you to the "Fascist Period" page at the *History of Italy*. It will give you an overview of fascism in Italy, but you'll also want to read two other sections at this site, the two immediately following "Fascist Period" in the index. They are "Rise of Fascism" and "Fascist Expansionism."

JAPAN—TOKUGAWA ERA

Best Search Engine: http://www.google.com/

Key Search Terms: Tokugawa + history

Tokugawa Japan
http://www.wsu.edu/~dee/TOKJAPAN/TOKJAPAN.HTM
high school and up

This series of essays on Tokugawa Japan covers the period from 1603 to 1868. From the home page, click on "Contents" at the left-hand side of the page. The list of links to essays includes the following topics: "Warring States Japan," "Oda Nobunaga," "Toyotomi Hideyoshi," "Tokugawa Ieyasu," "Life in Tokugawa Japan," "Tokugawa Neo-Confucianism," "Kokugaku: Japanese Studies," and "Mootori Norinaga."

JAPAN—ASHIKAGA

Best Search Engine: http://www.google.com/

Key Search Terms: Ashikaga + history

Washington State University: World Civilizations: Ancient Japan: Ashikaga Shogunate
http://www.wsu.edu/~dee/TOKJAPAN/TOKJAPAN.HTM
high school and up

This URL takes you to the home page for Tokugawa Japan. Click on the first topic—"Warring States Japan"—and you'll see a link pop up for the Ashikaga Shogunate and the Kamakura Shogunate. Read the section on the "Warring States," and then follow the link, which takes you to a page on the Ashikaga and Kamakura Bakufu, which is part of the section called "Feudal Japan."

The histories of these various governments is sometimes hard to follow, as they tend to be quite intertwined. Don't despair. Just keep reading, and use the "Glossary of Japanese Terms" that's provided in the contents page for each section.

JAPAN—KAMAKURA (SEE JAPAN—ASHIKAGA)

JAPAN—MEIJI RESTORATION

Best Search Engine: http://www.google.com/
Key Search Terms: Japan + Meiji + history
                       Meiji Restoration + history

JapanGuide.com: Meiji Period
http://www.japan-guide.com/e/e2130.html

Here's a no-nonsense survey of this period in Japanese history. Following the Tokugawa era, the Meiji Restoration saw the return of imperial power to the emperor Meiji. This page gives an excellent overview of significant events and people of the period, which lasted from 1868 to 1912.

Links within the site take you to other encyclopedia-type essays at *JapanGuide.com*. In addition, you'll find links to other Japanese eras, which might support your research. There is a general history overview if you need to get the big picture without spending a lot of time. And don't miss the two links at the bottom of the page. One is an informative site about the Meiji period; the other is an open-air museum for preserving and exhibiting architecture of the Meiji period.

KOREAN WAR

Best Search Engine: http://www.google.com/
Key Search Terms: Korean War + history
                       Forgotten War + history
                       DMZ War + Korea + history

Korean War Project (1950–1953)
http://www.koreanwar.org/
middle school and up

Although dedicated to providing a service to Korean veterans and their families, this site is also full of goodies for the student researcher. It features an excellent search engine, so that you can easily look up specific battles, generals, fronts, and much more. If your interests lie more with personal documentation of the battle, there are personal accounts of battle, diary entries, poems, casualty lists, and lots of information on those missing in action.

Try "DMZ War" or Heartbreak Ridge" for up close personal accounts of two different battles, but "Reference" is the section of this site you'll probably be most interested in. It's divided into sections, based on the types of resources. There's a section for the "Air Force," "Army," "Archives, Museums, and Libraries," "Associations and Groups," "Awards and Medals," "Books," "Casualty Listings," "DMZ 1953–2000," "Genealogy," "Government," "History," and more. You'll find different types of resources, everything from personal home pages of veterans to archives of Korean War material to Web sites of memorials.

Korean War 50th Anniversary Homepage
http://korea50.army.mil/
middle school and up

The official Web site for the Department of Defense commemoration of the anniversary is the fine place to start looking for information. The site is much more than a list of events scheduled for the official commemorative period, which runs from June 25, 2000, through July 27, 2003. It offers an impressive collection of material that includes a time line of the war, a list of Medal of Honor recipients, biographies, and maps.

The Korean War: A Radio Man's Story
http://www.dnaco.net/~csmartin/kwar.html
middle school and up

If you're looking for a smaller and more personal resource, try the Web site of Cecil H. Martin, a veteran of the Korean War. Features of the site include a poem by Martin, his personal history, and many photographs taken by him during his tour in Korea.

LABOR MOVEMENTS

Best Search Engine: http://www.google.com/
Key Search Terms: Labor movement + history
                        Socialism + labor movement
                        Child labor + history

Hard Labor: The Unions Who Fought for the First Monday in September
http://kids.infoplease.lycos.com/spot/labor1.html
middle school and up

This is an excellent article on the history of the labor movement in the United States. There are sections on the "AFL-CIO," "Craft Guilds and Industrial Unions," "Labor Legislation," "The Teamsters," and more.

Links within the article take you to biographies of key individuals or articles on related topics.

This is a relatively brief treatment of the topic, but it provides an excellent introduction. If you want to continue exploring the labor movement, use the links to Web sites on related topics. You'll find links to the Industrial Workers of the World Web site, a site on the Taft-Hartley Act of 1947, and a site on mothers in the workplace.

The Triangle Shirtwaist Factory Fire
http://www.ilr.cornell.edu/trianglefire/
middle school and up

On March 25, 1911, a fire broke out on the top floors of the Triangle Shirtwaist Factory in New York City, killing 146 workers, mainly young women, recent immigrants of Italian and European Jewish background. The scandal that followed brought the unhealthful, inhumane conditions of sweatshops to people's attention.

This Web site provides a very complete overview of the tragedy, including newspaper articles, photographs, political cartoons, and other historical information. Also helpful are tips for those writing a high school research paper on this topic.

LATIN AMERICA—COLONIAL

Best Search Engine: http://www.google.com/

Key Search Terms: Latin America + colonial + history

                       Latin America + colonialism

1492: An Ongoing Voyage
http://www.ibiblio.org/expo/1492.exhibit/overview.html
high school and up

Here's a multicultural site with both background material and primary resources on the Americas before and after Columbus came to call. The multimedia approach of the site is to interweave primary and secondary material—both images and texts—to explain what life was like in the Americas and how life was affected by Columbus's explorations.

The site features original maps, copies of ancient manuscripts, original photographs, and excerpts from diaries. It provides links to other resources, such as ancient calendars of the Mayas and drawings of Venetian sailing directions.

Not all parts of Latin America are represented at this site, but you'll find it's particularly strong on resources that reveal Mexico's history and the history of the Andean region. Click on "Middle American Cultures" for an introduction to this region, then follow the links to see the resources connected to this subject. If you're interested in another part of Latin America, scroll down the outline to see if there's a section of the site that covers that geographical region.

Don Mabry's Historical Text Archive
http://historicaltextarchive.com/sections.php?op = viewarticle&artid = 99
high school and up

Travel back in time to look at colonial South America through the eyes of one of its infamous explorers. This letter from the power-hungry Lope de Aguirre reveals his lust for gold and riches, which drove him to murder the leaders of his Peruvian expedition in search of El Dorado and to conquer a Spanish-settled island off the coast of Venezuela. He was eventually killed by his own men.

The letter collected here in the "Historical Text Archives" contains threats, demands for money, information about colonial Spanish corruption, and geographic details of lands and rivers never explored before Aguirre.

To read additional primary source material from this period of Latin American history, click on "Latin America: Colonial" at the bottom of the page. You'll see a list of various resources on "Colonial Lima," "Colonial Brazilian History," "Latin American Colonial Transportation," and much more.

LATIN AMERICA—INDEPENDENCE

Best Search Engine: http://www.google.com/
Key Search Terms: Latin America + independence
                     Latin America + revolution
                     Independence movements + South America
                     Independence movements + Central America

Research Sites for Latin American History
middle school and up
http://courses.ncsu.edu/classes/hi300001/bkmarks.htm

This gateway site contains links to sites that address many Latin American topics, including independence movements. Although you may find useful information under other headings, the best place to start exploring is "Independence Era, 1810–1826." You'll find sites here on Venezuela and Argentina. Scroll down the page a bit, and you'll see dozens of resources on the Mexican Revolution, Cuban Revolution, and revolutions in Nicaragua, El Salvador, and Peru.

Latin American Network Information Center
http://www.lanic.utexas.edu/
middle school and up

For good basic information on all the Latin American countries, try this site from the University of Texas. Start with the database of countries, and click on the country of your choice, then scroll down to the "History" section. You'll find a number of links to various types of history resources. Don't be scared off if the title of a site is given in Spanish. Many of these sites are bilingual and have an English option once you reach the home page.

In addition to the "History" section, you'll find a wealth of other information on every topic you can think of, from "Indigenous People" to "Literature," "Politics," and "Religion."

LIBERALISM

Best Search Engine: http://www.google.com/
Key Search Terms: Liberalism + history
                            Liberal Party + history
                            Liberalism + socialism
                            Enlightenment + liberalism

Liberalism
http://library.thinkquest.org/3376/Genktk5.htm
middle school and up

Here's your best bet for an overview of liberalism. This essay covers the concepts of liberalism and the philosophers, politicians, and writers associated with this form of political thought. You'll also read about the connection between liberalism and utilitarianism, the founding of the Liberal Party in England, and the new liberals of the twentieth century.

Hyperlinks within the essay take you to relevant essays on the Enlightenment, Adam Smith, John Stuart Mill, and other subjects. Many of these are highly recommended, in-depth ThinkQuest articles in their own right and contain further links themselves. So you can, for example, click on "John Stuart Mill" for an excellent essay about his life and work, and then click on "utilitarianism" for an essay about that philosophy.

Internet Modern History Sourcebook: Liberalism
http://www.fordham.edu/halsall/mod/modsbook18.html
middle school and up

For a collection of primary source material on liberalism, try the *Internet Modern History Sourcebook*. It's also a good place to look for primary sources on feminism, just in case you're also interested in that topic.

MACEDONIAN EMPIRE

Best Search Engine: http://www.altavista.com/

Key Search Terms: Macedonian Empire + history

Macedonia + partition

Macedonian state + history

Tsar Samuel + Macedonia + history

Macedonian History
http://www.geocities.com/~makedonija/history.html
middle school and up

This attractive site covers all of Macedonian history, from ancient Macedonia up through the independence of the republic of Macedonia. You'll find separate sections on "Philip of Macedon," "Settlement of the Slavs," "Tsar Samuel," "Macedonian Uprisings," "Balkan Wars" and "The Partition of Macedonia," "Aegean Macedonia," "Establishment of the Macedonian State in WWII," and more. The site is nicely illustrated with maps and photographs, and there's an easy-to-read chronology for placing major events and people in time.

History of Ohrid: Samuel's Empire
http://www.ohrid.org.mk/eng/istorija/samuil.htm
middle school and up

This concise narrative is an excellent introduction to the period in Macedonian history when the Macedonian provinces were united into one Macedonian slavic state known as Samuel's Empire, or the Macedonian Empire. The essay covers the period from 969 through the fourteenth century.

MALI (AFRICAN EMPIRE) (SEE SONGHAY)

MAMLUK EMPIRE

Best Search Engine: http://www.google.com/
Key Search Terms: Mamluk empire + history
                        Mamluks + Egyptian history
                        Egypt + ancient history

Major Powers in Egypt in the Second Half of the Eighteenth Century: The Mamluks
http://www.cad.strath.ac.uk/~ayman/BHME/txt/egypt32-txt.html
middle school and up

Though brief, this history of the Mamluks is informative and interesting to read. It chronicles the rise of the Mamluks from war slaves to rulers of their own empire. Links within the essay take you to essays on other topics, such as the Ayubids, Fatimids, Mongols, Crusaders, and other related topics. This is an excellent introduction to the Mamluks and should be your first stop if you're just getting acquainted with this medieval empire.

The Art of the Mamluks
http://www.islam.org/Culture/atm/atm.htm
middle school and up

This little site is really an excerpt from a book of the same title. It contains exquisite images of Mamluk artwork, including illuminated manuscripts and metalwork and accompanying text that is both simple and informative. A brief introduction to the Mamluk empire precedes the gallery of images.

MARSHALL PLAN

Best Search Engine: http://www.google.com/
Key Search Terms: George C. Marshall + history
                        Marshall Plan + history
                        European Recovery Program + history

George C. Marshall: The Plan
http://www.lcsys.net/fayette/history/plan.htm
middle school and up

Created by Friends of George C. Marshall Inc., this site details the history of the Marshall Plan and incorporates many primary resources, including the text of the "Marshall Plan Speech," which was given at Harvard University on June 5, 1947.

In a section following the overview of the Marshall Plan, numerous other speeches by government officials and diplomats are listed. There's also a section for articles that address George C. Marshall and the plan that earned him the Nobel Peace Prize, and a list of links at the bottom of the page to sites such as *The Marshall Plan European Cooperation Links*, the *George C. Marshall International Center,* and the *National Archives Library.*

MARXISM

Best Search Engine: http://www.google.com/
Key Search Terms: Marxism + history

Karl Marx + history

Engels + Marxism + history

Trotsky + Marxism + history

Marxism Central
http://csf.colorado.edu/mirrors/marxists.org/
high school and up

This is Marxism Central, a history of the revolutionary working class. Click on "Marxist History" on the home page for a list of subject areas covered at this site. You'll find sections on the "Paris Commune," "Early Soviet History," "The Spanish Revolution and Civil War," "History of the Cuban Republic," "History of Algerian Independence," and "USA: The Black Panther Party." Click on "Paris Commune," for example, and you'll find an excellent time line of events, an organizational overview of the commune, and links to other sections of the site that address the civil war in France and post-commune France.

In addition to containing all the major texts (in English) by Marx and Engels, you'll find hundreds of other texts at this site by Lenin, Trotsky, and others. There's also a non-English archive, with lists of texts collected in a variety of other languages. Just click on "Marxist Writers" on the home page to search for texts by an author's name. The site also contains an "Encyclopedia of Marxism" and an "Encyclopedia of Trotskyism."

Marxist.org Internet Archive
http://www.marxists.org/
middle school and up

For primary sources on the period of Russian history that began with the Russian Revolution and spanned most of the twentieth century, this site is the oldest and most comprehensive on the Internet. You'll find old photos, biographies of key individuals, and an extensive archive of the works of major Marxists.

The Marxist Glossary
http://www.uta.edu/english/cgb/marx/terms.html
middle school and up

This is a thorough collection of terms to help you navigate the theory once you've mastered the history of Marxism.

MAYANS

Best Search Engine: http://www.google.com/
Key Search Terms: Maya + history
                       Chichen Itza + history
                       Tulum + history

The Maya Astronomy Page
http://www.michielb.nl/maya/astro.html
middle school and up

In addition to the article on astronomy, with detailed sections on Venus, the sun, the moon, the ecliptic, and the Milky Way, you'll find nicely illustrated pages on Mayan mathematics—they are credited with the discovery of zero—Mayan writing, and the Mayan calendar.

Maya Links
http://www.kstrom.net/isk/maya/maya1.html
middle school and up

Though this site serves largely as a collection of links to other Maya sites, its maps' page and another page on traditional Mayan storytellers and their tales make this site worth the visit. Just go to the navigation bar at the bottom of the page and click on "Maps" or "Culture" to learn more. If you're just exploring the Mayan civilization and want to browse to have your curiosity aroused, this is the place to go. There's no keyword search option, but there's lots to captivate you if you have the time to wander.

You'll find links to in-depth descriptions of Mayan history and culture, pages on Mayan astronomy and the Mayan calendar, even a page devoted solely to the Mayans' use of corn.

Mystery of the Maya
http://www.civilization.ca/civil/maya/mminteng.html
middle school and up

"Maya Civilization," "Exhibits on the Plaza," "People of the Jaguar," and "IMAX Film" are the four sections of this wonderful site, which was created in association with the IMAX film of the same name from the Canadian Museum of Civilization.

Each of the three main sections of the site includes an introduction and then links to numerous topics. Under "Maya Civilization" you'll find "Cities of the Ancient Maya," "Cosmology and Religion," "Astronomy," and "Peoples, Geography, and Language," to name a few of the offerings. Look under the "Exhibits" section for Maya exhibits created in conjunction with the film. You'll find a reproduction of the sarcophagus of the priest-king Pacal and a scale model of a Maya settlement used in the making of the film among other things.

The "People of the Jaguar" is an exhibit focusing on authentic Mayan pottery decorated with figures and glyphs, as well as certain objects recreated for the IMAX film. A Jaguar god mask is among the artifacts you'll see.

MESOPOTAMIA

Best Search Engine: http://www.altavista.com/
Key Search Terms: Mesopotamia + history
                        Ancient Babylon + history
                        Assyria + history

Mesopotamia
http://www.penncharter.com/Student/meso/index.html
middle school and up

Look here if you're most interested in learning about day-to-day life in Mesopotamia. There are useful, brief introductions to culture, daily life, government, industry, and social levels. You can read about clothing, jewelry, and pottery under "Daily Life," for example, and about the gods people worshipped under "Culture." The *Ancient History Sourcebook* (see above) is more comprehensive and in-depth, but if you want something simple and short, start here. Once you pick a topic to focus on, use the *Sourcebook* for in-depth research.

Brief History of Assyrians
http://www.aina.org/aol/peter/brief.htm
middle school and up

This basic site gives an excellent overview of Assyria and its people. Start here if you're just beginning to explore this topic and want to focus on Assyria. The table of contents includes "Geography," "Racial Type," "Language," "Religion," and "History of Assyrians," which is broken into six periods, starting with the first Assyrian civilization in 2400 B.C. and ending with the Assyrian diaspora from 1918 to the present. Graphics include a large, helpful map, a picture of the Assyrian alphabet, and charts portraying the world Assyrian population and the religious affiliations of Assyrians.

Chronology of Ancient Mesopotamian History
http://www.angelfire.com/tx/gatestobabylon/whymeso.html
middle school and up

This site provides a chronological chart showing periods in Mesopotamian history and cultural progress made during those periods. For example, the second period listed is 3500 B.C.E., the Uruk Period, which produced the first pictographic texts. The time line covers the Sumer, Assyria, and Babylon and ends in 539 B.C.E. when Babylon was captured by Cyrus.

Following the time line is an excellent overview of ancient Mesopotamian history, written by an archaeology professor at University College London. This text will serve as a great introduction, if you're not already familiar with Mesopotamia.

Ancient History Sourcebook: Mesopotamia
http://www.fordham.edu/halsall/ancient/asbook03.html
high school and up

In addition to covering Sumer, Assyria, and Babylon, this comprehensive site has links on the following topics: "Ancient Near East"; "Akkadians"; "Kassites and Hittites"; "Chaldea/Neo-Babylonia"; "Sumerian Cities: Ebla, Ugarit, and Emar"; "Phoenicia"; and "Carthage," as well as links to general subjects, such as "Art and Architecture," "Gender and Sexuality," and "Modern Perspectives on Mesopotamia."

Click on "Gender and Sexuality," for example, and you'll find an old Assyrian marriage contract as well as the Code of the Assyrians from

1075 B.C.E., which deals with gender and sexuality issues in ancient Assyria.

This site is highly recommended and should cover just about any Mesopotamian topic on your list.

MEXICAN REVOLUTION

Best Search Engine: http://www.google.com/

Key Search Terms: Mexican Revolution + history

Diaz dictatorship + Mexico + history

Mexican Revolution
http://www.northcoast.com/~spdtom/rev.html
high school and up

Here's a comprehensive Mexican Revolution site that's oriented toward students and teachers. Useful resources include an extremely detailed time line, a list of key individuals with brief biographies, a page devoted to the presidents of the revolution with brief biographies included, and sections on the "Constitution of 1917," "The Plan of San Luis Potosi," and "The Cristero Rebellion." These are all listed under "Research," which is where you'll also find a section on "Student Help," as well as links to other useful sites.

The Mexican Revolution
http://www.mexconnect.com/MEX/austin/revolution.html
middle school and up

Want to read a brief summary of the revolution? Try this page, which is part of a much larger Mexican history site. The narrative is easy to read and will give you the basics that you need for understanding the significance of the revolution without testing your attention span.

Postcards of the Mexican Revolution
http://www.netdotcom.com/revmexpc/
high school and up

For insight into a little-known practice during the civil war, take a look at this unique site. The opening paragraph at the site explains what you'll find better than I can: "Much of Mexico's history for the decade of 1910–1920 was recorded by hundreds of photographers on postcards. Using glass plate cameras and early cut film cameras, primitive by today's standards, the photographers faced injury and death to obtain negatives which would be printed on postcard stock and sold to the soldiers and general public on both sides of the U.S.-Mexican border. Some of the views were obviously posed, and others showed the death and destruction resulting from the violence of a nation involved in a bloody civil war."

The site contains images of a handful of used and unused postcards with interpretive text alongside each one and translated text for those that were actually used.

MINOANS

Best Search Engine:	http://www.google.com/
Key Search Terms:	Minoan + history
	Sir Arthur Evans + Crete
	Crete + ancient history
	Minotaur + Crete
	Knossos + history
	King Minos + Minoan

Minoan Civilization
http://www.dilos.com/region/crete/min_cul.html
middle school and up

This site provides a good overview of Minoan history. Although it is a commercial site (part of the *Dilos Holiday World* travel site), you won't have any trouble avoiding the sales pitch to buy cruise tickets from Dilos. The site consists of 15 sections that discuss different aspects of Minoan history and culture, including the history of finding and excavating Cretan archaeological sites. There are illustrations of what Minoan cities would have looked like and photographs of artifacts from the ancient sites. You'll even find material about the mythical history of ancient Crete, such as King Minos and Ariadne of Knossos. What makes this Web site excellent, though, is its sections that use the archaeological sites as a jumping-off point to delve into Minoan history.

You'll probably want to start your exploration of this Web site by reading the essay on Minoan civilization on the home page. This piece discusses Minoan history from 2600 B.C.E. to 1000 B.C.E. Once you're ready to focus on a specific topic related to ancient Cretan civilizations, use the pull-down menu at the left-hand side of the home page. You can read essays on the following topics: "Minoan Palaces," "Sir Arthur

Evans," "Knossos," "Phaestos," "Archanes," "Gournia," "Iraklion Museum," "Ariadne," "Zeus-Europa," "Theseus," "Dikti Cave," "Labyrinth," and "King Minos." Each essay contains links that you can follow to learn more about a specific topic that is mentioned. Those of you who want to view Minoan artifacts should definitely check out the section on the "Iraklion Museum."

Prehistoric Archaeology of the Aegean
http://devlab.dartmouth.edu/history/bronze_age/
high school and up

All of you archaeology buffs will love this detailed Web site from the Classics Department at Dartmouth College. Although *Prehistoric Archaeology of the Aegean* covers more than Minoan history and culture, a good deal of the site is devoted to Minoan topics. You probably won't find another Internet site that provides the sheer amount of information that this one does. The only downside is that the site is a bit dry (and probably too advanced for middle school and some high school students). It also contains no visual aids to help explain the text. Despite these drawbacks, *Prehistoric Archaeology of the Aegean* is a unique resource that can play a central role in your research. Just make sure to read a more basic introduction to Minoan history, such as the one you'll find at the *Dilos* site, before you delve into this one.

Prehistoric Archaeology of the Aegean is arranged into online lessons that each cover a discrete topic. You don't need to explore the entire site. The lessons that might be relevant to your research include: "Lesson 5 (The Early Minoan Period: The Settlements)"; "Lesson 6 (The Early Minoan Period: The Tombs)"; "Lesson 10 (Middle Minoan Crete)"; "Lesson 12 (Minoan Architecture: The Palaces)"; "Lesson 13 (Minoan Domestic and Funerary Architecture of the Neo-palatial and Post-palatial Periods)"; "Lesson 14 (Late Minoan Painting and Other Representational Art)"; "Lesson 15 (Minoan Religion)"; and "Lesson 18 (The Nature and Extent of Neo-palatial Minoan Influences in the Aegean and Eastern Mediterranean Worlds)." Once you've selected a lesson from the table of contents on the home page, you can pick and choose to read sections of the lesson from the lesson menu.

One thing to keep in mind is that this site focuses on the archaeological remains of Minoan culture. While it uses these objects as the starting point for a broader discussion of Minoan history, this site (unlike *Minoan Civilization*) doesn't stray far from the archaeology. So you won't find material on mythical figures like King Minos, and you won't read about what later Greek authors thought of Minoan culture.

MONASTICISM

Best Search Engine: http://www.google.com/
Key Search Terms: Monasticism + history

Monks + Middle Ages

Saint Benedict + monks + history

Celtic + monasticism + history

Western Monasticism
http://www.newadvent.org/cathen/10472a.htm
high school and up

This *Catholic Encyclopedia* article is an excellent overall history of monasticism in the West. You'll find sections on the "Pre-Benedictine Period," "The Spread of St. Benedict's Rule," "The Rise of Cluny," "Period of Monastic Decline," and "Monastic Revival." The writing is a tad stilted, which may be due to problems in translation, but the information is excellent and accessible to those without a background in the subject.

The Keepers of Knowledge: How Knowledge and Learning Survived in the Middle Ages
http://historymedren.about.com/library/weekly/aa010798.htm
middle school and up

If you can ignore the annoying commercial windows that keep opening at this site, you'll find a nice little treat in this concise essay on the history of monasticism during the Middle Ages. Read this for a good overview of how and why the monastic life developed. Hotlinks throughout the essay take you to essays on double monasteries, Saint Benedict, the Book of Hours, and other relevant topics.

Celtic Monasticism
http://www.faculty.de.gcsu.edu/~dvess/ids/medieval/celtic/celtic.shtml
middle school and up

This site is devoted to the exploration of the spirituality and history of Celtic monasticism. In addition to the excellent "Introduction to Celtic Monasticism," you'll find links to "Holy Wells," "Burial Grounds and Circles," and more than a few virtual tours of Celtic monastic sites, such as Iona, Lindisfarne, and Glendalough. Hotlinks within the text take you on these tours.

MONGOL EMPIRE

Best Search Engine: http://www.google.com/
Key Search Terms: Mongol Empire + history

Kublai Khan + history

Genghis Khan + Mongol Empire

The Historical Mongol Empire
http://www.geocities.com/Athens/Forum/2532/
middle school and up

Here's a good starting point if you're just beginning to explore the Mongol Empire. This Geocities site provides an "Overview," an "In Depth History of the Mongol Empire," "Maps of the Empire," a "Timeline," and a section on "Genghis Khan." Each of these sections is accessible using the links in the menu at the left-hand side of the page.

The Land of Genghis Khan
http://www.nationalgeographic.com/genghis/index.html
middle school and up

Follow two veteran National Geographic writers as they trek across Asia, following in the footsteps of Genghis Khan. From the home page, just click on "Begin the Journey." This attractive National Geographic site offers you four sections to choose from—"Mongolia Today," "From the Field," "Biographical Basics," and "Map of the Empire." There's lots of additional resources and classroom ideas scattered throughout, and interesting images accompany the text. Just click on an image to read the caption that explains it.

This site is primarily focused on Genghis Khan, but you'll find links to other resources that explore his empire in more depth.

MUSIC

Best Search Engine: http://www.google.com/

Key Search Terms: Music + history

Classical music + history

Jazz music + history

DW3 Classical Music Resources
http://www.lib.duke.edu/music/resources/classical_index.html
middle school and up

This is your gateway to the world of music. *DW3 (Duke World Wide Web) Classical Music Resources* is the most comprehensive collection of classical music resources on the Web with links to more than 1,885 noncommercial pages/sites in over a dozen languages.

The site itself is comprised of 118 well-organized, subject-specific pages and features a powerful, easy-to-use internal search engine; numerous links to the Duke online catalog; and composer-specific pages and links organized by historical period for enhanced browsing. Since this is intended as an educational site, it contains few (if any) links to overtly commercial sites.

The home page opens to a menu with the following sections listed: "Composer Homepages," "Chronologies and Necrologies," "Nationally and Regionally Oriented Pages," "Organizations and Centers for Scholarly Research," "Electronic Journals and Newsletters," "Genre-Specific Pages," and "Databases."

HyperMusicHistory
http://musichistory.crosswinds.net/
middle school and up

Although this is actually a low-key commercial site, it contains excellent brief histories of jazz and classical music, as well as a history of instruments. Under "History of Classical Music," just pick your time period—Middle Ages, Renaissance, Baroque, Classical, Romantic, and Twentieth Century—and you'll be taken to an introductory article on the time period. A menu of subtopics includes, for the Baroque period, "Vocal," "Instrumental," "Characteristics," "Trends," and more.

In addition to the basic histories, you'll find "Classical Music News," "Jazz Music News," a "Glossary," a "List of Links," a "Composers Page," and much more.

Worldwide Internet Music Resources: National, International, and World Music
http://www.music.indiana.edu/music_resources/ethnic.html
middle school and up

So you're looking for the history of Bulgarian folk music? The sites listed above are great if you're interested in the classical music of America or Europe, but if your ear hears music from afar, you'll need to visit this index site, which organizes its links by country or region. You'll find several dozen countries or regions represented, many of them with numerous links. Some of the links will be in the language of the country, but many are in English.

In addition, there's a section on "Ethnomusicology Resources" at the top of this page. You'll see links to *Andean Wind Instruments, Khazana—Indian Music Recordings and Instruments,* and *TuneWeb,* an archive of traditional Celtic and American tunes.

NAPOLEONIC WARS

Best Search Engine:	http://www.google.com/
Key Search Terms:	Napoleonic Wars + history
	Napoleon + wars + history

NapoleonGuide.com
http://www.napoleonguide.com/index.htm
middle school and up

Although a commercial site with all the annoyances that entails, this guide to all things Napoleon serves up some wonderful fare if you're interested in the Napoleonic Wars. You won't, however, find one simple section on the wars.

The index of the site appears at the right on the home page. Scan down to the section on "Warfare," then under "Warfare" click on "Campaigns" to find essays on each of the First through Fifth Coalitions, the "Egypt Adventure," "In the Peninsula," "Into Russia," "1813: Germany," "France Invaded," "The 100 Days," and "The War of 1812." If you want to search by battle, click on "Battle" under "Warfare" for an alphabetical index. The essays you will find are detailed and well written with links to other areas of the site that provide more information.

In addition to the wars, you can research Napoleon himself, of course, the era of Napoleon, art, film, and games related to Napoleon, and many other military and related topics.

Napoleonic War Series
http://www.wtj.com/wars/napoleonic/
middle school and up

This wonderfully eclectic site will bring unusual as well as conventional resources to your fingertips. The site is divided into "Archives" and "Articles." Under "Archives" you'll find such things as "Napoleon's Correspondence," dispatches and orders from Napoleonic French Marshal Louis Davout, and recollections of several veterans of the French Revolutionary and Napoleonic Wars. Under "Articles," you'll find an overview of the French Revolutionary and Napoleonic Wars, a summary of the state of artillery at the end of the nineteenth century, and an article that chronicles the traumatic 1812 crossing of the Berezina River by the retreating French army.

NATIONALISM

Best Search Engine: http://www.google.com/
Key Search Terms: Nationalism + history

Nationalism Links
http://www.socresonline.org.uk/2/1/natlinks.html
middle school and up

Perhaps you're interested in Bosnian nationalism, or separatist movements in Texas, or Irish Republican history? You'll find all different forms of nationalism explored at this mega list of annotated links. And although this page has not been maintained in recent years, it's still the best gateway for exploring this massive subject.

The list of links was compiled by Paul Treanor in association with his article, "Structures of Nationalism," and is organized on the basis of the forms of nationalism described in his text: globalism, macro-cultural, nation state nationalism, ethno-nationalism, and localism. You'll find links to all the many places and types of nationalism you can imagine.

Nationalism
http://www.encyclopedia.com/articles/09011.html
middle school and up

This brief Encyclopedia.com article presents an introduction to nationalism, followed by sections on the necessary conditions for its development, and the history of nationalism, which traces elements of nationalism all the way back to the ancient Hebrews. You'll find links to key terms, such as "Machiavelli," "mercantilism," "Napoleon," "fascism," and "Indian National Congress."

Internet Modern History Sourcebook: Nationalism
http://www.fordham.edu/halsall/mod/modsbook17.html
middle school and up

This *Sourcebook* page on nationalism, unlike many *Sourcebook* pages, contains a useful brief introduction following the table of contents. The *Sourcebook* is devoted to collecting primary source material, so most of the links provided here are to texts—books, speeches, and government documents, among other types. But you'll also find the occasional link to a related Web page. The site is divided into sections on nationalism (general), cultural nationalism, liberal nationalism, and triumphal nationalism.

NAZISM (SEE ALSO GERMANY—NAZISM)

Best Search Engine: http://www.google.com/
Key Search Terms: Nazism + history
                                    Hitler + history

Nazism and World War II
http://www.cyberessays.com/History/45.htm
middle school and up

Here's an excellent overview of Nazism and World War II. It's a straightforward narrative that begins in 1919 and ends with the liberation of France in late 1944. It chronicles Hitler's rise to power and the sociopolitical context in which Nazism developed.

If you're looking for a straightforward resource that gives you the basics without going into lots of detail, this site should be the ticket.

Internet Modern History Sourcebook: Nazism
http://www.fordham.edu/halsall/mod/modsbook43.html
high school and up

To really understand Nazism, read the political texts that promoted its theories. Hitler's famous "25 Points," his speeches from 1921 to 1941, and even songs of the German army can be found among the primary source documents at this site. In addition, you'll find material about the Weimar elections and about the relationship between the church and the Nazis.

1920s (AGE OF ANXIETY)

Best Search Engine: http://www.google.com/
Key Search Terms: 1920s + Europe + history
                                    Interwar years + politics + Europe
                                    Anxiety + Europe + 1920s

1920s.net
http://www.1920s.net/index.htm
middle school and up

If you are looking for a fast and simple way to start learning about the tumultuous time of the 1920s, check out this easy-to-use Web site. Don't expect a nuanced or detailed view of the era. That is not this site's strength. What you will find are brief but thorough descriptions of the key political and cultural events that occurred in each European nation during the 1920s.

Although *1920s.net* will eventually provide an overview of the decade's world history, only the section on European is up and running right now. From the home page, select "Europe" from the menu on the left-hand side of the screen (or you can click on the continent on the map). You can then choose the country you want to study—either from the menu or from the map of Europe. You can access information about what happened in all the European countries, from Albania to Yugoslavia. The short essays about each country's events tend to emphasize political developments, although they do cover economic issues and cultural trends in a more cursory way as well.

The Age of Anxiety: Europe in the 1920s
http://www.pagesz.net/~stevek/europe/lecture8.html
high school and up

This Web site, which is part of the excellent *History Guide*, lets you know why the 1920s were an anxious time for Europeans. While it's a little more advanced than *1920s.net*, *The Age of Anxiety* explains more thoroughly the cultural, political, and economic upheavals of the 1920s.

The Age of Anxiety focuses on the intellectual history of the 1920s. Instead of just covering the events of history (in other words, the who, what, when, and where of a historical period), intellectual history examines the intellectual production from a certain period. Intellectual historians read novels and political philosophies, look at artwork and architecture, and even read how the historians of that period interpreted past events.

So, when you browse *The Age of Anxiety*, you won't find time lines or outlines. You will find two comprehensive essays that will introduce you to the intellectual history of the 1920s. It explains the backdrop of the period—the end of World War I. To help you understand the profound impact that World War I had on people and politicians, the site contains links that you can follow to read literature dealing with World War I. You can read a biography of Erich Marie Remarque and read excerpts of his novel about World War I, *All Quiet on the Western Front*. The same goes with the effect that World War I had on political philosophy. Select Paul Valery's name from the essay and you can read from his influential work, *The Crisis of the Mind*, which proclaimed the decline of Europe because of World War I.

You'll also be able to study the life and works of the people who shaped the 1920s—Lenin, Mussolini, and Hitler, as well as the philosophers who influenced them, such as Oswald Spengler, Richard Wagner, and Karl Marx. You can look at the startling new artwork that emerged in the 1920s, from the modernist architecture of Mies van der Rohe to the abstract paintings of Paul Klee. It's all just a click away. You only need to follow the links from the main essay. Remember to select "Part II" when you have finished reading the first page.

The Inter-War Years
http://interwaryears.8m.net/index.html
middle school and up

This site, which is simple and easy to use, takes the opposite approach to learning about the 1920s than *The Age of Anxiety*. Use *The Inter-War Years* for a fast overview of the events that took place between World War I and World War II all across the world. There are no biographies of key people, no excerpts from important intellectual works, and nothing but the most basic information. Nevertheless, *The Inter-War Years* is a great resource to use to review the chronology of the period. Because it covers the 1930s, the site also allows you to put the political events of the 1920s into a broader historical context. *The Inter-War Years* is also a snap to use. From the home page just select the year that interests you. You'll get a comprehensive chronology of the year's events.

NORTH ATLANTIC TREATY ORGANIZATION

Best Search Engine: http://www.google.com/
Key Search Terms: NATO + history

NATO History
http://www.stratnet.ucalgary.ca/outreach/Module1/Readings/1949–1989/
    NATO_History/NATO-history.html
middle school and up

This joint project of CMSS High School in Calgary, Alberta, Canada, and the Centre for Military and Strategic Studies is perfect for the student researcher who wants a more in-depth look at NATO's history. You'll find the site brimming with good information that's well organized and attractively displayed. Choose a decade you'd like to explore—the 1950s, 1960s, 1970s, or 1980s—and use the questions at the bottom of each section to quiz yourself on the reading once you're done.

The Origins of NATO
http://www.state.gov/www/regions/eur/nato/9904nato_index.html
middle school and up

Created to mark the fiftieth anniversary of NATO, this State Department site contains a detailed historical narrative on NATO and a superb chronology of agreements, declarations, and negotiations, which can be found below the foreword and preface on the home page. The historical narrative is broken down into sections, which are listed on the home page under the table of contents, in case you want to read only part of the history. Or you may prefer to use the previously mentioned CMSS High School site for history, and refer to this site just for its chronology.

NUBIA/KUSH

Best Search Engine: http://www.altavista.com/
Key Search Terms: Nubia + history
                        Ancient Egypt + history
                        Black culture + ancient history
                        Kush + history
                        Meroe + ancient Sudan
                        Napata + Nubia

Ancient Nubia
http://library.thinkquest.org/22845/
middle school and up

Everything you want to know about Nubia can be found in this spiffy, fully searchable site. There are sections on geography and topography, climate and natural resources, and archaeological history, as well as a general introduction to ancient Nubia. There's also a wealth of information on Nubia during the Bronze Age, including sections on the A-Group culture, the C-Group culture, the Kerma culture, and the colonial period. Click on the "Kingdom of Kush" to explore the Napatan, Meroitic, X-Group, and Christian periods. And if this isn't enough for you, try reading it all in another language. The page can be translated into French, German, Italian, Spanish, and Portuguese.

The Nubia Salvage Project
http://www-oi.uchicago.edu/OI/PROJ/NUB/NUBX92/
    NUBX92_brochure.html
high school and up

This great site from the Oriental Institute Museum at the University of Chicago provides images of artifacts from Nubia interspersed with a brief history of the land and its people, as well as a description of Nubia today. A basic chronology will help you keep track of the different periods in Nubian history. The *Ancient Nubia* site packs more punch than this basic offering, but it's worth a stop to check out the artifacts.

OLMECS

Best Search Engine: http://www.google.com/

Key Search Terms: Olmec + history

Mexico + ancient history

Mystery of the Olmec
http://www.time.com/time/magazine/archive/1996/dom/960701/
   archaeology.html
middle school and up

Find out about the first great culture of Mesoamerica in this *Time* magazine article, which was written to publicize a 1996 exhibit of Olmec art at the National Gallery in Washington, D.C. There's a brief mention of the exhibit, but the majority of the article addresses the culture of the Olmecs, including discussions of their politics, architecture, social structure, artwork, and more.

Olmec Civilization, 1200 B.C.–600 A.D.
http://www.crystalinks.com/olmec.html
middle school and up

This page from the *Ancient and Lost Civilizations* site offers a good historical overview of the Olmec, with sections on their geography, mathematics, farming, writing, society, cultural centers, ball games, stone heads, and other artwork. Interesting, high-quality images accompany the text.

OPIUM WARS

Best Search Engine: http://www.google.com/

Key Search Terms: Opium wars + history

China + Britain + opium wars

Lin Tse-hsu + China + history

Opium Wars
http://www.wsu.edu:8080/~dee/CHING/OPIUM.HTM
high school and up

This informative page on the opium wars is from Washington State University's excellent online world civilizations course. The page provides a basic summary of the history leading up to the war, which is followed by sections on Lin Tse-hsu, a key player in the opium trade conflict; a section titled "The War"; and one on the *Illustrated Gazatteer of Maritime Countries*, which is considered the first systematic attempt to educate the Chinese in Western technologies and culture.

> *Mr. Dowling's Electronic Passport: Chinese History: The Opium Wars*
> http://www.mrdowling.com/613-opiumwars.html
> middle school and up

Mr. Dowling's Electronic Passport never fails to provide unique information, and this page on the opium wars is no exception. You'll find two side-by-side historical summaries of the opium wars, one written by a Chinese person, the other written by a British person. Surrounding these accounts is a brief outline of the opium wars. What makes the page especially useful is the availability of links to other Chinese history topics. At the top of the page, you'll see "Dynasty," "Confucius," "The Boxer Rebellion," and numerous other links for easy reference.

OTTOMAN EMPIRE

> Best Search Engine: http://www.google.com/
>
> Key Search Terms: Ottoman Empire + history

> *Islam UK: The Ottoman Empire (1300–1922)*
> http://www.bbc.co.uk/religion/religions/islam/history/ottoman/index.shtml
> middle school and up

Part of the larger BBC site, *Islam UK,* this Ottoman Empire page contains an introduction as well as sections on "The Recipe for Success," "Constantinople," "Other Religions," "The Sultan's Life," "The Golden Age," and "Decline." Track the empire from its glorious rise to its gradual decentralization and decline. You'll find useful links throughout the site, as well as lots of interesting information on Islam if you're interested in exploring the religion.

> *The Ottomans*
> http://www.wsu.edu:8080/~dee/OTTOMAN/CONTENTS.HTM
> middle school and up

From the contents page, select from the following sections: "Origins," "Suleyman," "Selim II," "The 17th and 18th Centuries," and "European Imperialism and the Balkan Crisis." You'll also find "The Ottoman Reader," a "Gallery of Ottoman Culture," a "Glossary of Ottoman Terms and Concepts," a "Glossary of Islamic Terms and Concepts," and "Internet Resources on Islam." Although the gallery and Ottoman glossary were still under construction when we visited, the rest of this site at Washington State University contains superb information.

PALESTINE

Best Search Engine: http://www.google.com/
Key Search Terms: Palestine + history
                        Yassir Arafat + history

Quick Palestine Timeline
http://www.palestinehistory.com/qtime.htm
middle school and up

First of all, this time line is more than a time line. It's really a summary of Palestine's history in the twentieth century. The time line is organized around major agreements and movements, so you'll find several years lumped together with an explanation of the significant events that happened during those years. In addition, you can access, through links at the bottom of the page, complete time lines for the years 1996–2001. For summaries of specific periods in Palestine's history, this site offers the best resources.

Palestine-Net: Chronology of Palestinian History
http://www.palestine-net.com/history/bhist.html
high school and up

You won't find a more complete time line of Palestine's history anywhere on the Web. This one begins in 600,000 B.C., with the earliest human remains found in the area, and continues up through the Second Intifada in 2000. For the most part, this chronology is not for the casual student of Palestinian history, but if you need to see events laid out in chronological order, or if you're interested in a particular year or span of years, this is an excellent reference tool.

Mr. Dowling's Electronic Passport: Conflicts in the Middle East: Israel
http://www.mrdowling.com/608-israel.html
middle school and up

Are you confused about the source of the conflict between Israel and the Palestinians? If so, let Mr. Dowling clear things up. This page provides a straightforward, evenhanded summary of the conflict, beginning with the declaration of Israel as an independent Jewish homeland in 1948. You won't find all the nuances and details here, but you will get the basic story straight.

PAPACY

Best Search Engine: http://www.google.com/

Key Search Terms: Papacy + history

Popes + history

Papacy + Middle Ages

Papacy + Reformation

Papacy
http://www.encyclopedia.com/articlesnew/09803.html
middle school and up

This brief Encyclopedia.com article defines the papacy in broad terms, which may be helpful to you if you're looking for some very basic information. But if you want to explore the history of the papacy, you'll need to scroll to the bottom of the page where you'll find links to articles on the papacy in various time periods—in the early church, the Middle Ages, the Reformation, the eighteenth and nineteenth centuries, and the twentieth century. Here's your history divided neatly by era. None of these articles is terribly long, but the information is useful, and you'll find hyperlinks within the articles that let you explore related subjects in more depth.

The Internet Medieval Sourcebook: Empire and Papacy
http://www.fordham.edu/halsall/sbook1l.html
middle school and up

This *Sourcebook* page collects primary source material that addresses the history of the relationship between emperors and popes. Check it out, if for no other reason than to read the excellent introductory essay, which explains how the history of Western culture has been shaped by the conflicts of long-dead popes and emperors.

PELOPONNESIAN WAR

Best Search Engine: http://www.google.com/

Key Search Terms: Peloponnesian War + history

Athenian empire + history

Sparta + history

Thucydides + Peloponnesian War

Delian League + history

Pericles + Peloponnesian

The Peloponnesian War
http://www.multimania.com/sdelille/gdpa.html
middle school and up

If you are only going to visit one Web site about the Peloponnesian War, make sure that this is the one. Although this site has almost no original content of its own, it does provide links to hundreds of other Internet sites that cover nearly every aspect of the history of the Peloponnesian War. If you're looking for maps, chronologies, general overviews, ancient writing that discusses the war, scholarly papers, discussion groups—virtually anything about the Peloponnesian War—this site will take you where you can find what you need. As an added bonus this site is well organized, so that you can find quickly the material that you need. Give credit to the site's creator, Sven Delille, who updates and reviews the recommended sites to make sure the material is current.

The Peloponnesian War is composed of eight main sections that you can access from the main menu on the home page: "Ancient Sources"; "Thucydides"; "The War in General"; "Particular Points"; "Inscription"; "Reviews"; "Bibliographies"; and "Discussions." Within each of these broad areas, you'll find links to dozens of Web sites. If you're just beginning your research on the Peloponnesian War, you might want to go to "The War in General" section first. Here you'll be referred to some excellent sites, including those that provide maps, chronologies, and general overviews of the Peloponnesian War. Simply scroll down the list of English-language Web sites and you'll see links to scholarly lectures on the war, tactical analyses by the Naval War College, and Thomas Martin's brilliant essay on the Peloponnesian War and its aftermath at the *Perseus Project* site. If you are attempting to research a specific facet of the history of the Peloponnesian war, check out the "Particular Points" section from the main menu. For instance, if you're in the market for material about a specific battle, the Peloponnesian League, or the Athenian plague, scroll through the links in this section.

In addition to making available these fantastic explanatory sites, *The Peloponnesian War* can also put a wealth of primary material at your fingertips. When you go to the section on "Ancient Sources," you can read texts by Thucydides, Xenophone, Aristophanes, and Plutarch, among others. (If you happen to be fluent in Greek or Latin, you can even read the texts in their ancient language.) The section on "Thu-cydides" can refer you to dozens of resources about Thucydides and his famous book on the Peloponnesian War. If you actually want to view some primary documents, go to "Inscriptions," which contains photo-graphs of epigraphical inscriptions on documents from the first to the third century that are related to the Peloponnesian War and Thucydides.

If you are interested in reading reviews of books published about the Peloponnesian War, you'll love the "Reviews" section, which contains links to reviews of books—both scholarly and popular—on the topic. If you somehow haven't found what you need at this site, visit "Bibliog-raphies" for links to bibliographic resources. In the "Discussions" section you'll learn how to subscribe to mailing lists and discussion groups about Thucydides and the Peloponnesian War.

Peloponnesian War
http://www.historyforkids.org/greekciv/war/pelopwar/oleg.htm
middle school and high school

As terrific a site as Sven Delille's *Peloponnesian War* is, it can be a bit overwhelming, especially for younger students, to have to choose from such a vast array of material. If you need a more basic site—but one that is still comprehensive and top-notch—you'll want to visit this Web page, which is part of Portland State University's *Greek Civilization for Middle Schoolers*.

To find your way around this Web site, the easiest thing to do is simply to scroll down the home page. What you'll find is a brief but thorough review of the Peloponnesian War that covers the escalation of tensions between Athens and Sparta, the First War, the Sicilian Expedition, the fall of the Athenian Empire, and the results of the Peloponnesian War. As you read along, you'll notice links to follow if you need more infor-mation about a specific term used. Click on "Aegean Sea," for instance, and you'll be able to access a map showing you its location. Select "Pericles" and you can access a two-page biography on this Athenian leader.

More advanced students should not plan to use this Web site as their primary research tool. It will provide basic information about the Pel-oponnesian war and its legacy, but it can't provide the level of detail as most of the sites recommended by Sven Delille. Nevertheless, Portland State's site is a good place (especially for younger students) to learn about the Peloponnesian War.

PERSIAN EMPIRE

Best Search Engine: http://www.altavista.com/
Key Search Terms: Persian empire + history

                                   Zarathustra + history

                                   Persian Wars + history

The Persian Empire, 550–330 B.C.
http://campus.northpark.edu/history/WebChron/MiddleEast/Persia.html
middle school and up

A good and not overly detailed time line of the Persian empire, beginning with Zarathustra and ending with Alexander the Great conquering the empire. Some of the significant people and events listed in the time line hyperlinks to sites that provide more information.

The Persians
http://www.wsu.edu/~dee/MESO/PERSIANS.HTM
high school and up

Once again this Washington State University site, which was created for a course on world civilizations, provides a stellar historical overview, this time of Persian empire history. This site is much more in-depth than the time line listed above, but it's still aimed toward beginning students of the subject. Links along the left-hand side of the page take you to the "World Cultures Glossary" or to separate articles on related topics, such as "The Hebrews: After the Exile" and "Ancient Greece: The Persian Wars."

PERSIAN WARS

Best Search Engine: http://www.altavista.com/
Key Search Terms: Persian Wars + history

                                   Persian empire + history

                                   Croesus + Persian Wars

Ancient Greece: The Persian Wars
http://www.wsu.edu/~dee/GREECE/PERSIAN.HTM
high school and up

Part of the Washington State University site reviewed above (see **Persian Empire**), this page on the Persian Wars provides an excellent summary of the wars that the Greeks considered to be their most important. Nothing like Herodotus's version, the history here is written in a simple narrative style that you'll find easily accessible. And the site as a whole is chock-full of stellar ancient civilization material, so if you're interested in other ancient Greek topics, follow the links and you won't be disappointed.

The Persian Wars
http://history.boisestate.edu/westciv/persian/
middle school and up

If you're looking for more than just a summary, try this Boise State University page. The contents listed on the home page provide links to 22 Persian War topics, arranged chronologically, beginning with Croesus and Daria I and ending with Salamis and Plataea. The essays attached to each link are relatively brief and pleasantly written. Occasional photos and other resources interspersed with the text provide a bit of visual interest and diversion if you need to take a wee break from reading.

PHOENICIANS

Best Search Engine:	http://www.google.com/
Key Search Terms:	Phoenicians + history
	Canaanites + history
	Levant + Phoenicians

The History and Culture of the Canaanites and Phoenicians
http://www.geocities.com/SoHo/Lofts/2938/histcult.html
middle school and up

This page is part of *Qadash-Kinahnu,* a Canaanite-Phoenician temple on the Web, with more than 85 rooms to visit—all of them related to the Phoenicians. Start with the URL listed here to get the history and culture of the Phoenicians. The site starts at about 3000 B.C.E. and covers up to about 300 B.C.E. You'll find information on their ethnic, cultural, and linguistic origins; the cities they founded; the geography of the region; urban life; and trade, among other subjects.

Once you've acquainted yourself with Phoenician history, follow the links back to the home page of *Qadash-Kinahnu,* where you'll find links to the rest of the rooms in the temple, which are dedicated primarily to the study of Levantine and Near Eastern paganism. Lots of information here on the deities and myths of the Phoenicians if this strikes your fancy.

A Bequest Unearthed, Phoenicia
http://phoenicia.org/index.shtml
middle school and up

According to the preface on this site, which received a Britannica Internet Guide Award, "these pages are a compilation and repository of studies about the origin, history, geography, religion, arts and crafts, trade, industry, climate, mythology, language, literature, music, politics, wars, archaeology, and contribution to world culture of an ancient Canaanite people of the Middle East called the Phoenicians." That just about says it all.

You might find, like we did, that the organization of text and graphics is a little chaotic, but the content here is fascinating and worth the difficulty of finding your way through the maze. A long list of about 50 subjects covered on the site include such topics as anthropology, Cadmus, dentistry, Homer, the Torah, Tunisia, the Y chromosome, and wars, for example. While some of the material presented here is clearly subjective, most of it is well grounded in academic research. And the author of the page makes no effort to mask his opinions, so you always know when you're reading something subjective. In addition he provides a nice introduction to the site, which explains his approach to compiling Phoenician history.

While the previous site on the Phoenicians provides a good concise history, this site will lead the way as you explore beyond the basic history and discover a myriad of topics.

POLYNESIAN EXPLORATIONS

Best Search Engine: http://www.google.com/

Key Search Terms: Polynesian + history

Polynesians + navigation + history

1000 B.C.–800 A.D.: The Polynesians
http://www.studyworksonline.com/cda/content/article/0,1034,EXP118_
    NAV2–5_SAR99,00.html
middle school and up

If you're looking for a simple introduction to the Polynesian explorers, this is the site for you. There aren't a bunch of links to distract you, and the writing is geared toward students just beginning to study the Polynesians, so you can start right at the beginning with a section on the origins of the Polynesians. From there, this attractive StudyWorks page proceeds to cover the Polynesian colonization of islands and, especially, their means of exploration. The site is really focused on early navigation and mapping, so you'll read fascinating text on Polynesian boats, celestial navigation, wave navigation, and sea bird navigation.

Wayfinders, A Pacific Odyssey
http://www.pbs.org/wayfinders/index.html
middle school and up

If you're interested in sea exploration or Polynesian history, this site will surely captivate you. It's a PBS Web site companion to a film of the same name, and it will help you learn more about Pacific Island geography, culture, history, archaeology, linguistics, and celestial navigation. You can even ask questions of the experts who provided background information for the film.

From the home page, click on "Polynesian History and Origin" to begin your journey. From there, you can go to "Wayfinding," a page that explores the ancient art of navigating on the open seas with only nature as your guide—the stars, sun, sea swells, etc. Another page called "Sharing Stories" asks you to contribute your answers to questions about community and culture and gives you the opportunity to read how other site visitors have answered the same questions. "Ask the Experts" lets you tune in to Real Audio interviews with the experts who consulted on the making of the film. There's also a place for you to write in a question of your own which will be answered by the experts.

PREHISTORY

Best Search Engine:	http://www.google.com/
Key Search Terms:	Prehistory + human evolution
	Prehistory + art
	Prehistory + dinosaurs
	Prehistory + early humans

The Long Foreground: Human History
http://www.wsu.edu/gened/learn-modules/top_longfor/lfopen-index.html
high school and up

Part of an online learning module from Washington State University's excellent world civilizations course, this page links you to an overview of human evolution, a hominid species time line, and an essay on human physical characteristics. You'll find interesting and helpful illustrations in addition to the top-rate, introductory text. One chart compares the skulls of various primates; another shows the gibbon, gorilla, chimpanzee, orangutan, and pygmy chimp side by side, with links to more in-depth information about each species.

The time line also provides links to further information about each species listed in the chronology. The final section on physical charac-teristics breaks down traits into categories and explores each one in depth. You can click on links to information about brain size, human skin as a heat diffusion device, the throat and position of the larynx, and other specific topics.

*NM's Creative Impulse, The Development of Western Civilization I, World
    History, Prehistory*
http://history.evansville.net/prehist.html
middle school and up

If you want to branch out beyond the topic of human origins and evolution, this prehistory index contains history links to sites that ex-plore places, events, and dinosaurs, as well as people. It also contains a treasure trove of links on art and architecture—think cave paintings, rock art, megaliths, and more—as well as links to sites that deal with literature and drama, music and dance, and daily life and culture links.

For an index site, this one is actually quite manageable in size, and the links are well maintained and screened for quality. You're not likely to run across a dud here. And the page is neatly organized by category, so if you know you're looking for information on the earliest musical instruments, you can scroll down to "Music and Dance," and find links to sites such as *Music of the Ages* and *Neanderthal Flute*.

PUNIC WARS

Best Search Engine:	http://www.google.com/
Key Search Terms:	Punic Wars + history
	Rome + Carthage + history

Mr. Dowling's Electronic Passport: Rome: The Punic Wars
http://www.mrdowling.com/702-punic.html
middle school and up

This site, complete with a colorful map, summarizes the history of the three wars Rome fought against Carthage, a city in northern Africa, in the third century B.C. In addition to the top-rate text, you'll find an interactive quiz for testing yourself when you're done, and a link to the electronic passport to Carthage, which provides some additional infor-mation about the wars. A list of Rome-related links at the top of the page makes further exploration of Rome easy.

QURAN (KORAN)

Best Search Engine: http://www.google.com/

Key Search Terms: Quran + history

                      Koran + history

                      Islam + history + religion

                      Muslims + history + religion

The Qur'an
http://www.wsu.edu:8080/~dee/ISLAM/QURAN.HTM
middle school and up

Here's a good basic introduction to the origins and content of the Qur'an, Islam's holy text. Part of a Washington State University online learning module on Islam, this page is written for those with little background in Islam. What's especially nice about this introduction is its objective approach and the fact that it provides you with links to selections from the Qur'an, translated into English, so that you can read the book for yourself.

Al-Islam.org
http://www.al-islam.org/
middle school and up

Features at this site include a "Beginner's Guide" and sections entitled "About Islam," "Allah and the Holy Koran," "The Infallibles," "Beliefs and Practices," and "History and Current Events." This page, which is searchable and includes a subject index, is part of the Ahlul Bayt Digital Islamic Library Project, an extensive site that could take days to explore. Stick to the sections mentioned here, and you'll find plenty of resources on the history of the Qur'an, as well as some interesting contemporary information about Muslims and the practice of Islam in the world today.

REFORMATION, THE

Best Search Engine: http://www.google.com/

Key Search Terms: Reformation + history

                      Martin Luther + history

                      Counter Reformation + history

                      John Wesley + Reformation

                      John Calvin + wars

The Reformation Guide
http://www.educ.msu.edu/homepages/laurence/reformation/index.htm
middle school and up

This gateway to Web resources on the Reformation contains a list of about 20 topics, including Martin Luther, John Calvin, the Radical Reformation, the English Reformation, the Counter Reformation, a gallery of people in the Reformation, and a gallery of places related to the Reformation. Each of these major topic links takes you to a page that contains a brief introduction to the topic and then a much longer list of specific topics. Click on "English Reformation," for example, and you'll discover a storehouse of links to relevant topics—John Wesley's sermons, "The London Baptist Confession of 1689," Fox's *Book of Martyrs,* and many more.

In addition, from the home page, you can venture out a bit into non-Reformation links on Bible translations, Bible study aids, Christian theology, Christian classics, early church documents, and ancient history.

Discovery and Reformation
http://www.wsu.edu/~dee/REFORM/
high school and up

Here's another one of those wonderful Washington State University online learning modules. This one covers "The Portuguese," "The 'New World,'" and "The Spanish Empire" (under the "Discovery" heading) as well as the following Reformation topics: "The Northern Renaissance," "Martin Luther," "Ulrich Zwingli," "John Calvin," "Protestant England," "Counter-Reformation," and "Religious Wars." What makes these Washington State University pages so good is the quality of the text. (The pages themselves are a little bit frustrating to navigate until you get the hang of them.) But the writing is captivating, authoritative, and comprehensive without being laborious. And you'll often find intriguing illustrations and links to related resources, too.

At this Reformation page, you'll find a glossary of Reformation terms and concepts, a gallery of the Reformation and Northern Renaissance, a list of other Reformation resources on the Internet, and readings in Reformation culture.

RENAISSANCE, THE

Best Search Engine: http://www.google.com/
Key Search Terms: Renaissance + history

                                    Renaissance + art + history

Italy + Renaissance

Leonardo da Vinci + Renaissance

Galileo + Renaissance

(For the English Renaissance see also *Perseus Project* under Ancient Greece: Culture and Science)

Virtual Renaissance
http://library.thinkquest.org/3588/Renaissance/
middle school and high school

Meet Giovanni Renaissanci and other interesting characters as you journey back in time at this fun Thinkquest site. Although the Web technologies found here are somewhat rudimentary, the spirit behind the site is creative and the diversity of the material covered is impressive.

Click on "Town" first to gather clues about your new environment. Here you can visit the local tavern, attend school, and talk to some traveling musicians. After you've become familiar with the place, choose your next stop from a list of places that includes the Cathedral of Santa Maria, the Globe Theatre, the Courthouse, the Hospital of the Innocents, the Sistine Chapel, and the Tower of London, to name a few. In addition to lots of great original material, this site also contains many valuable links to other Renaissance-related sites.

Web Gallery of Art
http://gallery.euroweb.hu/
middle school and up

This is an outstanding site for Renaissance and Reformation art history. Spanning the years between 1200 and 1700, the site presents more than 3,500 reproductions of European paintings and sculptures. Useful biographies can be found on all the more significant artists, and each artwork is annotated. The site is fully searchable and contains a section for guided tours, in case you'd like more interpretive assistance.

The Galileo Project
http://es.rice.edu/ES/humsoc/Galileo/
middle school and up

This is an award-winning hypertext site on the life and work of Italian astronomer Galileo Galilei. Find information—both text and pictures—on his family and his career. A section called the "Observing Gallery" contains accounts of his discovery of Jupiter's moons, as well as information on contemporary astronomers. You can even read detailed descriptions of the instruments Galileo used in his experiments and observations.

European Renaissance/Reformation
http://www.execpc.com/~dboals/rena.html
middle school and up

Part of the *History/Social Studies Web for K–12 Teachers*, this is an extensive list of sites on everything from Leonardo da Vinci to medieval Renaissance wedding information. The links are not organized in any helpful way, so it's somewhat laborious to find what you're looking for, but if you'd just like to browse a list of sites related to the Renaissance and Reformation, this is a good one. The links are good and the sites appropriate for high school and early college students.

ROMAN EMPIRE (SEE ALSO PERSEUS PROJECT UNDER ANCIENT GREECE)

Best Search Engine: http://www.google.com/
Key Search Terms: Rome + history
                        Julius Caesar + history
                        Claudius + Roman empire

Rome Project
http://www.dalton.org/groups/rome/
middle school and up

Winner of several awards for excellence in design and presentation, the *Rome Project* is The Dalton School's database of primary and secondary resources about the Roman republic and empire. A list of sections on the home page includes "Literature," "Military," "Archaeology," "Political," "General," "Philosophy," "Drama," "Religion," "Search Engines," and "Maps of the Roman Empire."

Students will find thousands of links to Greek and Latin classics, images of archaeological sites, translations of plays, law codes, and more. The site also contains plenty of reference material, such as time lines and chronologies, maps, and glossaries of military equipment.

The Forum Romanum
http://library.thinkquest.org/11402/?tqskip=1
middle school and up

When the center of the world was Rome, the center of Rome was the Roman Forum, and that is the subject of this Thinkquest site, designed by students from The Netherlands in 1997. The following sections will help you explore not only the Forum but also the Roman empire in which the Forum thrived—"Introduction," "The Forum,"

"History and Religion," "Daily Life," "Biographies," and "Anecdotes and Stories."

You'll also find a quiz to test your knowledge once you've perused the site. The index serves as a nice dictionary to Roman terms and concepts, and there's a search function so that you can look up topics of interest.

Roma
http://www.mclink.it/n/citrag/roma/doc/history/est_000.htm
middle school and up

Here you'll find a comprehensive look at the history of Rome from the legends that surround its foundations by Romulus, Remus, and Aeneas to the last emperors. The periods of the republic as well as the empire are treated in detail and divided into various time periods based on significant wars and government leaders.

Even though it is quite large, the site is well organized and easy to navigate. For information on the empire, look under "The Roman Empire" section and choose from links that include the "Julius-Claudius Dynasty," "The Flavian Dynasty," "The Antonini Dynasty," and "The Last Emperors." Each of these is further subdivided into specific individuals or topics.

ROME: REPUBLIC (SEE ALSO ROME PROJECT UNDER ROMAN EMPIRE)

Best Search Engine: http://www.google.com/
Key Search Terms: Rome + republic + history
                     Roman + civil wars + history

Roma
http://www.mclink.it/n/citrag/roma/doc/history/est_000.htm
middle school and up

Here you'll find a comprehensive look at the history of Rome from the legends that surround its foundations by Romulus, Remus, and Aeneas to the last emperors. The periods of the republic as well as the empire are treated in detail and divided into various time periods based on significant wars and government leaders.

Even though it is quite large, the site is well organized and easy to navigate. For information on the republic, look under "The Republic" section and choose from links that include "The Expansion of Rome across Italy," "The Conquest of the Mediterranean," and "The Civil Wars." Each is further subdivided into specific topics.

ROYAL GENEALOGIES

Best Search Engine: http://www.google.com/
Key Search Terms: Royal genealogy + history

                        Royal families + history

                        British + royal family + history

Directory of Royal Genealogical Data
http://www.dcs.hull.ac.uk/public/genealogy/royal/catalog.html
middle school and up

This searchable database of royalty from ancient times to the present is focused on the British royal family, but because of the intermarriage that has occurred over the ages, just about every ruling family in the Western world is represented here. The catalog contains sections on the following—"The Ancient Near East," "The Hellenistic World," "The Roman and Byzantine Worlds," "The Barbarian West," "Europe," "Islamic Dynasties," "India," "The Far East," "Africa," and "The New World." To date, the only complete sections are "The Roman and Byzantine Worlds," "The Barbarian West," "Europe," and "Islamic Dynasties," but these contain the genealogical dates for more than 30,000 people.

Under each of these sections, you'll find between 5 and 10 links. Click on "Europe," for example, and there's "British Isles," "Ireland," "France," and "The Low Countries" among other links. Choose "British Isles," and you're given five more links—"Monarchs of Britain," "Monarchs of Scotland," "Monarchs of England," "The Principality of Wales," and "The Peers of the Realm." Click on "Monarchs of England" for links to more than 50 royals. Each link contains basic information about the person's life and death, as well as links to the members of his or her immediate family.

This is an exhaustive site, and one that is meticulously compiled for the serious scholar.

Genealogical Gleanings
http://www.uq.net.au/~zzhsoszy/index.html
middle school and up

For Africa, Asia, Oceania, and the Middle East, try this database of royal family lineages. The index is organized by country, and then by family within the country. The amount of information given for each individual in the database varies and there isn't as much emphasis placed on ancient members of these families, but there's a wealth of personal history here. Under "Africa," for example, click on "Thembu Royal Family," the family of President Nelson Mandela, and you'll be given links to the listings for 716 individuals from 274 families.

RUSSIA—GENERAL

Best Search Engine: http://www.google.com/

Key Search Terms: Russia + history

Russian History on the Web
http://www.russianhistory.org/
middle school and up

This is an extremely valuable gateway site for students of Russian history. The critically evaluated Internet resources you'll find here include index sites, sites with bibliographic information, sites for collaborating with others (such as discussion lists and professional organizations), primary source sites, secondary source sites, and a list of tendentious pages, which are mentioned as a warning to students and researchers.

Under "Indexes," for example, you can choose from three categories—"General," "Historical," and "Special Topics." If you choose "Special Topics," you'll find annotated links to four very intriguing sites—"Medieval Russia Links and Research," "Imperial Russian Web Ring," "Eastern Front Web Ring," and "Medieval Slavic Studies." Each of these is an index page itself, which will guide you to useful pages on their chosen topic.

RUSSIA—KIEV RUS

Best Search Engine: http://www.google.com/

Key Search Terms: Kievan + Russia + history

                          Kiev Rus + history

                          House of Rurik + history

                          Russian Empire + history

Russian History
http://www.departments.bucknell.edu/russian/history.html
middle school and up

Another general Russian index site, but this one boasts some offerings that beginning students of Russian history will find quite valuable, such as links right upfront to a "Chronology of Russian History," a "History of Russia and the Former USSR," and a "Genealogy of the Russian Nobility." You'll also find numerous other key topics in Russian history. Some are in Russian, but most of these resources are in English.

Go to "Chronology of Russian History," and click on "The Kievan and Appanage Periods" for a detailed chronology of Kiev Russia, complete with embedded links, that covers the years from 859 to 1240. Here you'll read about the House of Rurik, the period of the Kievan Russian Empire that was destroyed by the Mongol-Tatars, and then the recentralization of the defeated empire with the rise of Moscow.

RUSSIAN REVOLUTION

Best Search Engine: http://www.google.com/

Key Search Terms: Russian Revolution + history

October Revolution + Russia

February Revolution + Russia

Lenin + Russian Revolution

Trotsky + Russian Revolution

Bolsheviks + history

Vladimir Lenin
http://members.nbci.com/1870/
middle school and up

It can be a challenge to find a Web site that provides comprehensive coverage of the Russian Revolution and that isn't too biased. There are an inordinate number of Web sites about a facet of the Russian Revolution that have an overt political agenda. This one on Vladimir Lenin is one of the better ones that you'll find. From its title, you could probably guess that it does a good job on the topic of Lenin. It has short and long biographies of Lenin, digital copies of his works, a massive photograph archive, and even audio clips of Lenin speaking. But the site also gives a detailed review of the events of the Russian Revolution. As a result, you'll find this site helpful if you want general information about the Russian Revolution or if you want specific material about Lenin.

The site is divided into five main sections: "The Life of Lenin," "Photographs," "The Works of V. I. Lenin," "Links," and "Bibliography."

You'll find links to the sections "The Life of Lenin" and "Photographs" on the left-hand side of the home page. At the bottom of the home page (in much smaller font) are the links to the other three sections.

The best place to find plenty of information about both Lenin and the Russian Revolution is in the section "The Life of Lenin," which contains dozens of biographies (or excerpts from larger biographies) on Lenin and his role in the Russian Revolution and other events in Russian history. You can take your pick from these resources, but if you do want a full picture of the Russian Revolution, don't overlook the biography by Nina Gourfinkle. To access this, simply select "A Full Biography" from the links near the top of the page. Gourfinkle devotes four online chapters to the events of the Revolution. Definitely read the chapters "1905," "The Revolution in Progress," "The Sealed Coach," and "October 25, 1917." If you'd like a more multimedia approach to studying Lenin's life, then check out the video and audio clips of him giving speeches. You'll see these links at the top of the section's page. (You can even listen to audio clips of Lenin's favorite music). Near the bottom of this section's page are links you can follow to read Trotsky's obituary of Lenin. Trotsky writes extensively about the Russian Revolution in this document.

After you've read all about Lenin's life, do you want to know what he looked like? No problem if you do, because this Web site has one of the largest online collections of Lenin photographs. Select "Photographs" from the home page, and then pick the year that interests you. You can also opt to view photos of Lenin's signature and of his giving speeches.

Those of you hard at work on a research paper will appreciate the site's large collection of primary documents written by Lenin. Select the "Works of V. I. Lenin," and you'll be taken off-site to the *V. I. Lenin Library*, which makes available to you dozens of documents written by Lenin. You can view the "Complete List" of Lenin's work, or skip to "Selected Works," which houses his best-known treatises. The *V. I. Lenin Library* also has a handy "Subject Index" so that you can look for documents on a specific topic.

If you haven't found everything you need at the *Vladimir Lenin* site, check out the "Links" section, which recommends additional online resources, and the "Bibliography" of print material. Be aware that the links are disappointing, though. They are mostly to other (inferior) sites on Lenin and to sites run by various communist or socialist groups. You won't find links to any sites on the Russian Revolution.

Marxist.org Internet Archive
http://www.marxists.org/
middle school and up

For primary sources on the period of Russian history that began with the Russian Revolution and spanned most of the twentieth century, this site is the oldest and most comprehensive on the Internet. You'll find old photos, biographies of key individuals, and an extensive archive of the works of major Marxists.

RUSSIA—PETER/CATHERINE

Best Search Engine: http://www.google.com/
Key Search Terms: Romanov + history

Peter + great + history

Catherine + great + history

Romanov Timeline
http://www2.sptimes.com/Treasures/TC.2.3b.html
middle school and up

This page from the *Romanov Timeline* covers the eighteenth century and includes brief essays on Peter the Great, Peter II, Catherine I, and Catherine the Great, as well as many other lesser-known Romanovs.

The contents page contains pictures of each royal with a link to the biographical essay. Links within the essays take you to other *Romanov Timeline* pages on such topics as the Orthodox Church and dragoons.

Catherine the Great Links
http://www.wasa.uk.net/history/links/Russia/Catherine_II.html
middle school and up

This is a good, selective list of links to the Catherine the Great pages. The links are well organized under the following sections: "Primary Sources," "Monographs and Articles," "General Sources," "Biographical References," "Bibliographical References," "Chronology," "Culture," "Philosophy, Philosophers, and the Enlightenment," "Portraits," and "Miscellaneous." Each link is briefly annotated. Try the biography link, "Catherine the Great," which has a table of contents with about eight different topics including "A Wedding in St. Petersburg," "The Birth of the Tsarevich Paul," "Peter Deposed," and more. The site also contains a Catherine the Great FAQ page.

RUSSIA—NINETEENTH CENTURY

Best Search Engine: http://www.google.com/
Key Search Terms: Russia + history + nineteenth century
    Russia + imperial period
    Russia + golden age

Russia in the Nineteenth Century
http://www.departments.bucknell.edu/russian/fn9015/1800Russ.html
middle school and up

This article gives a good introduction to Russia's golden age of culture. Broken down into two sections—1800–1860 and 1860–1900—the narrative combines economic, political, social, and cultural history. Links within the text allow you to explore key topics in more depth. These include "Alexander Pushkin," "Napoleonic Wars," "The Decembrists," "Slavophiles," "Alexander II," and quite a few other hotlinks. Some are brief definitions of the topic; others are entire Web sites or sections of sites devoted to the topic.

Follow the link for Lobachevsky, for example, one of Russia's great mathematicians, and the biographical page that pops up gives you comprehensive information on his life and death, as well as links to other topics related to him, most of them dealing with mathematics.

Survey of Russian History
http://www.gened.arizona.edu/atheneum/imperialrussia.htm
middle school and up

This excerpt from the survey of Russian history by John Garrard covers the years 1801 to 1917 and gives particular attention to the politics of the time, with lengthy sections on Alexander I, II, and III, and Nicholas I and II.

The writing is clear and easy to follow, even if you don't have a background in Russian imperial history, and this page makes a nice partner to the previous site which covers the political history only briefly. If you're looking for in-depth information about the czars without getting bogged down in every detail, this is the page for you.

RUSSO-JAPANESE WAR

Best Search Engine: http://www.google.com/
Key Search Terms: Russo-Japanese War + history
    Treaty of Portsmouth + history

Russo-Japanese War
http://www.encyclopedia.com/articles/11252.html
middle school and up

This brief *Encyclopedia.com* article will give you an overview of the Russo-Japanese War and provide you with links to other *Encyclopedia.com* articles on related topics, such as Manchuria, Korea, Admiral Togo, President Roosevelt, and the Treaty of Portsmouth. In addition to the historical overview, there's a "Bibliography" link at the bottom of the page.

Russo-Japanese War Factbook
http://www.skalman.nu/russo-japanese/
middle school and up

For a look at this war from a military perspective, check out this little site. It contains loads of data on the naval strength and personnel on both sides. Click on "Link" for a list of other topics related to this war. You'll find links entitled "Russo-Japanese Conflict: Its Causes and Issues," "Russo-Japanese War Ramblings," the "Russo-Japanese War Research Society," and the "Treaty of Portsmouth," among others. Some of these are academic articles, such as "Some of the Issues of the Russo-Japanese Conflict," from the *Yale Review*; others are written by amateur historians with a particular interest in military history. You'll find an assortment of resources, but all are worthwhile and informative.

SASSANIDS (PERSIA)

Best Search Engine:	http://www.google.com/
Key Search Terms:	Sassanids + history
	Persia + ancient history

The Sassanids
http://www.historyforkids.org/learn/westasia/history/sassanids.htm
middle school

Here's an excellent site for beginning students of Persian history. The writing is simple and clear, and the text contains numerous links to related topics, such as the Persian empire, Zoroastrians, Greeks, and Romans, among others. Part of the *Western Asia* history site, this page on the Sassanids is one of about 15 such pages on western Asia topics such as the Sumerians, Hittites, Greeks, Alexander the Great, and the Maccabees.

All you'll get here is a brief introduction to the Sassanids, but that could be enough to get you interested in pursuing Persian history further.

SCIENTIFIC REVOLUTION

Best Search Engine: http://www.google.com/
Key Search Terms: Scientific revolution + history
Renaissance + science + history
Galileo + history

Science during the Renaissance
http://www.geocities.com/CapeCanaveral/hangar/6739/timeline.html
middle school and up

This multilayered time line covers the years from 1400 to 1676 and contains links to eight in-depth articles on specific subjects listed in the time line, such as "Tycho Brahe, a Man Defined by the Cosmos" and "The Gutenberg Bible, or Greed and Lawsuit." It also includes images and publication facts for many of the great events and books of the period. It contains such entries as the one for 1498—"the first tooth-brush is used by a Chinese man" and one for 1560—"a solar eclipse is recorded in Europe," as well as other more expected entries, such as "Galileo assembles his first astronomical telescope," which is found under the year 1608.

This is an excellent site for inspiration, if you just want to browse on the subject of the scientific revolution, or if you want to see events in chronological relation to one another. The articles are excellent resources, as well, and do not need to be read only in the context of the time line.

The Galileo Project
http://es.rice.edu/ES/humsoc/Galileo
middle school and up

This is an award-wining hypertext site on the life and work of Italian astronomer Galileo Galilei. While much of the site pertains specifically to Galileo, there are also some excellent resources here on the early scientific revolution. Under "Additional Resources" on the home page, go to "Table of Contents for Topics," which is a list of links to people, places, and things that were important during Galileo's time. You'll find links to the Medici family, Johannes Kepler, and Pope Urban VIII under "People." Under "Things," you'll find "Collegio Romano," "The Hydro-static Balance," "Sunspots," and "Tides," for example.

If you want to read about Galileo, there's a wealth of information here—both text and pictures—on his family and his career. A section called the "Observing Gallery" contains accounts of his discovery of Jupiter's moons, as well as information on contemporary astronomers.

You can even read detailed descriptions of the instruments Galileo used in his experiments and observations.

SCYTHIANS

Best Search Engine: http://www.google.com/

Key Search Terms: Scythians + history

Eurasia + ancient history

The Scythians
http://www.silk-road.com/artl/scythian.shtml
middle school and up

Here's an excellent introduction to the Scythians, the ancient people famous for their early use of horses, whose kingdom reached its height in the fourth century B.C. Sections in this article include "Land of Myth and Gold," "History," "Language," "Taming the Horse," "Life Style in the Steppes," "Religion," "Rites of Death," and "Animal Art Style." A couple of colorful maps will help you place the Scythians, and there are several nice illustrations and a quote from the historian Herodotus to round out the page.

SEVEN YEARS WAR

Best Search Engine: http://www.google.com/

Key Search Terms: Seven Years War + history

Treaty of Paris + history

Seven Years War
http://www.infoplease.kids.lycos.com/ce6/history/A0844575.html
middle school

This Infoplease site on the Seven Years War is a great place to get your basic historical overview of the conflict. Concise and simple, this article is divided into the following sections, which are accessible by links on the home page—"Introduction," "Nature of the War," "The War Begins," "Conduct of the War," and "Peace." There's also a bibliography at the end.

Links embedded within each section help you explore key events and people in greater depth. These include "The War of the Austrian Succession," "Peter III of Russia," and the "Treaty of Paris," for example.

The Seven Years War Website
http://www.militaryheritage.com/7yrswar.htm
middle school and up

This Web site, home of "The Discriminating General," contains articles, uniform and service charts for regiments, and replicas covering this period of conflict, all written and organized by aficionados of military history. There are also sound clips and video clips for those who enjoy multimedia resources and a list of reenactment Web sites and events around the country.

Click on "Article" for example, and you'll find numerous articles under each of the following categories—"Army Life," "Battles," "British Regiments," "French Regiments," and "Uniforms and Equipment." Go to "Internet Links" for a list of about 15 links to articles on very specific Seven Years War topics, such as "The Battle of Quiberon Bay: An English View" and "Captain Knox's Account of the Fall of Quebec."

Use this site for more esoteric information once you've studied the basic history. And if you're interested in the military details of the war, this is a great place to look.

SHINTO

Best Search Engine:	http://www.google.com/
Key Search Terms:	Shinto + history
	Japan + religion + history

Shinto Religion
http://www.comedition.com/AAAA/Religion/ShintoReligion.htm
middle school and up

This comprehensive Shinto site is part of a larger site called *Religion at All American Family,* which is an excellent resource if you're looking into any religion and want to read a diversity of carefully selected resources. At the Shinto page alone, there's a wealth of useful information. Annotated links on the home page will take you to a variety of sites. Follow the link for "Shinto Documents," where you can read excerpts from key texts of the Shinto religion, including the creation story and the generation of key gods. There's a link to the "International Shinto Foundation" and to "The Way of the Gods," which is a photographic journal of Shinto shrines and festivals with a basic overview of the religion.

The best place to start your exploration of Shinto is by clicking on "Shinto: The Way of the Gods," which will take you to a nicely illustrated essay from the online magazine *Trincoll*. Or scroll down just a little on the home page and follow the link to "History, Beliefs, and Practices." This *Religious Tolerance* site goes into more detail about the various forms and practices of Shinto and gives more attention to current practice than to history, although you will find a brief historical overview at the top of this page.

Ancient Japan
http://www.wsu.edu/~dee/ANCJAPAN/CONTENTS.HTM
high school and up

For a more academic and in-depth history of Shinto, this is the best site. On the home page, click on "Shinto" under "Ancient Japan," which will take you to a concise but very informative essay on the history of Shinto. You'll also find links to Shinto "Creation Stories" and to the "Japan Glossary." Back at the home page, you can choose to read other *Ancient Japan* topics, such as the essays on the Nara and Heian periods, or go on to one of the numerous topics under "Early Japanese Buddhism" and "Early Japanese Culture."

Scroll down to "Additional Resources" and you can choose to view the "Gallery of Ancient Japan," the "Ancient Japan Timeline," the "Japan Atlas," or "Internet Resources on Japan."

SINO-JAPANESE WAR

Best Search Engine: http://www.google.com/
Key Search Terms: Sino-Japanese War + history
                        China + Japan + history
                        Manchurian Incident + history
                        Rape of Nanking + history
                        Comfort women + Sino-Japanese War

Sino-Japanese War
http://www.encyclopedia.com/articlesnew/11925.html
middle school and up

For the most evenhanded account of this highly controversial war, it's best to stick with a basic encyclopedia article to get your introduction. From there you can move on to read accounts of the war by Chinese or Japanese sources and to get an understanding of why this war remains such a painful topic.

The *Encyclopedia.com* article begins with a section called "Origins," which is followed by "Outbreak of War" and "World War II." Although this is a brief overview, you will find links to other relevant topics, such as the "Manchurian Incident." Once you're familiar with the basic outline of the war, move on to the sites described below to understand some of the issues concerning this war that remain contentious.

Alliance for Preserving the Truth of Sino-Japanese War
http://www.sjwar.org/
middle school and up

While this is not an objective view of the war, the sentiments represented here are central to an understanding of the Sino-Japanese War and the conflicts that have lingered since the close of World War II.

The table of contents contains sections on "Key Facts of Japan's War Crime," "Japan Is in Denial" and "Is History Repeating Itself?" In addition you'll find the following articles: "Biochemical Warfare—Unit 731," "Sex Slave—Comfort Woman," and "Rape of Nanking." There's also a "News and Reference" section with press releases and news stories about these topics.

SLAVERY AND SLAVE TRADE

Best Search Engine: http://www.google.com/
Key Search Terms: Slavery + history

Slave trade + history

Africa + slave trade

Slave kingdoms + history

British History 1700–1930: The Slave Trade
http://www.spartacus.schoolnet.co.uk/slavery.htm
middle school and up

This comprehensive site contains a wealth of compelling information on the slave trade including 30 "Slave Accounts," a section on "The Slave System," with links to such topics as "African Slave Trade," "Cotton Plantations," "Slave Markets," "Slave Breeding," and "Runaways;" and a section called "Slave Life," with links such as "House Slaves," "Marriage," "Whipping," and "Slave Music." There are also sections on "Events and Issues," "Women's Anti-Slavery Society," "Anti-Slavery Group," "Legislation," and "USA Campaigners against Slavery," which boasts nearly 50 links to people such as Elizabeth Cady Stanton and Walt Whitman.

The organizers of this site have done a wonderful job of combining secondary and primary sources. Go to the section on the "African Slave

Trade" under "The Slave System" and you'll first read a historical over-view of Europeans trading slaves from Africa, beginning in the four-teenth century. This account is followed by excerpts from two different slave narratives, a Scottish explorer's account of his travels in Africa, and another European man's book about the African slave trade.

The Slave Kingdoms
http://www.pbs.org/wonders/Episodes/Epi3/slave.htm
middle school and up

Not long after charting Africa's shores, Europeans began to trade with West African tribes—the Europeans traded guns and gold for human slaves. This Web site, which is part of the larger PBS site that is a companion to the television show, *The Wonders of the African World*, is one of the few top-notch sites that gives the history of the slave trade from the perspective of African history. *The Slave Kingdoms* focuses on the western African kingdoms that flourished because of their role in the slave trade.

The site combines essays, interviews, photographs, maps, and video clips to tell its story. For an excellent overview about the slave trade, select "Continue" at the end of the paragraph under "Confronting the Legacy of African Slave Trade." Return to the home page when you're ready for the site's in-depth features: "Wonders," "Retelling," "Gates' Diary," and "Cultural Close-Up." Select the topics that interest you from the menu at the bottom of the home page.

"Wonders" contains a history of two West African tribes that grew rich and powerful from the slave trade—the Ashanti and the Dahomey. "Retelling" has a wealth of fascinating material. You can watch an in-terview of a current Ashanti leader explaining the Ashanti role in the slave trade, as well as an interview of Martine de Souza, a descendant of one of the most infamous slave traders. There's also a written firsthand account of growing up in Ghana with the legacy of the slave trade, and the perspectives of African Americans who visit Africa and must con-front the history of the slave trade. "Gates' Diary" is less helpful. It contains the written reflections of the show's narrator, Henry Louis Gates, on how the slave trade has affected African Americans. "Cultural Close-Up" has a short profile on the Gbeto warriors of western Africa.

SOCIALISM

Best Search Engine:	http://www.google.com/
Key Search Terms:	Socialism + history
	Marxism + history

Labor movement + history

Karl Marx + socialism

Democratic Socialists + history

Socialism
http://hsb.baylor.edu/html/gardner/CESCH04.HTM
middle school and up

For an index of socialism sites on the Web that's been critically reviewed, try this one from an economics professor at Baylor University.
If the list were annotated, the index would be even more useful, nevertheless it's a good gateway if you want to browse among the best socialism sites on the Web.

Modern History Sourcebook: Crib Sheet: Socialism, Marxism, Trade Unionism
http://www.fordham.edu/halsall/mod/SOCIALISM.html
middle school and up

Paul Halsall of the *Internet Modern History Sourcebook* has put together
crib sheets, brief bulleted summaries, of a number of topics in his sourcebooks, and this one is particularly helpful. In addition to its chronological outline of socialism's evolution, it contains a nice diagram on the
origins of Marxism. Take a look at this upfront if you're just beginning
to study socialism, and decide where you want to go from here. Do you
want to read more about the origins of socialism in the French Revolution? Or the philosophies of Marx, Engels, and others? Or Labour
Parties in England? The possibilities are too numerous to list, but once
you've checked out this crib sheet, you'll have a roadmap for further
exploration.

The Labour Movement
http://www.spartacus.schoolnet.co.uk/socialism.htm
middle school and up

This encyclopedic site from Britain's *Spartacus Encyclopaedia* won't
give you a historical overview in one brief article, but it will provide
you with links to excellent resources on many of the people, organizations, movements, and events at the core of socialism's history. Scroll
down the home page and you'll see sections on "Pre-Socialist Radicals,"
"Socialist Writers and Philosophers," "Political Organisations," "Labour
Journals and Newspapers," the "Christian Socialist Movement," "Fabian
Society," "Social Democratic Federation," "Independent Labour Party,"
"The Labour Party 1906–1950," and "The Zinoviev Letter."

The biographies of key socialists at this site are quite in-depth and contain links to related topics also found in the encyclopedia, so your explorations might proceed from Mary Wolstonecraft's biography to the hyperlink on the "Unitarian Society" to "factory reform."

Socialist Party U.S.A.
http://sp-usa.org/history/

The Socialist Party's Web site provides an excellent history of the party, which contains sections on "The Early Years" (1901–45), on "The Post War Years" (1945–68), on "Dissent and Division" (1968–73), and "Building Anew: The Socialist Party Today." Links within the article will take you to the Web sites of other key organizations, such as the Industrial Workers of the World and the Communist Party.

Now the history of the party is not identical to the history of the movement, but there is much overlap, and you will necessarily follow the history of the movement as you read about the party.

SONGHAY (GHANA, MALI)

Best Search Engine: http://www.google.com/
Key Search Terms: Ancient Africa + history
Songhay + history
Ancient Ghana + history
Kingdom + Mali + history

Ancient Africa
http://www.penncharter.com/Student/africa/index.html
middle school and up

Here you'll find an in-depth look at the three major civilizations of ancient Africa—Ghana, Mali, and Songhay. Sections on culture, daily life, geography, government, industry, social levels, and more will let you learn about each civilization in relation to the others.

Click on "Government" to read about the first leader of the Songhay empire or go to "Daily Life" if you're interested in their religion, the types of houses they built, or the stories they told.

West African Kingdoms
http://www.bbc.co.uk/worldservice/africa/features/storyofafrica/
    index_section4.shtml
middle school and up

Part of the BBC's *Story of Africa* site, this section on West African kingdoms contains pages on ancient Ghana, Kanem, Mali, Songhay, and the Hausa States, among other subjects. You'll love the multimedia presentations and the colorful illustrations.

Using the menu at the right, just pick the kingdom you want to explore, and click. You'll arrive at a separate page for each kingdom that explores, in a general overview, its complete history. Additional resources are woven into most pages. You'll find, for example, that within the ancient Ghana page is a link to an audio recording of someone reading a quote from Al-Bakri, a tenth-century geographer, that describes the opulence surrounding the king of Ghana.

Civilizations in Africa: Songhay
http://www.wsu.edu:8080/~dee/CIVAFRCA/SONGHAY.HTM
middle school and up

This site provides a brief history of what is often called the greatest empire in African history, the Songhay, covering the period from the early fourteenth century to the early seventeenth century. Look here to get your chronological and geographic bearings if you're just starting out on an exploration of the Songhay.

SOVIET UNION—GENERAL

Best Search Engine: http://www.google.com/

Key Search Terms: Soviet Union + history

Soviet Leaders
http://www.artnet.net/~upstart/soviet.html
middle school and up

Winner of a Britannica Internet Guide Award, this site chronicles eight leaders of the Soviet Union with detailed time lines of each one's life. And I mean detailed. You won't find much missing from these chronologies that include personal as well as political events of significance.

In addition to each of these chronologies, the site has a minute-by-minute chronology of the 1991 coup that resulted in the dissolution of the Soviet Union, a page on the Soviet-U.S. summit in Geneva, which took place in November of 1985, a page defining "perestroika," and a page of 73 slogans from the Great October Socialist Revolution.

SOVIET UNION—STALINIST

Best Search Engine: http://www.google.com/

Key Search Terms: Stalin + Soviet Union history

Stalinist Russia + history

Stalinization + Soviet Union

Revolution of 1917 + Soviet Union + Stalin

Stalin's Russia
http://mars.acnet.wnec.edu/~grempel/courses/stalin/
high school and up

Subtitled "A Study in Totalitarianism and Autocracy," this site offers the lectures of history professor Gerhard Rempel. Twenty lectures in all cover such topics as the "Revolution of 1917," "The Purge," "War Communism," "Stalin vs. Trotsky," "Comintern Founded," "Stalin as Warlord," "The Cold War," "Terrible Ivan," "De-Stalinization," and more. Each of these topics receives a thorough treatment, so be prepared for a little reading when you visit this site. The time invested is well worth it, though, if you want an in-depth understanding of Stalin's Russia.

In addition to the lectures, the page has a quiz and copies of exams for testing your knowledge, a page of links, a map, a list of films on the subject, and a personal page called "My Gulag," which discusses Dr. Rempel's father's experience with the gulag. There's a link at the bottom of this page for a cybertour on the gulag, which is highly recommended. "A Journey into the Heart of Our Own Gulag" weaves together the private and public histories of the gulag, using the letters and personal histories of Dr. Rempel and his family.

SOVIET UNION—POST–WORLD WAR II
EXPANSION

Best Search Engine: http://www.google.com/

Key Search Terms: Soviet Union + post World War II + history

Soviet Bloc + expansion + history

The Soviet Period, 1917–1991
http://www.departments.bucknell.edu/russian/chrono3.html
middle school and up

This is a chronology of the entire Soviet period, but it's no ordinary chronology. You'll find that nearly every entry has at least one, if not more, links to other sources that provide all kinds of historical information on the events and key players of the Soviet Union.

The chronology is divided into sections—the 1917 Revolutions, Lenin, Stalin, Kruschev, Brezhnev, Andropov, Chernenko, and Gorbachev. Go to the section that interests you, or start at the top and read through the entire chronology. If you want to research post–World War II expansion in the Soviet Union, scroll down to the late 1940s and begin reading from there. You'll want to follow the links on Kruschev, Gagarin, the Berlin Wall, the Cuban missile crisis, and Brezhnev, for example. Some of the topics actually have several links.

SOVIET UNION—DISSOLUTION OF

Best Search Engine: http://www.google.com/

Key Search Terms: Soviet Union + 1991 coup + history

Soviet Union + dissolution + history

Perestroika + Soviet Union + history

1991 Coup
http://www.artnet.net/~upstart/1819aug.html
middle school and up

Want to see just how the Soviet Union fell apart? This impressive site offers a minute-by-minute chronology of the four days, August 18 to August 22, 1991, that forever changed the shape of the Soviet Union.

The time line is literally minute by minute, so give yourself plenty of time when you visit this site. There's a lot to take in.

Beyond the Fall: The Former Soviet Bloc in Transition, 1989–1999
http://www.time.com/time/btf/home.html
middle school and up

If you'd like a visual experience of the Soviet Bloc's dissolution, try this photographic essay. For 10 years following the collapse of the Berlin Wall, *Time* contract photographer Anthony Suau traveled the lands of the former Soviet bloc. In hundreds of powerful images and audio commentaries, he documents the region's people as they leave behind their old lives and look toward an uncertain future.

Read the "Introduction" for an essay that gives some background history on the Cold War and its eventual demise, while also weaving in the personal perspective of its creator. Then just follow the arrows at the bottom of each page for a tour of the exhibit.

SPAIN—GENERAL

Best Search Engine: http://www.google.com/

Key Search Terms: Spain + history

                            Spanish Empire + history

History of Spain
http://www.sispain.org/english/history/index.html
middle school and up

This exhaustive history of Spain begins with the first human settlements and moves through sections on the Romans, Visigoths, Muslims, and Catholic monarchs, the discovery of America, the Spanish Empire, the Bourbons and the Enlightenment, the Peninsular War and the Constitution of 1812, the nineteenth century, the loss of the colonies, the First World War, the Second Republic, the Spanish Civil War, the Francoist dictatorship, the democratic transition, and parliamentary monarchy. This is an excellent gateway site to the history of Spain—easy to navigate and authoritative.

SPAIN—MOORISH

Best Search Engine: http://www.google.com/

Key Search Terms: Spain + Moors + history

                            Muslims + Spain + history

Mr. Dowling's Electronic Passport: The Middle Ages: The Moors
http://www.mrdowling.com/703-moors.html
middle school and up

Part of a larger world history site, this brief essay gives you in a few short paragraphs the entire history of the Moors in Spain. Don't miss it. It's a superb overview, complete with excellent hotlinks for delving deeper into various aspects of the topic. The site is superbly organized with links to other Middle Ages topics at the top of the page, and links to world history topics other than the Middle Ages located in a bar at the left.

Muslim Spain and European Culture
http://www.xmission.com:8000/%7Edderhak/index/moors.htm
middle school and up

If you're focused on the culture and arts of the Moors in Spain, check out this site. The narrative is really the story of the rise of the Moors, and the accompanying images are beautiful.

SPANISH ARMADA

Best Search Engine: http://www.google.com/
Key Search Terms: Spanish Armada + history
                       Spanish empire + armada + history
                       King Philip + Spanish Armada
                       Queen Elizabeth + Spanish Armada

The Spanish Armada
http://www.newadvent.org/cathen/01727c.htm
high school and up

This entry from *The Catholic Encyclopedia* provides a good general overview of the events leading up to the defeat of the Spanish Armada by Queen Elizabeth's forces in 1588, as well as the consequences of that defeat. Links within the text take you to entries on key personalities and subjects, like the King of Spain, Philip II, and Protestantism.

A section on Catholic cooperation rounds out the entry.

The Spanish Armada
http://tbls.hypermart.net/history/1588armada/
middle school and up

Heads up, you ship aficionados and anyone interested in the military and naval aspects of this topic. While this site contains good general information, what makes it stand apart from other sites are the search-able database of ships and the sections on "King Philip's Invasion Plan," the "Spanish and English Fleets," and "Ways of Fighting at Sea in the 1580s." Records of the more than 300 ships involved in the armada campaign can be searched by keyword or by record number in the data-base. Detailed descriptions of these ships include what they carried, how they were equipped for battle, their origins, their purpose during battle, and their fates, if known.

SPANISH CIVIL WAR

Best Search Engine: http://www.northernlight.com/
Key Search Terms: Spanish Civil War + history
                      Anarchy + Spain + history
                      Fascism + Spain + history
                      Francisco Franco + Spain
                      International Brigades + Spain + civil war

About the Spanish Civil War
http://www.english.uiuc.edu/maps/scw/scw.htm
middle school and up

This comprehensive site from the University of Illinois's English Department has done a terrific job of bringing together a wide array of materials about the Spanish Civil War. It contains material that provides historical background on the war, as well as a detailed chronology of the key events of the Spanish Civil War (including plenty of information about the International Brigades). It also has an excellent photo collection and samples of the propaganda posters used by both sides of the conflict. To top it off, the site has primary documents related to the war in addition to several scholarly essays that provide a more nuanced view of the topic.

To access this site's offerings, use the menu on the home page. If you want more basic historical information about the Spanish Civil War, you'll first want to visit the "The Spanish Civil War" and "Chronology of the Spanish Civil War" sections. "The Spanish Civil War" covers the context in which this bloody conflict took place, contains an overview of the major events, and descriptions of the key players, a review of the role of the International Brigades, and a bibliography. The "Chronology" consists of a fairly detailed time line accompanied by maps and photographs. While the "Chronology" does go a little heavy with details about the Abraham Lincoln Brigade, you'll find it more than adequate for learning the important events of the Spanish Civil War.

Once you're ready for some primary material, check out the "Spanish Civil War Photo Essays" and the "Spanish Civil War Posters." These visual collections will add a whole new facet to your understanding of this subject. If you want primary texts, the site includes "Spanish Civil War Letters," "Barcelona in 1936" (an excerpt from George Orwell's *Homage to Catalonia*, which is based on his experiences fighting in the war), and Ernest Hemingway's "On the American Dead in Spain."

This site also provides material that takes a scholarly look at specific topics. "The Aura of the Cause" examines the role of photography in the Spanish Civil War. "Old Soldiers" (an article originally printed in *Harper's*) uses a reunion of International Brigades as the starting point for discussing the Spanish Civil War's impact. "An Anarchist Perspective on the Spanish Civil War" (an excerpt from Eddie Conlon's *The Spanish Civil War: Anarchism in Action*) analyzes the anarchist viewpoint in the war, as well as the role the ideology played in shaping the conflict. There are also two essays about key players: "About Durutti" (on Buenaventura Durruti) and "About Francisco Ferrer."

Spanish Civil War Index
http://www.users.dircon.co.uk/~warden/scw/scwindex.htm
middle school and up

Researching a topic as broad as the Spanish Civil War can sometimes be a fairly vexing task. With so many factions, alliances, and key players involved, it can be tough to keep the details straight! This Web site puts the important events of the Spanish Civil War at your fingertips. Don't expect the breadth of resources that you found at the *About the Spanish Civil War* site. There are no primary documents or multimedia collections here, but you will find a thorough review of the Spanish Civil War.

Although it's not a glamorous site, the *Spanish Civil War Index* provides a quick overview of the different factions in the war—from the Carlists and the Catholic Church to the Anarcho-Syndicalists and the Socialists. Simply select "The Politics of the Spanish Civil War" from the short menu on the home page to read this synopsis. The site also contains one of the best time lines on the Spanish Civil War that you'll find on the Internet. Select "The Main Events of the Spanish Civil War" from the main menu and you can access a detailed chronology (along with brief descriptions) of the important events. It's especially strong in describing battles and their impact on the ultimate outcome of the war. Check out the "Introduction" from the main menu for an ultra-quick review of the topic.

SPANISH EMPIRE

Best Search Engine: http://www.google.com/
Key Search Terms: Spanish Empire + history

Spanish Empire + explorations + history

The Rise and Fall of the Spanish Empire
http://www.sispain.org/english/history/rise.html
middle school and up

To get your dates straight, just check this time line of the Spanish Empire. It's brief but it covers the highlights, starting with the unification of Spain under Charles I and ending in 1714 when Philip V of France became king of Spain. It's part of a larger history. (See **Spain— General History** for complete review.)

The European Voyages of Exploration: The Fifteenth and Sixteenth Centuries
http://hist.ucalgary.ca/tutor/index.html
middle school and up

This excellent Web site from the University of Calgary will introduce you to the topic of the Spanish empire's earliest exploration of Africa. The site focuses on the two countries that led the way in European expansion—Spain and Portugal—and discusses not only Africa, but Brazil, the Caribbean, the Americas, and Asia as well. It allows you to place the voyages in their historical context and to learn *why* Spain and Portugal were drawn to these explorations, what they hoped to accomplish, and what the consequences of their actions were.

Since the site is structured as an online tutorial, you can either choose the topics from the menu on the home page that interest you or follow the entire narrative by clicking on "Proceed with the Tutorial" at the bottom of each screen. The "Introduction" provides good background material on the Spanish Empire's motivations in exploring the rest of the world. And the history sections have much substantive information. Also don't overlook the sections about "Iberian Pioneers," "Spain," and "Knowledge and Power." These sections explain the history of Spain (which again will help you make sense of what prompted Spain to explore), as well as the political, economic, and social conditions in Spain at the time they launched voyages.

Once you've gotten a sense of the factors that propelled Spain to take to the high seas, you can select from any one of the places the Empire explored to learn more about its actions in those countries.

SUMER

Best Search Engine:	http://www.altavista.com/
Key Search Terms:	Sumer + history
	Mesopotamia + Sumer
	Sumerians + history

Mr. Dowling's Electronic Passport: Mesopotamia: The Sumerians
http://www.mrdowling.com/603-sumerians.html
middle school and up

Mr. Dowling's historical overview of the Sumerians is perfect for those of you encountering this ancient civilization for the first time. The page provides only the basics, but it's part of a larger section on Mesopotamia, where you can also read about "The Fertile Crescent," "Numbering Years," "Writing," "The Hammurabi," "The Assyrians," and other topics. As with all of Mr. Dowling's pages, this one provides an interactive quiz, where you can test yourself to see what you've learned while visiting the site.

THIRTY YEARS WAR

Best Search Engine: http://www.google.com/
Key Search Terms: Thirty Years War + history
                        Europe + Thirty Years War

The Thirty Years War
http://www.historylearningsite.co.uk/thirty_years_war.htm
high school and up

This comprehensive site on the Thirty Years War, which is really a series of wars in Europe between 1618 and 1648, is geared toward students taking the United Kingdom's A-Level examinations. There are three major sections of the site: "The Causes of the War," "The Course of the War," and "The Impact of the War." Under each you'll find links to numerous topics. Each link takes you to an article of medium length with quite a few embedded links to relevant topics.

The coverage here is quite systematic, and the organization of the site is easy to follow. Although the site doesn't offer much in the way of primary sources, the articles provide an excellent historical overview of the Thirty Years War.

Thirty Years War
http://www.pipeline.com/~cwa/TYWHome.htm
middle school and up

This site provides summaries, in varying detail, of the military and diplomatic developments of the Thirty Years War. The summaries are more basic than the site listed above and thus appropriate for someone just beginning to read about this period in European history.

Start by reading the text on the home page for an introduction and brief overview of each stage of the war. If you want to continue after that, look to the menu at the left, scroll down to "Links to Detailed Narrative," and choose the topic that interests you. Choices include "The Bohemian Rebellion (1618–19)," "The Danish War (1624–27)," and "The French and Swedes Alone (1635–38)," to name just a few.

In addition to the text offered on this site, there are several links to maps on the site, additional Web resources listed, and a bibliography. There's also a search mechanism if you want to look up a topic.

TRADE AND TRADE ROUTES

Best Search Engine: http://www.google.com/
Key Search Terms: Trade + history

Trade routes + history

Silk Road + history

Spice trade + history

Ancient Routes
http://www.ancientroute.com/
middle school and up

Devoted to exploring the ancient trade routes around the Mediterranean, this site covers the fall of the Roman Empire, the beginnings of Christianity, and up to but not including the rise of Islam. Although the creators of the site have not yet finished with all the routes, the following are presently available: "The Amber Road," "King's Highway," "Silk Road," Royal Road," and the "Lower Road." What each of these routes covers is explained at the link.

To journey best, we recommend that you choose one of these preplotted routes and learn by exploring the subjects that interest you along the way. There are many subjects linked to each route, and each link is within the site. But, if you prefer, there's also an index of subjects available that you might want to check. We chose to explore the "King's Highway," a long trip across the Sinai Desert, through Jordan into Syria, Damascus, Palmyra, and ending at the Euphrates. Maps and illustrations abound, so don't worry about getting lost, but you may find there's more territory to cover than you were expecting. These are lengthy journeys, and the site creators have taken care not to miss any important topics along the way.

Silk Road Foundation
http://www.silk-road.com/toc/index.html
middle school and up

This stellar multimedia site will make you wish you could journey back in time to travel the Silk Road yourself. The table of contents listed at the left-hand side of the home page includes the following sections: "Studies," "Articles," "Lectures," "Culture," "Travel," "Bibliography," "Maps," and "Timeline." Click on "Studies" to read in-depth articles on two of the major stops along this trade route—Xinjiang and Dunhuang.

Under "Articles," you'll find a chronology of Silk Road history, as well as abstracts of articles about the Silk Road from journals such as *Antiquity* and *The Journal of Indo-European Studies,* as well as many others

One of the most interesting articles at this site is found in the section called "Travel." Click on this section, then scroll down to the bottom, and click on "Ancient Travelers," which will bring up an extensive article about dozens of the most famous people to travel the Silk Road. A brief biography about each ancient traveler acquaints you with the details of his or her travels, as well as basic biographical information, such as birth and death dates.

For fun, don't miss the "Culture" section, where you can hear music from the Silk Road or read a Tajik folk tale, for example.

Timeline—A Brief History of the Fur Trade
http://www.whiteoak.org/learning/timeline.htm
middle school and up

Here's an attractive, annotated time line of the fur trade in North America, beginning with the French Era, 1600–1760, and covering the British Era, 1760–1816, and the American Era, 1816–50. What you'll find here is a brief description of the most significant events in the 250 years during which the fur trade flourished.

If you want to do more than just read about the fur trade, backtrack to the home page (link at the bottom of opening page) for the White Oak Learning Center and Trading Post, where the year is 1798, and the fur trade is booming. This living history site, located in the North Woods of Minnesota, offers some fun interactive resources for students studying this period of American history.

A Comparative Chronology of Money from Ancient Times to the Present Day
http://www.ex.ac.uk/%7ERDavies/arian/amser/chrono1.html
middle school and up

This site begins with the dates 9000–6000 B.C. and describes domestic cattle as the earliest form of money in many societies. The final entry, after 20 pages of chronology, is for 2002—"New *Euro* coins and notes to be introduced by the European Union."

Eclectic in nature, this chronology is fascinating to read because it incorporates so many places and events. The development of coins, the growth of the banking industry, and the origins of the words "money" and "mint" are all accounted for here.

The site also includes essays on money, including one titled "History of Money," a page called "Money—Past, Present, and Future," and a search function, in case there's a specific topic you want to look up here.

UNITED NATIONS

Best Search Engine: http://www.google.com/
Key Search Terms: United Nations + history
                        UN + history
                        World War II + United Nations

About the United Nations/History
http://www.un.org/aboutun/history.htm
middle school and up

For a very brief summary of the origins of the United Nations, read this page at the United Nations official Web site. This account begins with the establishment of the first international organizations to cooperate on specific matters, which is to say that it begins with the founding of the International Telegraph Union in 1865 and the Universal Postal Union in 1874. The history ends with the establishment of the United Nations on October 24, 1945.

Once you've read this little history, you might want to hunt around the rest of the UN Web site. Use the link at the bottom of the history to return to the home page for the mother site. In the menu at the left, you'll see a link for "About the United Nations." Click on that link for the following sections: "Background Information," "Main Documents," "Who's Who," "Member States," and "Staff Services." Under "Background Information," which is where the history page is located, you'll find other sections of interest, such as "Basic Facts about the UN" and "UN in Brief" and "Organization Chart of the UN System," just in case you want to get a visual perspective on how all the departments of the UN are related to one another.

There's much, much more to explore at this site, so if you're looking for more than just history, browse the menu on the home page to get the complete offerings. The site is available in Arabic, Japanese, Spanish, French, and Russian, in addition to English.

The United Nations and Related Sites
http://www.unhistory.org/Links/UN.Links.htm
middle school and up

This page on the United Nations WWW server contains links to all United Nations online resources, as well as a number of related resources. Included here are more than 50 organizations—groups like the UN High Commissioner for Refugees, the UN Children's Fund, and the International Monetary Fund.

URBANIZATION (SEE ALSO INDUSTRIAL REVOLUTION)

Best Search Engine:	http://www.google.com/
Key Search Terms:	Urbanization + history
	Cities + history
	Industrial revolution + cities + history

Lower East Side Tenement Museum
http://www.thirteen.org/tenement/index.html
middle school and up

If you're interested in urban housing and immigration, you'll find much to explore at this multimedia site. An actual tenement building that has been preserved as a National Historic Site, 97 Orchard Street stands as a testament to the urban poor who once inhabited its five floors. You can take a virtual tour of the building in Manhattan's Lower East Side as it was in 1870, when the building was first erected, or in 1915, just 20 years before it was boarded up. Just click on a window of the building, and enter the life of one of the families who inhabited the room. There are 11 dramatizations in all, including Russian, German, Polish, Greek, and American families, among others. There are also two QuickTime movies that will let you explore inside of the tenement apartments. If you don't have QuickTime, not to worry. You can download it from this site.

For in-depth information, click on "History" on the home page to read about the history of housing for the urban poor, including detailed sections on the efforts of reformers. Or, if you're into architecture and archaeology, you'll enjoy the "Restoration" section, where you can click through 13 layers of wallpaper that were peeled off just one room at 97 Orchard Street.

The Urbanization of America
http://www.ecb.org/tracks/mod9.htm
middle school and up

This lesson on urbanization is one of lessons at *Tracks*, a Web site that offers multimedia learning resources to help students explore American history and geography. The lesson is really a collection of links to topics like "Ellis Island," "Angel Island," "Teenage Immigrants," "The Pullman Strike of 1894," "The Life of Henry Ford," and much more. In addition to the links that address the effects of immigration, industrialization, and urbanization, you'll find a "Teacher's Resources" section and an excellent links page with links to some of the best general U.S. history sites.

VEDAS, THE

Best Search Engine:	http://www.google.com/
Key Search Terms:	Vedas + history
	Vedic age + history
	Vedas + ancient India

Washington State University: World Cultures: Ancient India: The Vedas
http://www.wsu.edu/~dee/ANCINDIA/ANCINDIA.HTM
high school and up

For a clear, concise introduction to the history of the Vedas, the ancient India module at Washington State University's online world cultures course can't be beat. The URL above will take you directly to the contents page for the ancient India module. You'll want to scroll down to the section on "Ancient Indian Religion" and click on "The Vedas" to begin your exploration. If you've got plenty of time, however, start with the "Pre-Vedic Age" to understand the context in which the Vedas developed. After reading "The Vedas," you'll want to click on "Next" at the bottom of this section to read about "The Vedic Age" and then "The Vedantic Age." These sections will give you an excellent overview of the Vedas and their influence on ancient India's history.

Back at the *Ancient India* home page, you'll see a section called "Resources" at the bottom of the page. Use this to access an ancient atlas, a glossary of ancient India terms and concepts, a gallery of ancient India images, and a list of other helpful resources.

Veda and Dharma
http://www.spiritweb.org/Spirit/veda.html
middle school and up

Here you can dive right into the practice of Vedic religion. You won't find the type of historical summary that the Washington State site offers, but you will learn the significance of the Vedas and how they're used in everyday life.

This extensive page on the Vedas is part of the massive *SpiritWeb* site, where you'll find links to all things spiritual. You'll also find introductions to other ancient Indian spiritual texts and to some of the traditional teachings of Hinduism.

VIETNAM WAR

Best Search Engine: http://www.google.com/
Key Search Terms: Vietnam War + history
                        Gulf of Tonkin + Vietnam
                        Protest + history + Vietnam

The Vietnam Conflict
http://www.deanza.fhda.edu/faculty/swensson/ewrt2vn.html
middle school and up

For an extensive and eclectic Vietnam gateway site, try this "academic information portal for education and research" from Professor John K. Swenson at De Anza College. The contents listed on the home page include approximately 40 different topics. You'll find the "Domino Theory," "School Web Sites," "Maps," "Native Americans," "Special Forces," "Poems," "Widows, Widowers, and Children," a "Glossary," and much more.

Click on "Coming Home" for example, and you'll get a list of links to a variety of resources addressing the subject of soldiers returning to America. Click on "Agent Orange" for fact sheets, research results, and personal experiences related to the chemical and its use in the war.

The Wars for Viet Nam: 1945–1975
http://vietnam.vassar.edu/
middle school and up

This is your best stop for an academically oriented historical overview. This site from Vassar College provides excellent resources original to the site, as well as links to historical documents and other Vietnam-related Web sites. Three sections are listed upfront on the home page that correspond to these offerings—"Overview," "The Documents," and "Other Viet Nam Links."

Read the overview to get your history straight. The article addresses, among other topics, the Geneva Peace Accords, the National Liberation Front, the Gulf of Tonkin Resolution, the War in America, and the Nixon years. Links within the article take you to other sites, where specific subjects are dealt with in more depth, and illustrations vividly bring the text to life.

Under "Documents," many complete texts related to the war can be found. If you're looking to incorporate some primary sources into your research, this is a good place to check.

The "Links" page is both comprehensive and well organized, so that you can easily locate exactly the type of site you need.

Images of My War
http://www.ionet.net/~uheller/vnbktoc.shtml
middle school and up

Would you rather read a personal history of the war? Here is one veteran's detailed autobiography. Although the site begins with sections on his life before the war, the majority of the site traces Ron Heller's experiences during the war. A U.S. Army Ranger who served between 1968 and 1970, Heller does an excellent job of introducing his memoir and of recording his recollections. A photo album and chronology accompany the text.

VIKINGS

Best Search Engine: http://www.google.com/
Key Search Terms: Vikings + history
                                    Sweden + Vikings
                                    Medieval history + Vikings

The Viking Home Page
http://www.control.chalmers.se/vikings/indexframe.html
middle school and up

Here's a good Swedish index site on Vikings. What makes this one particularly nice is that it's selective about the links it includes. You won't find an endless number of links, but the ones you do find will be good. The page is organized by topic and includes the following sections: "General Information"; "Before the Vikings"; "Viking Ships"; "Saga, Eddas, and Runes"; "Warfare"; "Food and Beverage"; and "Vikings of Today," to name just a few.

If you're just looking for a good introduction, try the "Viking Network" (under "General Information") where you can "get to know the

Vikings." You'll find that the text is in Swedish and English, side-by-side, which is great if you just happen to be studying Swedish and want to practice your reading skills.

ORB: The Online Reference Book for Medieval Studies
http://orb.rhodes.edu/
high school and up

This ambitious site serves as an online textbook for medieval studies. The site contains an encyclopedia with essays, bibliographies, images, documents, and links to other sources; a list of essential medieval topics, a textbook library, a collection of resources for the nonspecialist, and a list of external links. There's a good living history site on the Vikings, which can be found by clicking on "Of General Interest" on the home page, and then following the links for living history sites.

WARFARE (SEE ALSO ARMS AND ARMOR)

Best Search Engine:	http://www.google.com/
Key Search Terms:	Warfare + history
	Ancient Greece + warfare
	Twentieth century + warfare + history

Warfare in Hellas
http://cal044202.student.utwente.nl/~marsares/warfare/
high school and up

Researching warfare in ancient Greece? This *Hellas.Net* page examines the history of warfare, starting with the Battle of Meggido in 1460 B.C. and covering such topics as "Prehistoric Warfare," "The First Armies," "The Age of Chariots," "The Appearance of Cavalry," "The Roman Legion," "Siege Warfare," and "Naval Warfare." Each of these topics is covered in significant depth. Just follow the links from the home page to the individual articles.

Following the "History of Warfare" are sections on "The Greek Army," "The Persian Army," "The Macedonian Army," "Mercenaries," "The Persian Wars," "The Struggle for Hegemony," "The Rise of Macedon," and "The Era of the Diadochs." Each of these sections is subdivided into numerous topics, just as in the "History" section.

Hellas.Net is still under construction, although the sections on "Warfare" and "History" are 99 percent complete. Just beware that if you try to access other sections, you may not be able to. Do keep it in mind, however, if you're looking for an ancient Greece resource in the future.

Top-notch information and user-friendly design make this one of the Web's best, if not quite finished, sites.

Images of War
http://www.ibiscom.com/cbpintro.htm
middle school and up

Using photographs to document the progression of warfare during the twentieth century, this feature on the EyeWitness Web site offers an interesting perspective on the evolution of the soldier. Images include "Machine Gun Crew" and "Wounded" from 1918; "Rescue," "Crossing the Rhine," and "Fleeing in Terror" from 1945; as well as photographs from the wars in Korea and Vietnam. Quotes, captions, and analysis accompany the presentation, and all images can be enlarged. This is an excellent vehicle for exploring history, technology, and the arts.

WITCHCRAFT

Best Search Engine:	http://www.google.com/
Key Search Terms:	Witchcraft + history
	Salem witch trials + history

The Witching Hours
http://shanmonster.lilsproutz.com/witch/
middle school and up

An award-winning starting point for research into the European witch trials of the medieval through Enlightenment periods, this site is organized around a number of topics, each of which has its own drop-down menu for searching. There's "Documents on the Witch Craze," "Magic, Spells, and Potions," "The People of the Witchcraze," "Punishment, Torture, and Ordeal," and more.

Click on "The People," for example, and you'll find a list of links to essays within the site on "The Stedinger-Political Witches," "Judaism and Conspiracy Theories," "From the Mouths of Babes: Children and Witchcraft," and other intriguing topics.

The information here is well documented, and a link to an extensive bibliography of sources can be found at the bottom of the home page. There are also lists of other links, a question and answer forum, and a FAQs page.

Witchcraft Hysteria
http://www.nationalgeographic.com/features/97/salem/newintroframe.html
middle school and up

This interactive site on the American witch trials brings the terror of the time right to your fingertips and is sure to engage even the most hardened researcher. Just click, if you dare, on "Experience the Trials" for a first-person perspective on what it was like to be accused as a witch.

If you'd rather take a safer approach, use the drop-down menu in the upper right-hand corner of your screen to choose which section of the site you'd like to explore. There's the "Introduction," "Prologue," and "Epilogue" to read, then you can submit a question at "Ask the Expert," or send a postcard to a friend at "Send a Postcard." If you'd like to participate in a forum on parallels to the Salem witch trials in modern history, click on "Forum."

WOMEN—ACHIEVEMENTS

Best Search Engine:	http://www.google.com/
Key Search Terms:	Women + achievements + history
	Women + science + history
	Women + math + history

National Women's Hall of Fame
http://www.greatwomen.org/
middle school and up

This site celebrates the courage and determination of U.S. women from many different walks of life. It presents fascinating biographies of a number of women, from Bella Abzug to "Babe" Didrikson Zaharias. "The Learning Center" provides teacher resources and educational activities designed to increase students' understanding of women's struggle for equal rights and their contributions to American culture.

Biographies of Women Mathematicians
http://www.agnesscott.edu/lriddle/women/women.htm
middle school and up

Do any of you still think math is for boys? If you do, this treasure trove of women who excelled in the field of mathematics is sure to change your mind. The site, which can be viewed chronologically or alphabetically, includes images and biographies of nearly every female mathematician of the past three centuries. Students may be surprised to discover that, more than 150 years ago, Ada Lovelace, the daughter of Lord Byron, wrote a plan that today is regarded as the first computer program!

Women of NASA
http://quest.arc.nasa.gov/women/intro.html
middle school and up

This excellent presentation is designed to encourage young women to explore careers in math, science, and technology. It provides personal profiles of more than 100 women who work for the National Aeronautics and Space Administration (NASA) as pilots, writers, psychologists, scientists, educators, engineers, technical assistants, secretaries, flight controllers, and more! Students can read about their personal lives, educational and vocational backgrounds, and job requirements and responsibilities. The site also hosts a chat forum that offers weekly online events, ideas for integrating the site into a school curriculum, and a number of other resources.

WOMEN—SUFFRAGE

Best Search Engine: http://www.google.com/
Key Search Terms: Suffrage movement + U.S. + history
                      Seneca Falls Declaration + history
                      Equal Rights Amendment
                      Women's movement + U.S. + history

Living the Legacy: The Women's Rights Movement 1848–1998
http://www.Legacy98.org/
middle school and up

Are you looking for a Web site that takes you through the history of the women's rights movement in America? If so, pay a visit to *Living the Legacy*. Although the site is pretty drab looking, it contains an excellent essay that charts the key developments in the women's rights movement from 1848 to 1998. The essay doesn't spend too much time on any one person or event. Instead its purpose is to give you an overview of the movement as a whole. Also be sure to check out the site's women's rights time line. Think of these two resources as a terrific starting point for your research on this subject.

It's easy to get to these documents. Select "History of the Movement" and "Detailed Timeline" from the home page's main menu. The rest of the site is focused on contemporary women's issues and organizations, so you probably can skip the other sections.

Seneca Falls Declaration
http://civnet.org/resoures/teach/basic/part3/17.htm
middle school and up

The Seneca Falls Convention of 1848 had a profound impact on women's rights movements in both the United States and Great Britain. The convention's participants (who included Lucretia Mott and Elizabeth Cady Stanton) drafted the Seneca Falls Declaration, which called for women's suffrage and a reform of marital and property laws. This Web site lets you read the full text version of the Seneca Falls Declaration. (For an interesting comparison read the Seneca Falls Declaration and the Declaration of Independence together.) Although there's a short introduction to the primary document, you might want to explore a Web site such as *Living the Legacy* to learn the historical context of the Seneca Falls Convention.

All Men and Women Are Created Equal
http://www.angelfire.com/hi2/drme/women1848.html
middle school and up

Since in 1848 it was considered unseemly for a woman to conduct a public meeting, the Women's Rights Convention in Seneca Falls was actually chaired by a man—James Mott, husband of Lucretia Mott, one of the convention's organizers.

You'll learn details like this and more in this interesting article by Constance Rynder, a professor of history at the University of Tampa. She tells in this captivating narrative that upon arriving at Wesleyan Chapel—the convention site—on the morning of Wednesday, July 19, the organizers discovered the door locked. Since no one had a key, Elizabeth Cady Stanton's nephew had to climb in through an open window and unlock the front door.

If you're researching the Women's Rights Convention and want to get an up close, personal look, you'll love Rynder's approach. It's full of the energy that those attending the convention felt about their cause, and it accurately conveys the importance of the convention in the overall history of the women's rights movement.

Votes for Women
Selections from the National American Woman Suffrage Association Collection, 1848–1921
http://lcweb2.loc.gov/ammem/naw/nawshome.html
middle school and up

This outstanding Web site allows you to look at original documents from the women's suffrage campaign. *Votes for Women* is part of the Library of Congress's *American Memory* project. Like other Library of Congress exhibits, this one is a step above most other Internet sites.

Votes for Women contains digitized copies of 167 books, pamphlets, and artifacts that document the women's suffrage movement. The texts were originally housed in the libraries of Susan B. Anthony, Elizabeth Cady Stanton, and other leaders of the suffrage movement. The collection contains a wonderful array of material. You'll find the transcripts of speeches given by Lucretia Mott and Elizabeth Cady Stanton, newspaper clippings about the suffragists, the minutes from the meetings of different organizations, the banner from a suffrage parade, and loads more. To locate documents, you can conduct a keyword search (best for tracking down a specific item), or you can browse the collection by author or subject. You'll see these three choices at the top of the screen.

The Web site also has some interpretive material to help you fully understand the documents. In the middle of the home page you'll see a link for a time line, "One Hundred Years towards Suffrage: An Overview." This detailed time line conveys the important people, events, setbacks, and organizations related to the suffrage movement.

Chronology of the Equal Rights Amendment: 1923–1996
http://now.org/issues/economic/cea/history.html
middle school and up

This Web page, which is part of the National Organization for Women (NOW), chronicles the history of the Equal Rights Amendment (ERA). The ERA was first introduced in Congress in 1923, and has since been introduced in every Congressional session since then. The ERA passed Congress in 1972, but it failed to get 38 states to ratify it.

The history of the ERA is closely connected with the broader history of the women's movement. Use this Web site to learn about both. To navigate the site, simply scroll down the screen. If you want to focus on a specific in ERA history, select it from the table of contents on the home page. You can follow links from within the text to learn more about important people, events, and dates. You'll be able to access thorough biographies of figures such as Alice Paul, Susan B. Anthony, and Patricia Ireland. You can also read the text of the ERA and get an overview of the history of NOW.

WOMEN—WAR

Best Search Engine: http://www.google.com/
Key Search Terms: Women + war + history

Military Women Veterans
http://userpages.aug.com/captbarb/
middle school and up

"Captain Critical" provides an impressive collection of online material on America's women veterans. The site documents, through text and images, the role of women in the military from the American Revolution up to Bosnia and current conflicts.

An eclectic array of information includes sections on "The Military Academies," "Women Who Were Spies," "Women Military Pilots," and other subjects that provide a special angle on women who have served.

What Did You Do in the War, Grandma?
http://www.stg.brown.edu/projects/WWII_Women/tocCS.html
middle school and up

Linda Wood, a librarian at South Kingstown High School in Rhode Island, presents this unique project. Ninth graders interviewed Rhode Island women who lived during World War II. The more than two dozen accounts that resulted are both moving and fascinating. They provide an intimate look at the mood and events of the time. Some remarkable young storytellers reveal some remarkable women. Don't miss a word!

WORLD WAR I

Best Search Engine: http://www.google.com/
Key Search Terms: World War I + history
                       Great War + history

Trenches on the Web
http://www.worldwar1.com/
middle school and up

Trenches on the Web is a comprehensive resource of World War I materials brought together and organized in a user-friendly manner. Click on "Reference Library" to peruse the site map and take in the depth and breadth of this awesome collection of information: time lines, articles, primary sources, virtual reality activities, and much, much more.

Visitors can also get an overview of the site by clicking on "Selected Tours of this Site." Your options include "The Arts and the Great War," "The Soldier's Experience," or "First-Hand Accounts."

Teachers and students of the Great War will find this site full of useful information, and best of all, there's a great search function to help you find it. The site is truly oriented toward helping students navigate its vast number of resources and participate in learning activities with these resources. Check out the "Media Room," where you can listen to music from the era, or join the "Discussion Forum" if you want to share ideas with others.

The Great War
http://www.pbs.org/greatwar/
middle school and up

This Web companion of the PBS series of the same name provides some wonderful resources perfect for augmenting classroom instruction on World War I. The section "Interviews" alone offers a wealth of first-hand accounts of Europe from all sides of the war. The time line is no longer available, but click on "Maps and Locations" and "Start Interactive Gallery" for a fabulous collection of facts and images on the war presented in chronological order.

WORLD WAR II

Best Search Engine: http://www.google.com/

Key Search Terms: World War II + history

Nazis + war

Holocaust + history

Homefront + World War II + history

World War II
http://www.skalman.nu/history/ww2.htm
middle school and up

For the overall history of World War II, this index of sites is comprehensive and well organized. There are three sections: "General," "Allied," and "Axis," with regions or countries listed under each. If you're interested in the war in Europe, look under "General" and click on "Europe." You'll see an Angelfire site called "World War II in Europe," which provides an excellent overview. You'll also find many links to sites dealing with significant European battles and campaigns—the Battle of Britain, the London Blitz, and Normandy, for example.

Unfortunately, the links provided at this site are not annotated, but the titles of links tend to be quite descriptive (perhaps the site creator has embellished the names of sites to make them more explanatory). In any case, you'll find a wealth of information collected and organized here.

World War II Resources
http://www.ibiblio.org/pha/index.html
middle school and up

This site collects primary source documents on the war, and its collection is huge and varied. You'll find diplomatic documents, the Pearl

Harbor attack hearings, numerous chronologies, including one of international events during the war, the speeches of Franklin D. Roosevelt during the war, and much more.

The links are usually to other sites, where the documents are located. This site is part of the World War II Web ring, so you'll find it easy to access the Web ring and many more World War II links.

Decoding Nazi Secrets
http://www.pbs.org/wgbh/nova/decoding/
middle school and up

This NOVA site is a companion to a PBS special that offers an intriguing look into espionage and breaking the code of Nazi messages. Not only can students learn the facts behind World War II ciphering, they can also send their own coded messages using Shockwave technology.

World War II: An American Scrapbook
http://www.tqjunior.thinkquest.org/4616/
middle school and up

This ThinkQuest entry uses interviews from primary sources to present a picture of life during the Second World War from the vantage point of the United States. Lesson plans on "Rosie the Riveter's Recipes," "It's My Right," and "HIStories-HERstories" are extensions of the content presented on the site and are designed with middle-school students in mind. The site also challenges students to investigate their families' involvement in the war and to submit their stories to the site.

What Did You Do in the War, Grandma?
http://www.stg.brown.edu/projects/WWII_Women/tocCS.html
middle school and up

Linda Wood, a librarian at South Kingstown High School in Rhode Island, presents this unique project. Ninth graders interviewed Rhode Island women who lived during World War II. The more than two dozen accounts that resulted are both moving and fascinating. They provide an intimate look at the mood and events of the time. Some remarkable young storytellers reveal some remarkable women. Don't miss a word!

ZIONISM

Best Search Engine: http://www.google.com/
Key Search Terms: Israel + history
                      Zionism + history

Jews + Palestine + history

Balfour Declaration + history

The Creed of an American Zionist
http://www.theatlantic.com/unbound/bookauth/zionism/steinbrg.htm
high school and up

The movement to establish a separate Jewish homeland in Palestine has been and remains extremely contentious, and there are numerous Web sites that chronicle this conflict, but most of them are far from objective. This article by Rabbi Milton Steinberg is not objective either, but he admits that right upfront. He willingly exposes his biases, so that you know what you're dealing with when you read his article.

With that in mind, read this wonderful article by Rabbi Steinberg, published in *The Atlantic* magazine in February 1945. It does a wonderful job of explaining the concepts of Zionism, as well as the conflicts amongst Jews about Zionism. It's particularly revealing concerning American Jews.

Chronology of Selected Events in the History of Modern Zionism and Israel
http://www.adl.org/Israel/advocacy/chronology.asp?xflag=3

This chronology may help you get the big picture. It begins on February 14, 1896, with the publication of Theodore Hertzl's treatise "The Jewish State" and covers quite a bit of ground before ending on June 1, 2001, with the terrorist attack at a Tel Aviv nightclub that killed 21 Israeli youths. At this page, in the left-hand column, you'll also find a link to a "Glossary of Key Terms and Events in Israel's History."

ZOROASTRIANISM

Best Search Engine:	http://www.google.com/
Key Search Terms:	Zoroaster + history
	Zoroastrianism + history
	Zoroaster + history
	Zoroaster + Indian history

Who Are We Zoroastrians?
http://coulomb.ecn.purdue.edu/~bulsara/ZOROASTRIAN/wawz.html
middle school and up

Part of the Zoroastrianism page at Purdue University, this site offers an excellent introduction. Sections on the "Background," the "Zoroastrian Doctrine," "Living a Zoroastrian Life," "The History," and "The Pharsis," to name a few, provide all the basics.

For more in-depth research, click on "Back to the Home Page" and choose the Zoroastrian page. From here, you can join one of several Zoroastrian mailing lists, or just read other articles on the subject. There's one, for example, on the Zoroastrian calendar that covers its historical development and its religious content.

Zoroastrianism
http://www.hindubooks.org/sudheer_birodkar/hindu_history/
    zoroastrianism.html
high school and up

This is a more extensive history of Zoroastrianism, with quite a bit of biographical information on Zoroaster that is not contained in the Purdue University site. Sections include "The Life Story of Zoroaster," "The Great Achemienian Empire," "The Greek Invasion and the Parthians," "The Sassanians—Zoroastrianism at Its Zenith," "The Arab Onslaught," "The Coming of Islam," and "The Parsis in India." Although the writing is wonderfully clear and accessible to those without a background in the subject, there is a summary provided at the bottom of the article, just to review the major points covered.

This resource is one part of a chapter in an online book called *Hindu History—A Search for Our Present in History*. If you follow the link to the table of contents, which is found at the top of the page, you'll see many other chapters and sections of chapters on Hindu history that might be of interest.

3

———∞∞∞———

Materials and Resources for World History Teachers

Each of the sites reviewed below reflects the unique needs of world history teachers. Without a doubt, some of these sites will be ones you will want to bookmark on your computer. We've arranged the sites in this section into two broad categories: "Web Resources" and "Hands-on Opportunities." Keep in mind, however, that sites earmarked for teachers are by no means off-limits to other audiences. Parents who are home-schooling their kids, for instance, can use these sites to develop excellent at-home activities, lessons, and field trips. See also the general sites listed in "The Basics" section in Volume 1 of this set.

WEB RESOURCES

Historical Map Web Sites
http://www.lib.utexas.edu/Libs/PCL/Map_collection/map_sites/hist_sites.html

This University of Texas site links you to historical maps all over the world. Choose a part of the world you wish to search, and then choose a link. The sites listed are not annotated, so sometimes it may be difficult to know whether the site will work for you, but there's a wealth of good information. You may not even need to travel beyond this site's borders. Just click on "Historical Maps from Our Collection" to search the University of Texas library site first.

The History Net: Where History Lives on the Web
http://www.thehistorynet.com/

Teachers looking for published articles on specific world history topics will want to check out *The History Net,* where you'll find every topic imaginable. Just use the menu along the left-hand side of the home page to choose your time period or subject, and let the search begin.

There's also a daily quiz, links to reenactments, seminars, exhibits, and "Today in History" sections that might be fun for use in your classroom.

H-Net Teaching
http://www.h-net.msu.edu/teaching/

The H-Net system maintains an array of sites on teaching, and this URL is a gateway to many of those sites. Each site includes edited, threaded discussions on topics of interest to list subscribers, as well as archives of previous discussions. You can find the following discussion lists at *H-Net Teaching:*

H-AfrTeach—Discussion about teaching African history and African Studies.

H-High-School—If you're a high school history or social studies teacher, you probably already know about this one. If not, check it out.

H-Teach—Here you'll find teachers at all levels engaged in enlightening discussions on a wide variety of topics.

HyperHistory Online
http://www.hyperhistory.com/online_n2/History_n2/a.html

For quick reference to maps, biographies, brief histories of people, places, and events, use the 3,000-year time line at *HyperHistory.* Use the menu at the left-hand edge of the page to choose "People," "History," or "Events." "History" links you to a number of time-period options. Choose one and your time line pops up, complete with color-coded text (green for science, technology, economy, discovery; yellow for religion, theology, etc.) Links to maps, biographies, and brief histories appear in blue on the time line.

History/Social Studies for K-12 Teachers
http://www.execpc.com/~dboals/boals.html

This site received a Britannica Internet Guide award, and it's easy to see why. An intriguing menu opens the site with buttons for many different social studies topics. Click on "American History" and find yourself with a list of standard topics, such as "Imperialism," "Vietnam," and "Civil Rights." But click on any one of these topics, and what you find is much more than just standard resources. Under "Civil Rights," 67 links, each one annotated, take you to such sites as *The Malcolm X*

Homepage and a page devoted to civil rights historic sites that can help you plan your next class field trip.

Internet Modern History Sourcebook: History and Music
http://www.fordham.edu/halsall/mod/modmusic.html

This section of the *Modern History Sourcebook* will connect you to musical texts and sounds that illustrate certain topics and times in modern history—from the Reformation up to Modern Europe. Themes include "Nineteenth Century Nationalism and Imperialism" and "Socialism as a Culture," just to give you a few examples.

Under the "Nationalism/Imperialism" link, you'll find "Songbook of the 65th Regiment," which contains songs of the British soldiers in New Zealand, and two excerpts from operas by Verdi, as well as numerous national anthems.

Medieval/Renaissance Food Home Page
http://www.pbm.com/~lindahl/food.html

Studying medieval Renaissance history in your class? Bring the period alive by preparing a medieval meal with your students. Research recipes, cooking utensils, and more at this comprehensive site. There are sections on "Primary Sources, Reference, Bibliography," "Articles/Publication," "Individual Recipes," and "Other Things that Might Be of Interest," which includes a cookbook from 1650 and a "Medieval Brewing" page.

Roman Life
http://www.dl.ket.org/latin1/things/romanlife/index.html

Use this site to find historical information on Roman life and directions for making your own Roman costumes. You'll find information on Roman names, the slave market, and Roman roads in the "Other" section. Under "Clothing" read about women's and men's clothing and hairstyles, and access directions to make a stola or tunic.

Schools of California Online Resources for Education—History/Social Science
http://score.rims.k12.ca.us/

Designed primarily for K–12 teachers in California, this site will be helpful to teachers in all states. Its system for rating recommended Web resources, using a 1–5 scale, assures that what you find here will truly be the cream of the crop.

Links include "Resources and Lessons by Grade Level," "Resources and Lessons by Topic/Keyword," "Virtual Projects & Film Trips," and "Online News Sources." Each Web site recommended by SCORE is evaluated by a team of educators who score it for accuracy, grade appropriateness, depth, and variety. If you click on "Resources by Grade Level," then choose "Grade 10 World History" and "Geography: The Modern World," you'll be given a number of different units to choose from, each one containing Web resources and activities. The resources are organized from best to worst, with the rating system explained at the top of the page.

The Viking Home Page
http://www.control.chalmers.se/vikings/indexframe.html

If you'd like to introduce your students to Viking culture, this page has lots to offer. Learn about sagas, eddas, runes, Viking ships, warfare, Viking music, Norse mythology, and much more. Links to groups that interpret this time period are also included. You can also make use of the general Viking history found at the site or get links to other major Viking sites on the Web.

HANDS-ON OPPORTUNITIES

AFS Global Educators Program
http://www.socialstudies.org/profdev/profdev1.html#opportunities

If you want to go abroad with one of the oldest and most established international organizations, AFS (American Field Service) is for you. Open to teachers, librarians, and education administrators at any stage of their careers, these programs take you for one month or an entire semester to China, France, Argentina, Mexico, South Africa, or Spain.

AFS aims to provide educators with intercultural experiences that will affect the way they teach and learn throughout their careers. Your experience will combine classroom teaching with cultural immersion, allowing you to gain insight into a different way of life and educational system. There are also opportunities to meet with community leaders and local government officials to exchange ideas on education and culture.

If you'd like more information or an application, just contact AFS using the e-mail address or phone number provided at the bottom of the page.

Dar al Islam: Teacher's Institute
http://www.daralislam.org/programs/reach/ti.cfm

These are one- or two-week institutes, held in Abiquiu, New Mexico, for secondary school teachers who want to learn more about the faith, civilization, and worldview of Islam. There are morning and evening lectures, study groups, and research opportunities in the library and media room. Teachers learn from top-notch academic and traditional scholars about how to more effectively teach their students about Islam.

The application deadline is in the early spring of each year. See the complete application instructions online. You may also want to read some of the newsletters or other publications available from this organization's Web site.

Federal Reserve Bank of New York: Educator-Oriented Initiatives
http://www.ny.frb.org/pihome/educator/initeduc.html

The Federal Reserve Bank of New York offers several programs of interest to world history teachers. "The Global Economic Forum," for educators at all levels, is a three-day summer program in which educators gain an international perspective on a wide array of economic issues by assuming the roles of policymakers from various nations.

"In the Shoes of a Fed Policymaker" is very similar, except that the focus is on the making of monetary policy in particular. This is a four-day program. For more information on these programs, which are held in New York City, visit the Web site. If interested in enrolling, you will need to contact the Federal Reserve Bank of New York by phone or e-mail.

Global Volunteers
http://www.globalvolunteers.org/

If you'd like your hands-on experience to involve doing some good for people in another part of the world, Global Volunteers can help you make it happen. They coordinate service-learning programs that offer educators the opportunity to participate in short-term human and economic development projects in more than 15 countries worldwide, including Mexico, Poland, Spain, Vietnam, Greece, Ecuador, Ireland, Ghana, Tanzania, Romania, and Italy. Projects typically involve building community facilities, painting and repairing homes, teaching conversational English, providing health care services, and assisting in environmental projects.

NEH Projects
http://www.neh.fed.us/projects/si-school.html

Summer institutes abound for teachers of history, but the ones offered by the National Endowment for the Humanities are among the best. The topics are intriguing, the locales diverse, and the stipends generous. Eligible applicants must teach full-time in an American K–12 school or, if teaching abroad, a majority of their students must be American.

Topics for the 2002 seminars and institutes included "The Vietnam

War: Morality and Politics," "Writing Africa: Comparative African and European Palavers and Perspectives," "The Epic and Saga Tradition in Medieval Ireland," and "Historical Interpretations of the Industrial Revolution in Britain." Check the Web site for upcoming topics, and start planning now. Applications are due by March 1 of each year.

St. Johnsbury Advanced Placement Summer Institute for Secondary Teachers
http://www.stj.k12.vt.us/other/apinstitute.html

Does Vermont in July sound good to you? If you teach Advanced Placement History, you just might want to consider the St. Johnsbury workshops. These workshops, which were founded 17 years ago, cover nearly every subject offered in Advanced Placement, European history and world history included. Four sessions are offered through the month of July, and all of them cover test development and reading, new developments with AP curriculum, developing AP assignments, and sharing problems and approaches in teaching.

See the Web site for more information. If interested, you'll need to e-mail the school for application details.

4

⟶ ∞ ⟵

Museums and Summer Programs for World History Students

In this chapter, we've scouted out the best Web sites for museums, organizations, and summer programs for world history students. This part of the book is designed to help you learn about world history in a more hands-on style. We'll describe Web sites where you can take a virtual tour of Paleolithic cave art in France, visit Chateau Versailles outside of Paris, or read the diaries of Vietnam veterans.

We've also found amazing sites that'll convince you to log off your computer—to experience Middle Eastern culture while living with a Jordanian family, attend a Governor's Scholars Program in your state, or explore Easter Island off the coast of Chile, where Internet connections are few and far between.

See also the general sites listed in "The Basics" section in Volume I of this set.

MUSEUMS

The Age of Enlightenment in the Paintings of France's National Museums
http://www.culture.fr/files/imaginary_exhibition.html

If you're studying the Enlightenment in France, you won't want to miss this online exhibit from the French Ministry of Culture. There are wonderful paintings from the Enlightenment, accompanied by an essay on the historical background of the period, an essay on the dominant Enlightenment painting styles, and a short genealogy of French royalty. Follow the links within each section for biographies of key people and images of the artwork discussed.

Anne Frank House
http://www.annefrank.nl/ned/default2.html

If you're studying World War II and the Holocaust, you've surely read *about* Anne Frank's diary if you haven't actually read the diary itself. This URL takes you directly to the English-language version of the Anne Frank House Web site, which is also available in Dutch and Spanish. Located in Amsterdam, the actual Anne Frank House is where the young girl wrote her famous diary while in hiding during World War II.

At this Web site, you can get a glimpse of the hiding place, read excerpts from Anne's diary, even look at pages from the original diary. There's interesting information on the publication of the diaries after Anne's death and on the public's reaction to the diaries. This is a beautiful and moving site, with lots of wonderful information for newcomers as well as aficionados.

The Cave of Chauvet-Pont-D'Arc
http://www.culture.gouv.fr/culture/arcnat/chauvet/en/

Divided into the following four sections—"The Cave Today," "Research," "Time and Space," and "Witnesses"—this Web site provides access to an archaeological discovery of a decorated Paleolithic cave. Explore the cave's images, learn about the discovery of the drawings, their authentication and preservation, or study the geographic and archaeological context of this particular cave art.

If you're studying prehistory, or are just plain fascinated by ancient cave art, this well-done site will take you deep into one of France's most significant discoveries and let you learn more about prehistoric humans and their art, as well as the work of archaeologists, whose job it is to study and preserve sites like this one.

Chateau de Versailles
http://www.chateauversailles.fr/en/

Studying French history? "Discovering the Places," "Meeting the People," and "Past and Present Life" are three of your main options when you enter the home page of the Chateau Versailles Museum. View drawings of Versailles at various times in history, read about its construction, study Marie Antoinette and Napoleon I, or view masterpieces from the Museum of French History, which is located in the Chateau. You can even read a sample day-in-the-life account of the Sun King (Louis XIV), beginning with his in-person alarm clock's (the First Valet de Chambre) arrival at 8:30 A.M. and ending with his 10 P.M. public supper.

This site also includes material in French for students and information for planning a visit to Versailles, should a trip to France be in your future. The site is available in French, English, or Spanish, so you can practice your language skills if you like.

Hellenic Culture
http://www.culture.gr/

This site plays host to a collection of cultural links on ancient and contemporary Greece. One entire section is devoted to "Museums, Monuments, and Archaeological Sites" of Hellas. Click on "Archaeological Sites," and you'll be given links to dozens of archaeological museums and collections, including the Acropolis museum, where you can view some of the most important pieces of art from ancient Greece. Under "Museums," you'll find museums devoted to cinema, theater, music, art, folklore, and more.

Library Exhibits on the Web
http://www.sil.si.edu/SILPublications/Online-Exhibitions/online-
    exhibitions-frames.htm

Here's a fun place to browse if you haven't narrowed down the topic of your research yet and are just looking for inspiration and ideas. The Special Collections Department at the University of Houston maintains this list of links to online exhibits curated by libraries. The majority of the exhibits have a historical theme, and all of them contain digital images and descriptions of text. Recent exhibits included in the list were *1492: An Ongoing Voyage* at Cornell University and *1918—Australians in France* at the Australian War Memorial. You can be sure that the exhibits listed here are worth the time it takes to visit.

Oriental Institute Museum
http://www-oi.uchicago.edu/OI/default.html

Part of the University of Chicago, the Oriental Institute Museum Web site offers a stellar virtual museum of antiquities from Egypt, Mesopotamia, Iran, Syria, Palestine, and Anatolia. The site is well organized and the quality of the images is exceptional, but this is a large site with lots to offer, so navigating can become confusing. Just use your browser's back button if you get lost.

In addition to the virtual museum, the site also boasts awesome "Photographic Archives" from the Institute's expeditions. Just follow the link from the Museum's home page. Under "Research and Projects," look for materials collected on individual digs sponsored by the institute. Finally, try "ABZU," the institute's index to Internet resources on the ancient Near East. You'll find lots to explore.

The Vietnam War Museum
http://members.aol.com/mraffin/vnmuseum.htm

You'll find diaries, photographic archives, original drawings and paintings, and a collection of Vietnam War stamps, among other offerings, at this Web site of the Vietnam War Museum in Chicago. If you're studying the war and want to read some memoirs to go along with the history in your textbook, this might be a good place to do it.

The site design is a bit haphazard, so it might take you a few times scrolling down the home page to find what you're looking for, but don't be discouraged. The links are all good, and the material collected here is worth your time.

SUMMER PROGRAMS

American University in Bulgaria
http://www.aubg.bg/

The American University in Bulgaria offers a Balkan Summer Studies Institute for students interested in southeast Europe. Courses offered include archaeology, computer science, history, interdisciplinary studies, literature, and sociology. The program includes travel throughout the region.

Just follow the links on the Web site for "Academic Programs" and then "Summer School."

AMIDEAST
http://www.amideast.org/

AMIDEAST offers a four-week summer program in Jordan. Lectures and site visits introduce participants to a country in the throes of change, yet rooted in cultural continuity. The program is designed for undergraduate students with varying degrees of education or experience in Middle Eastern Studies and the Arabic language. Language lessons will focus on spoken colloquial Jordanian Arabic. You do not need to have prior knowledge of Arabic. A homestay is included.

Follow the menu link for "Study Abroad," and you'll find this program in Jordan, as well as numerous other options.

Education World's Countdown to Summer: Free Summer Programs for Teens
http://www.education-world.com/a_curr/curr074.shtml

Interested in an academically enriching summer program in world history, even though you may not have the funds? Here you'll find a list of freebies, including Governor's Honors Programs. Although most states offer such programs, not all of them are free.

Each state's Governor's Scholar's Program differs a little from the next, but most are month-long, residential programs for academically motivated students who have just completed their junior year of high school. Apply online to the free programs listed here, or contact your state's Governor's Honors Program for more information.

Historic Preservation Internship Training Program
http://www2.cr.nps.gov/tps/hpit_p.htm

Are you one of those history buffs who never tires of visiting battlefields and historic landmarks? If so, this might just be your dream summer job. Open to undergraduate and graduate students, this program lets you undertake research and administrative projects within the National Park Service during the summer or school year. Its purpose is to help train America's future historians, archaeologists, architects, curators, planners, and archivists by fostering an awareness of the cultural resource management activities of the Park Service. Although this program takes place on American soil and is geared toward U.S. history, it's such a stellar training ground for historians of all types, that you might want to consider it, even if your area of expertise lies beyond U.S. borders.

Check the Web site for internships available next summer. You'll find them in museum management, cultural landscaping, architecture, archeology, and many other history-related disciplines with either the National Park Service, the Department of the Interior, or General Services Administration.

Institute for International Cooperation and Development
http://www.iicd-volunteer.org/

This organization trains and sends volunteers abroad for development aid work in Africa and Central and South America. Programs last between 6 and 19 months, so this is a little more than a summer commitment, but you'll have lots of opportunities to learn and grow through academic studies, training in practical skills, team work, international travel, and work in community development projects. Angola, Zimbabwe, Mozambique, and Brazil are some of the participating countries.

Check out the Web site to learn more about this international volunteer program. Just use the menu on the right-hand side of the page to access sections on "History," "Philosophy," "Solidarity Work," "Preparation Period," and "International Period," to name just a few of the topics covered.

If you're interested in teaching, you'll want to take a close look at how this program is structured. In addition to the work experience abroad, it includes an educational component for when you've returned from your overseas trip.

Peterson's Summer Opportunities
http://www.petersons.com/summerop/select/a068se.html

Here you'll find 168 sponsors with summer programs offering history. Most are traditional academic programs, so use this list if you're looking to beef up your transcript for college. Prestigious programs include the Enforex Spanish Language School, which offers Enforex Hispanic Culture: Civilization, History, Art, and Literature, a summer program that takes place in both Barcelona and Madrid—your choice. This is primarily a language program with optional activities in culture and sports.

Another travel-abroad option is the University of St. Andrews Scottish Studies Summer Program in . . . you guessed it . . . St. Andrews, Fife. Study Scottish history, culture, literature, music, and art, in an academically enriching environment. If your interest lies south of the border, way south, you can learn about Chilean culture with the Youth for Understanding International Exchange-Chile. You'll stay with a Chilean family while you study Chile's history and culture and then travel around Easter Island, the most remote island on earth.

If you want to stay in the States and beef up on your AP History skills, try The Discovery School at the University of California, Los Angeles. Its focus is precollege enrichment, with various options in history. The possibilities are too numerous to list. Check out the site yourself and dust off your backpack for new and exciting adventures.

Summer Program in Historic Preservation
http://www.usc.edu/dept/architecture/special/specialprogla.
    html#preservation

Two full weeks of classes designed to introduce you to the field of preservation is what you'll find at this University of Southern California program. If you're a college student, you may find that you can get credit for the work done here, but the classes are open to anyone with an interest in the subject.

In addition to classroom work, you'll visit such Los Angeles historic sites as the Gamble and Freeman Houses, Rancho Los Alamitos, the Workman and Temple Family Homestead Museum, and the Getty Conservation Institute. These field trips will serve as a context for examining a broad range of legal, economic, aesthetic, and technical issues associated with the documentation, conservation, and interpretation of historic structures, landscapes, and communities.

Tufts University/Talloires
http://ase.tufts.edu/frenchalps/

If European history is your focus, this Tufts University program will surely sound appealing. Situated in the Benedictine Priory of Talloires, the Tufts University European Center offers a variety of unique educational programs, designed specifically for high school, college, and adult students, so the first thing to do is click on the option that best describes you when you access the home page.

Students explore contemporary issues in education, archaeology, environmental studies, international relations, French language and culture, and European history. You'll have fun while you learn in various settings that include guided instruction, informal discussion, and first-hand encounters with the vast natural resources and people of this lively Alpine region. Although French is not required, some exposure to the language is useful.

University of Oslo International Summer School
http://www.uio.no/iss/

Some 500 students from all parts of the world gather at the University of Oslo in Norway every summer to study various subjects and experience Norwegian culture. Undergraduate and graduate courses are available in Scandinavian art, economics, history, international relations, literature, peace studies, politics, sociology, and special education. Classes are taught in English. Intensive Norwegian language study is available, but not required. Financial aid is also available.

Check the Web site to read more about the program and view the upcoming summer course catalog.

5

——∞——

Careers

Whether you're simply gathering information to help you turn your passion for world history into a livelihood or you're actively searching for
your first job in the field, the World Wide Web can play an integral
role in the development of your career.

Your idea of a perfect job using your background in world history may
involve teaching in a secondary or postsecondary school, working as a
museum curator, researching and writing books, or working in government, law, or journalism, for example—the choices are remarkably varied. Regardless of the specific field you're interested in, you'll discover
numerous Web sites with tools to help you determine your career aptitudes, match your academic interests with a university program, locate
funding for a research project, find online peers, register for professional
conferences or student workshops, and of course, you'll encounter numerous job database sites, including those specific to history-related
careers.

We've selected what we consider to be the best career-building history
Web sites, with the needs of upper-level high school and college students
firmly in mind. These sites, which include professional organizations and
societies, federal and state agencies, private companies, and nonprofit
groups, should give you a good jump start on your career.

See also the general sites listed in "The Basics" section of this volume.

PROFESSIONAL ORGANIZATIONS AND SOCIETIES

American Association of Museums
http://www.aam-us.org/

Scroll down the page and click on "Museum Careers" to read about what museums do and what types of work museum professionals perform. A handy list of common duties and positions will let you test your own interest against those of museum workers. This site also contains specific information on education and training for jobs in the museum world, as well as a section called "How to Find Internships and Employment." Nothing fancy about this professional association's site, but it will answer some basic questions for you if you're considering pursuing a career in museums.

American Council of Learned Societies
http://www.acls.org/

Dedicated to fostering the advancement of humanistic learning in the humanities and social sciences and to strengthening relations between the national societies devoted to these studies, the American Council of Learned Societies (ACLS) offers many different fellowship and grant programs to historians. The council also convenes and supports conferences and working groups in various fields.

Visit this Web site to learn more about ACLS activities and programs. Just follow the menu at the top of the page to learn about ACLS constituent societies, online scholarly resources, and ACLS publications, as well as its fellowship and grant programs.

The American Historical Association
http://www.theaha.org/

The Web site for the largest professional association for historians in the United States provides general information on the association, conferences, job lists, and the *American Historical Review*.

If you're interested in working in education, the American Historical Association (AHA) has created a Web site that should be one of your first stops when exploring career options in history. The site offers a job service, where you can peruse current job offerings in the field, most of them teaching positions. You'll also want to take a look at the primer on teaching history, with information for both secondary and post-secondary educators.

Go to the bottom of the page, and you'll find a databank of information aimed at historians pursuing a career teaching at the university level. Information and statistical reports on Ph.D. production, hiring, salary data, enrollment trends, and part-time employment can help you decide if this is a path you'd like to pursue. If you're already advancing along a career path in postsecondary history education, you may want to browse the AHA's extensive list of dissertations in progress, too.

The Association for Living History, Farm, and Agricultural Museums
http://www.alhfam.org/welcome.html

Like to play dress up and make-believe? If so, living history might just be for you. Living history museums attempt to breathe life into static exhibits, by recreating the work and the daily life of the people who populated particular historic environs.

The Association for Living History, Farm, and Agricultural Museums (ALFAM) is the professional association serving those who work in living history museums. In addition to the standard offerings of such associations—newsletters, conferences, regional meetings, and the like—you'll find links to more than 80 living history Web sites around the world, like the Agricultural Museum of the Rhineland in Germany and the Museum of Wooden Architecture in Novgorod, Russia. There's also "Living History HELP," a glossary and bibliography that will help you understand more about careers in living history museums. If you already know that you want to work in this field, use the site's extensive job listings to locate employment opportunities.

National Council for the Social Studies
http://www.ncss.org/

Defined as an information service for educators, this organization's Web site contains sections on conferences, standards, teaching resources, awards and grants, meetings, membership, and more. If you're considering a career as a teacher, you'll find lots to think about here, and if you're already headed down that career path, you'll be able to take advantage of all the resources offered. Click on "Professional Development" to learn more about educational and work opportunities as a world history teacher.

The Society of American Archivists
http://www.archivists.org/

North America's oldest and largest national archival professional association might be of interest to you if you enjoy identifying and preserving historical records. Check out this site to learn more about the variety of employment opportunities in the field and the education requirements you will need to meet to become an archivist.

Why Become a Historian?
http://www.theaha.org/pubs/why/blackeyintro.htm

Ten historians of varying backgrounds share insights into their chosen profession in this collection of essays written by historians for students. The pamphlet provides good food for thought if you're considering a career in history.

The easiest way to access it is to type in the URL provided above. The links from the American Historical Association Web site are too difficult to follow.

World History Association
http://www.woodrow.org/teachers/world-history/

In partnership with the Woodrow Wilson Leadership Program for Teachers, the World History Association is a great place to learn about what it's like to teach history at the secondary level. This Web site contains announcements, teaching materials, conference papers, a focus module on the Mongols, and reviews of books.

Although there's nothing directed specifically toward students interested in becoming world history teachers, this site is geared for teachers and will thus give you lots of insight into the world history teacher's life. Under "Announcements," you can read a report on the status of history in the nation's schools or glance over the minutes of the seventh annual meeting of this association. The teaching materials and focus module are wonderful examples of the type of curriculum world history teachers create.

FEDERAL AND STATE GOVERNMENT ORGANIZATIONS

Peace Corps Master's Program
http://www.peacecorps.gov/volunteer/masters/index.html

Trying to decide between graduate school and the Peace Corps? The Peace Corps has come up with a way that you don't have to choose. Thanks to partnerships with more than 40 campuses across the United States, the Peace Corps Master's International (MI) program allows you to incorporate Peace Corps service into a master's degree program.

Students apply to both the Peace Corps and the participating graduate school, and must be accepted by both. You would typically complete one year of graduate studies before starting a Peace Corps assignment. Your Peace Corps assignment then serves as the foundation for a thesis or other culminating project.

You can use the Web site to learn more about the participating graduate schools and the specific areas of study, which include history-friendly subjects such as education, intercultural relations, international education, international service, public administration and policy, creative writing, and communications.

State Historic Preservation Officers
http://www.achp.gov/shpo.html

These folks administer the national historic preservation program at the state level, review National Register of Historic Places nominations, maintain data on historic properties that have been identified but not yet nominated, and consult with federal agencies. They are designated by the governor of their respective state or territory.

This page is part of a larger Web site that belongs to the Advisory Council on Historic Preservation. In addition to the information about working in historic preservation, you'll find intriguing articles on current issues in historic preservation around the country, as well as a section on training and education.

U.S. Department of State: Student Programs Index
http://www.state.gov/www/careers/rstudprogindex.html

If you're interested in a career in foreign affairs, you'll want to visit the U.S. Department of State's comprehensive Web site.

The Department manages several student employment programs that can provide you with invaluable on-the-job experience in a foreign affairs environment. If selected for one of the programs, you could work in Washington, D.C., or at an embassy overseas. Positions are both paid and unpaid and are available during spring, summer, and fall.

Use the comprehensive Web site to learn details about the various programs, which include a cooperative education program; a graduate fellowship program; the Presidential management intern program; domestic and overseas student internships for university juniors, seniors, and graduate students; and student-worker trainee opportunities for high school, vocational school, and undergraduate students.

NONPROFIT ORGANIZATIONS AND SPECIALIZED WEB SITES

High School Journalism
http://www.highschooljournalism.org/

Because they often enjoy research and writing, many historians become journalists. At this cool site, you can chat with a pro about the ins and outs of working as a journalist or newspaper editor, or you can beef up on the basics you'll need for pursuing a career. There's a list of awards for high school journalism students, links to hundreds of journalism schools, and a plethora of scholarship info.

Test your journalism skills with the site's quick quiz. Questions like, "According to the *Associated Press Stylebook*, what is the abbreviation for Minnesota?" will give you clues to the type of knowledge you'll need to succeed in this field. The quiz changes every day, so if you don't like the results today, study and try again tomorrow.

History as a Career
http://www.ub-careers.buffalo.edu/cdo/chistory.htm

Part of a larger State University of New York Web site on careers, this page has solid information on 12 different career options for historians. Everything from government archivist, which we've covered a bit here, to advertising representative, which we haven't covered, is discussed. This is a good source if you need to brainstorm about possibilities.

History Departments around the World
http://chnm.gmu.edu/history/depts/

Are you applying to college and interested in majoring in world history? This searchable database from George Mason University will let you explore the offerings in world history at more than 1,200 locations around the world. Just follow the links for the college or university of your choice, and you'll be taken directly to its history department.

Index

Page numbers in bold indicate main discussion of a topic.

About the Authors

ELIZABETH H. OAKES is the author of more than 15 books, including *Career Exploration on the Internet* and *International Encyclopedia of Women Scientists*.

MEHRDAD KIA is Professor of History at the University of Montana.